D1422738

PELICAN BOOKS

A 217

JUSTINIAN AND HIS AGE

P. N. URE

JUSTINIAN AND
HIS AGE

*

P. N. URE

PENGUIN BOOKS

HARMONDSWORTH · MIDDLESEX

Penguin Books Ltd, Harmondsworth, Middlesex

U.S.A.: Penguin Books Inc., 3300 Clipper Mill Road, Baltimore 11, Md
[*Educational Representative :*
D. C. Heath & Co., 285 Columbus Avenue, Boston 16, Mass]

AUSTRALIA: Penguin Books Pty Ltd, 200 Normanby Road,
Melbourne, S.C.5, Victoria

AGENT IN CANADA: Riverside Books Ltd, 47 Green Street
Saint Lambert, Montreal, P.Q.

—

Made and printed in Great Britain by
Wyman and Sons Ltd, London, Fakenham
and Reading

—

First published 1951

Contents

*

List of Plates

*

List of Maps

*

Errata

*

Map 2
for Mediolandum *read* Mediolanum
for Ancora *read* Ancona

Map 3
for Persamenia *read* Persarmenia

Preface

*

THE object of this book is to put before the reader a portrait of a great emperor and an account of his age as we have it recorded by contemporary writers. The trustworthiness of the historians of antiquity is, of course, within limits, open to criticism, and scholars of the last few generations have done invaluable work in establishing and applying canons by which to test them. One unfortunate result however of such researches is that in modern histories of ancient times the stress tends to be laid on the results of minute critical study, and the general reader has often some difficulty in disinterring from this accumulation the contemporary narrative which it is intended to elucidate. It is generally agreed that the chief sources for the age of Justinian are in the main honest and truthful, and in the pages that follow I shall therefore as far as possible let these writers speak for themselves. We have some excellent works on Byzantine history in our language, notably J. B. Bury's *History of the Later Roman Empire from the death of Theodosius I to the death of Justinian* (A.D. 395–565), Macmillan 1923; Norman Baynes' *The Byzantine Empire*, Home University Library 1925, revised 1943 (with good bibliography); the same scholar's chapters on Justinian in the *Cambridge Mediaeval History*, and of course the great Gibbon's *Decline and Fall* (the best edition Bury's, with numerous supplementary notes). For anyone who is prepared to read the accounts of Justinian in any of these works this little book of mine will be quite superfluous, provided only that he has sufficient leisure and sufficient mastery of Greek and Latin to turn up all the references to the sources that are to be found in the footnotes and bibliographies of these scholarly works. For those who cannot do so it is hoped that this account of the life work of the most notable of the Byzantine emperors as presented to us by men who actually witnessed it may meet a real want. If it should lead a few of them to turn and equip themselves for a serious study of Byzantine history, the writer will indeed have been rewarded.

P. N. URE

The writer of this book did not live to see it in print. It has been left to others to see it through the press and to record, as far as they are able, the author's thanks to those who helped him. For generous co-operation in the search for suitable illustrations warm thanks are due to Mr George E. Bean, Professor John Garstang, Mr A. S. B. Glover, Dr Winifred Lamb and the Warburg Institute of the University of London. For preparing the photographs from which plates 14–16 were made and for information about some of the coins illustrated in them the writer was greatly indebted to Mr J. Allan of the Department of Coins and Medals in the British Museum. For permission to publish these plates thanks are due to the Trustees of the British Museum, to the Turkish Embassy for plates 3 and 8, to Fratelli Alinari of Florence for plate 11 and to the Compagnia Fotocelere of Turin for plates 9 a and b.

In the last stages of the production of the book I have had invaluable help from Mr J. A. Crook, who has most kindly read the whole of the proofs, and from Miss J. M. C. Toynbee, who has allowed me to take advantage of her expert knowledge of coins.

A. D. URE

CHAPTER I

Introduction: The Historical Background

*

FOR all whose roots are in Europe, whether they are citizens of one or other of the states of modern Europe, or have found new homes in the new worlds of North and South America, Australia and New Zealand, or have spread eastward from Russia into the vast spaces of Northern Asia, or have established themselves in North or in South Africa, it is imperative that some knowledge of the Roman empire should be part of the normal historical background. To make this claim is not to say that the Roman empire was a good thing. It is simply the statement of a fact; for it is a fact that our present-day civilization is an offspring of that of the empire of the Caesars. Only in the Far East in India and China do we find great civilized communities that have worked out their own salvation independently of the great Graeco-Roman experiment of the Mediterranean world. At a time when the whole world is struggling towards a new order which is bound to involve all these great regions in close contacts and collaboration, it becomes particularly important to take stock of our respective achievements in the long past which has created the absorbing present. Without such a survey of the roads along which we have come it is impossible to realize where we now stand and to get our bearings for the course which we are to make in the future.

Two facts in particular need to be stressed if we approach the history of the Roman empire from this point of view. The first is the unparalleled duration of the new order that was first outlined by Julius Caesar in his brief dictatorship and then consolidated in the long reign of Augustus. From the battle of Actium (31 B.C.), which made Augustus master of the whole Roman empire, to Romulus Augustulus, the last Roman emperor to sit on the imperial throne in Italy, is over 500 years, and for the greater part of that time the whole Mediterranean world and the countries adjoining, up to the Solway and Tyne in Britain, the Rhine in west Europe, the Danube in east Europe, the Euphrates in west Asia and the deserts in north Africa, all enjoyed the blessings of the pax Romana. In west Europe we naturally regard the end of the long line of Roman Caesars as the end of an epoch; and so it was in a very real sense. It was not till A.D. 800 that the Frankish king Charlemagne was crowned as Caesar by the Pope at Rome and started the line of German Caesars which ended only with the fall of the Hapsburg Kaisers and their offshoot the Hohenzollerns in 1918. For us the period between the end of the Roman line in 476 and the beginning of the German in 800 is rightly regarded as the dark age of Europe. But we are apt to forget that the eclipse of A.D. 476 was only partial. Ever since the first Christian emperor, Constantine, had founded at the old Greek city of Byzantium a second, eastern capital which came to be known either as New Rome or, more lastingly, as Constantinople (the city of Constantine) or more simply as just the city (*sten polin*, Istambul), there had been two capitals to the empire, and generally two emperors to share the growing burden of upholding it.

The Greek half of the empire proved itself much tougher than the Italian. The last of the Greek emperors perished with his empire defending a breach in the walls of Constantinople in 1453. When the news of the discovery of America first reached Europe there must have been people alive who could remember the days when a Christian emperor still reigned in Constantinople. For the last eight centuries of its existence the history of the eastern empire is largely the story of the struggle against Islam. But more and more it grew to be also the story of the estrangement between the east and west of Europe, between the Roman Christianity of the Gothic cathedral and the Gregorian chant on the one hand and the Orthodox Greek Christianity and Byzantine culture of the east on the other. The effect of this protracted schism between the Latin and Greek empires and churches was felt beyond the bounds of the empire. The peoples of west Europe, Saxons and Franks, Spaniards and Germans and also the western Slavs all fell within the sphere of Old Rome; but those of east Europe and notably the Slavs of the Balkan states and Russia, were civilized and converted to Christianity from New Rome: they are the inheritors of, and they have reacted against, the Byzantine tradition. This is a fact that should not be forgotten when people in west Europe are making a serious and honest attempt to understand a great people whose antecedents, and therefore whose whole outlook, must inevitably be different from our own.

The other great fact to be borne in mind about the Roman empire, east and west alike, all through the many centuries of its history, is its fundamental conservatism. It was born out of weariness produced by a century of savage civil war which had itself followed almost without a break on a century of wars of conquest. Between 280 and 146 B.C. the people of Rome had conquered by force of arms most of the lands that border on the Mediterranean. The fact that many of these wars of conquest had not been deliberately sought had not diminished either the loss of life or the strain on the survivors. The century of civil war had been still more disastrous and deplorable. The lack of both imagination and generosity that had led the senatorial class to crush by violence instead of guiding with understanding the generous young reformers Tiberius and Gaius Gracchus (133–121 B.C.) had paved the way for the bloodthirsty struggles between Marius and Sulla, Caesar and Pompey, and it was as a successful warlord that the dictator Julius Caesar, after the defeat of Pompey at Pharsalia in 48 B.C., had brought the whole Roman world under the sway of one supreme military commander. His murder in 44 B.C. had led to a fresh struggle between rival war lords, and the defeat of Antony and Cleopatra at Actium in 31 B.C. found a world too weary to long for anything but peace, quiet and security, that deep desire to be left alone to cultivate one's garden that finds its perfect expression in the *Georgics* of

Virgil. The poet was in his twenties when Julius was murdered; as a result of the civil wars his father had been dispossessed of his farm near Mantua, and the fact that it had been restored as the result of a personal appeal to the young Octavius no doubt had predisposed the poet to regard him as the coming saviour. He wrote his *Georgics* in the years that just preceded the crowning mercy of Actium and he must have been voicing the hopes and fears of masses of his fellow countrymen when he prays that the future Augustus may be spared to save a ruined race from a state of things in which right and wrong had changed places, countless wars raged over all the world, crime flourished in countless forms, no proper honour was paid the plough, the countryside lay desolate, the farmers had all been carried off from their farms, the ploughshare had been turned into the sword, here Euphrates and there Germany were mobilizing for war, neighbour cities were rushing to arms and the laws had been trampled underfoot.

The Roman empire was the answer to Virgil's prayer. For centuries the Roman legions kept their watch on the Rhine and the Danube, the Euphrates and the deserts of North Africa. Here or there the frontier might be modified or advanced, notably when Claudius annexed Britain and when Trajan extended the empire's borders in the east; but essentially it remained neither greater nor less in extent than in the days of Augustus. And within these frontiers the farmer received, if not the honour he deserved, at any rate consistent encouragement and protection. Neighbour cities no longer lived in a state of armed watchfulness against one another: all the communities and provinces of the empire were protected and administered by or through an all-pervasive and generally benevolent civil service. Something indeed had gone out of the world that some may feel to be the very essence of the good life. Aeschylus and Socrates, Isaiah and the writers of the Psalms, and probably many a republican Roman would have felt that somehow all was not as it should be with their descendants. There is something to be said for the dogma that bureaucracy is not enough.

Still, peace and the reign of law were rightly felt as blessings even when they ceased to be the miracle that they seemed to the young Virgil. The bureaucratic machine worked so smoothly that even a mad emperor like Caligula or Nero hardly affected the general prosperity. And for the greater part of the second century in particular Rome was blessed with a succession of singularly humane and enlightened emperors. 'If a man,' says Gibbon in a famous passage of his *Decline and Fall of the Roman Empire*, 'were called to fix the period in the history of the world during which the condition of the human race was most happy and prosperous, he would without hesitation name that which elapsed from the death of Domitian to the accession of Commodus' (A.D. 96–180). This is of course the verdict of an enlightened patrician of the eighteenth century. The preface to the first edition of his earlier volumes is dated 1 February 1776, the year after the outbreak of the American War of Independence; the last volumes appeared in 1781, eight years before the French Revolution. Still, a verdict first pronounced by Virgil and endorsed by Gibbon demands and deserves our serious consideration.

Towards the middle of the third century of our era the empire showed the first signs of cracking. In A.D. 251 a Roman emperor was crushed and killed by invading Goths; in 260 his successor was captured by the Persians, and died a captive in Persia. But the situation was restored by Diocletian and Constantine, and the empire did not begin to collapse seriously till after A.D. 400, when the legions withdrew from Britain, never to return, and Rome was sacked by the Goths (A.D. 410). Before the end of the fifth century all the western half of the empire had fallen to the barbarians – Vandals in Africa, Goths in Italy and Spain, Goths, Franks and Burgundians in Gaul, Angles and Saxons in Britain. Only east of a line drawn north and south through the narrow sea off Brindisi did a Roman emperor still hold sway – in the Balkans, Egypt, and the Asiatic provinces of the empire.

We have a good deal of first-hand information about

the state of things in these Western kingdoms. The great
Augustine died at Hippo (Bona, in what is now Tunis)
in A.D. 430 when the Vandals were besieging it; his *City
of God* was inspired by the human catastrophe that he
had lived to witness. Boethius, whose *Consolations of
Philosophy* was translated by both Alfred and Chaucer,
had been a minister of Theoderic, the Gothic king of
Italy, by whom he was put to death only three years
before Justinian's accession. The Franks we know from
the pages of Gregory of Tours, the very human bishop
who wrote their history in the following century. All
alike tell a dismal story of the distress of nations. Anything
less like the good life as conceived by Virgil or Gibbon
could scarcely be imagined. Medieval Europe was
painfully taking shape and the process was to be profoundly influenced by the Roman tradition. But the ideal
of the empire one and indivisible was never again to be
realized. East and West drifted apart and both alike lost
something vital in the process. But before this finally
happened the Emperor Justinian made one last effort
to regain the West and bring all the provinces of the
empire from the Atlantic to the Euphrates under the
one paternal sway of Roman law and Roman administration. It is the story of this attempt that is the subject
of the chapters that follow.

CHAPTER II

The Wars

*

'The Emperor Caesar Flavius Justinianus, Alamanni-
cus, Gothicus, Francicus, Germanicus, Anticus, Alani-
cus, Vandalicus, Africanus, Pious, Happy, Renowned,
Conqueror and Triumpher, Ever Augustus.' Preface
to the *Digest*, A.D. 533.

THE disintegration of the empire had been steadily proceeding for over a century when Justinian in A.D. 527
began the double task of bringing the lost provinces back
to the one fold and of setting the fold itself in order. Everything shows that he was a man who felt strongly that he
had a divine mission for both tasks. 'Governing under
the authority of God our empire, which was delivered to
us by His Heavenly Majesty, we prosecute wars with
success, we adorn peace, we bear up the frame of the
State, and we so lift up our mind in contemplation of the
aid of the Omnipotent Deity, that we do not put our
trust in our arms nor in our soldiers nor in our leaders in
war nor in our own skill, but we rest all our hopes in the
providence of the Supreme Trinity alone, from whence
proceeded the elements of the whole universe, and their
disposition throughout the orb of the world was derived.'
(Justinian, *Constitutio* 'Deo Auctore', explaining the plan
of the *Digest*.)

Justinian's laws are dealt with in Chapter VIII, but
as one object of these pages is to introduce the reader to
the contemporary documents on which our knowledge of
the emperor and his times is based it seems appropriate
to start our account of his wars by quoting the military
titles that he himself affixed to his name in the decree
which announced the completion of his famous *Digest* of
Roman law and the brief confession of faith with which
he began the decree that explains the plan of the work.

They may serve too as a reminder that the wars and the laws were part of one grandiose plan.

For the wars themselves we must turn first and foremost to Procopius, the remarkable historian whose history of them is largely the account of an eye-witness. Of his quality as a writer and historian we will speak later (Chap. IX). It may suffice for the moment to emphasize that Bury, the most notable of our modern Byzantine historians, declares him to have been the most excellent Greek historian since Polybius (*Later Roman Empire*, A.D. 395–565: II. p. 419), and that there is every reason to endorse this high praise

But let us allow the historian to introduce himself. This is how he prefaces his history. 'Procopius of Caesarea wrote the history of the wars which Justinian, emperor of the Romans, waged against the barbarians both of the East and of the West... that the long years might not for lack of record consign mighty deeds to oblivion and altogether blot them out; he thought that the remembrance of them would be a thing of some importance and of great help both to the people of the present day and to those who shall come hereafter, if ever again time should bring men into similar straits. For historical analogies can be of some profit to those who are preparing for war or are involved in struggles of other kinds; they reveal how earlier generations were affected by similar struggles and suggest what sort of issue those who are well advised may expect for that in which they are engaged. He was conscious that he was particularly qualified to write it for the simple reason that it had fallen to his lot to be chosen as adviser to the general Belisarius and in that capacity to have been present at practically all the events. He held that the proper qualification for an orator is cleverness, for a poet invention, but for a historian truth. For this reason he did not conceal the shortcomings even of any of those who were his greatest friends, but accurately recorded everything that befell everybody, whether it so happened that what they did was well done or otherwise' (*Wars* I. i. 1–5).

This is the language of the great historians of the fifth

century B.C. and we shall find that one of our difficulties in assessing the reliability of Procopius as a writer is that he consciously models himself on his great predecessors Herodotus and Thucydides. We shall have to admit that Procopius was attempting the impossible when in the Roman empire of the sixth century A.D. he set himself the task of writing history in the spirit of the great masters of Classical Greece. The atmosphere that he breathed was so utterly different from theirs. But for the moment we are concerned only with the narrative of the campaigns that were waged by Justinian's armies and the extent to which they were successful in recovering the lost provinces and consolidating the threatened frontiers, and within these limits he is generally admitted to be a remarkably good and trustworthy guide. He is certainly a lively one, and fortunately for us he is now easily accessible in the Loeb edition, in which the standard text of Haury is reprinted face to face with a good English translation by H. B. Dewing. The reader of these pages is strongly recommended to consult at any rate the right-hand pages of this most useful work. Anyone with any knowledge of Greek will find the left-hand pages still more fascinating.

Procopius himself begins with the Persian wars, which are the subject of his first two books (Vol. I of the Loeb edition). Our approach as Westerners is naturally from the west, and it will be more convenient to begin with the Vandalic wars that led to the recovery of northern Africa or Libya, as the whole of North Africa exclusive of Egypt was formerly called.

(a) *The Vandalic War and the Recovery of North Africa*

(Procopius, *Wars* III–IV)

The account of the Libyan campaigns is prefaced (III. i. f.) by a summary of the events that had led to the conquest of Libya by the Vandals in the general break-up of the empire that took place when Arcadius and Honorius were emperors of the East and West respectively. When these two unhappy brothers succeeded their father

Theodosius the Great in A.D. 395, the empire was still practically intact; Chapter i of Book III is devoted to an interesting account of the extent of the empire from the Straits of Gibraltar to the Caucasus. From one end to the other of the undivided empire was 347 days' journey. The emperor of the East held territory extending 120 days' journey with Cyrene and Dyrrachium (Durazzo or Dürres in Albania) as his western limits, the Western empire accounted for the rest. Procopius then proceeds (III. ii) to tell how in the reign of Honorius barbarians took possession of his lands. The most important of these barbarians were Goths, Visigoths and Vandals. 'These all differ from one another in name, as has been stated, but are distinguishable by nothing else at all; for they all have white skins and fair hair; they are tall and goodly in appearance, observe the same customs and similar religious practices, being all of the Arian faith, and have a single language called Gothic. My impression is that they were all originally of a single race, and only later got their distinctive names from their several leaders. This people dwelt of old beyond the river Danube' (III. ii. 3–6). Next follows an account of the capture of Rome by the Visigoth Alaric in A.D. 410, of the revolt of Britain from the Romans in A.D. 407, and of the withdrawal of the Visigoths into Gaul after Alaric's death, and of how the Goths (or Ostrogoths as they are more generally called) crossed the Danube and started on the migration that ultimately led to the founding of the Ostrogoth kingdom in Italy with its capital at Ravenna, whose further history, as we are here informed, is treated later, in the Gothic Wars (*Wars*, V–VIII).

Meanwhile the Vandals, from their home about the Maeotic Lake (Sea of Azov), 'being hard pressed by famine, migrated to the land of the Germans, who are now called Franks, on the river Rhine, bringing with them as allies the Alans, a Gothic race' (III. iii. 1, cf. the titles claimed by Justinian in the preface to the *Digest* quoted at the heading of this chapter). From there they moved on into Spain, where they were granted the right to settle by Honorius shortly before his death in A.D. 423. It was soon after this, when Valentinian III (A.D. 425–55) was emperor and his mother Galla Placidia (the forceful sister of Arcadius and Honorius whose tomb with its rich mosaics is still to be seen at Ravenna) was acting as regent, that the Vandals under their king Gizeric, Gaiseric or Genseric, crossed over from Spain into Africa (A.D. 429). The best part of what is now Algeria, Tunis, and Tripoli was torn by them from the Roman empire and became a Vandalic kingdom.

The name of Vandal has become synonymous with wanton destruction, and the history of Gizeric's treatment of the conquered Libyans illustrates the way they earned their reputation. 'Many were banished or put to death, for many serious charges were brought against them; but the one that was regarded as the most serious of all was that a person had money of his own and was concealing it' (III. v. 16–17). To prevent the conquered Libyans from having any centre at which to organize revolt, Gizeric demolished the walls of all the cities except Carthage. Later in his reign every year at the beginning of spring he made raids into Sicily and Italy, enslaving some of the cities, razing others to the ground, and plundering everything. The first of these destructive raids was made against Rome itself (III. v. 2, 8, 22–25). He seems indeed to invite comparison with his contemporary Attila the Hun, with whom on occasion he had negotiations (Bury I. 291).

Gizeric lived to a good old age, having ruled the Vandals thirty-nine years from the date when he captured Carthage. He died in A.D. 477 (III. vii. 29–30). He had completely defeated the great force sent against him by the emperor Leo in A.D. 467 (III. vi); but Leo's successor Zeno (474–91) came to an agreement with him, and signed an endless truce which was observed both by Zeno himself and by his successor Anastasius (491–518) (III. vii. 26). Gizeric is a classic example of the ruler who, after spending most of a long life in circumventing his enemies by craft and driving them out of their possessions by force, ended his days almost in the odour of sanctity – a precursor in some ways of characters like Frederick the Great and Bismarck.

The Vandals do not appear to have undergone any sudden conversion to the ways of gentleness and peace. Honoric, the son and successor of Gizeric, forced the Christians of Libya to change over to the Arian faith, and 'any whom he found not readily yielding to him he burnt, or destroyed by some other mode of death. There were many too whose tongues he cut out at the very roots: these men were still in my days going about in Byzantium enjoying the unimpaired use of their speech and feeling no ill effects at all from this punishment' (III. viii. 4). Gundamund, who in A.D. 484 succeeded Honoric, subjected the orthodox Christians to still more cruel tortures, though we are given no details; but his brother Trasamund, who succeeded him in 496, though likewise an ardent proselytizer in the Arian cause, is described (III. viii. 8f.) as a high-minded man who sought to win converts by offering them honours and offices or great sums of money, or, if they were criminals, remission of punishment. Hilderic, who succeeded him in A.D. 523, continued the mild policy of his predecessor and was a close friend of Justinian, who now controlled the policy of his uncle, the old emperor Justin (518–27).

Under the gentle Hilderic it looked as though an era might be beginning for North Africa in which the Vandals, in friendly relation with the emperor, might gradually and peacefully accept the ways, if not the allegiance, of the empire. Two individuals appear to have been mainly responsible for the catastrophic course that events actually followed, namely Gelimer the Vandal and Justinian. Both men were reacting, in very different ways, to a sudden change that had taken place in the international situation. The Vandals in North Africa had suffered their first great setback when the army of Trasamund was almost annihilated by the Moors (III. viii. 14–29). Under Hilderic they suffered another heavy disaster from the same quarter (III. ix. 3), and what was equally serious they quarrelled with the Ostrogoths of Italy. To Justinian, already emperor in fact and waiting to succeed his uncle, it must have seemed that he was being providentially summoned to the throne just at the moment marked out for the recovery of the Western provinces. But Gelimer the son of Geilaris the son of Genzon the son of Gizeric saw the same events with very different eyes. As second eldest male descendant of Gizeric he was heir to the Vandal throne, and he saw his inheritance being betrayed by his kinsman Hilderic into the hands of Justinian. Accordingly he conspired with the noblest of the Vandals, seized the supreme power, and imprisoned Hilderic and his chief officers (A.D. 530). Justinian, who by now had succeeded his uncle, at once protested; Gelimer replied by blinding Hilderic's chief general and putting the old king himself into stricter confinement, charging them both with planning flight to Constantinople. Procopius records a further exchange of protests between Gelimer and Justinian; but neither made the slightest concession to the other. Justinian patched up a peace with Persia and prepared for war with the Vandals.

The proposed war was not greeted with enthusiasm by the emperor's advisers. 'The praetorian prefect and the controller of the treasury and others who were charged with the collection of the public and imperial taxes were particularly distressed and anxious, for they reckoned that they would have to contribute immense sums to meet the needs of the war and that they would be granted no consideration or extension of time. And each of the generals, expecting that he would be given the command, shrank back in fear at the great danger of the fighting he would have to engage in, based upon his ships, on hostile territory against a great and mighty kingdom, always assuming that he escaped the perils of the sea and safely arrived there' (III. x. 3–4). The troops just back from the Persian war were equally unwilling to start a fresh campaign: the military prestige of the Vandals was still immense, and they seem, like their commanders, to have been hardly more afraid of the Vandals than of the sea they would have to cross before the campaign began. The praetorian prefect, John the Cappadocian, is said to have urged the difficulty of mastering Libya while Italy and Sicily were in alien occupation (III. x. 15). John's arguments made some impression on the emperor and checked his eager desire for the war; 'but one of the priests whom they call bishops came from the east and said he wished to have word with the emperor. And when admitted to his presence he declared that God had charged him in a dream to go to the emperor and re- prove him because, after undertaking to rescue the Christians in Libya from tyrants, he then for no reason had shrunk back. "And yet," He had said, "if he goes to war, I myself will help him and make him lord of Libya"' (III. x. 18–20). The bishop was probably preaching to the converted. At any rate the emperor began to organize a large expeditionary force of which Belisarius was to be generalissimo. Two incidents at the outset much helped the project. Tripolis revolted from Gelimer and aided by a small force sent by the emperor came over to his side, and Gelimer's governor in Sardinia also revolted and sought Justinian's help.

The main armada (III. xi) was made up of 10,000 foot soldiers and 5,000 horsemen; 500 ships were required to transport them, and 92 fast fighting ships escorted them. At last, in A.D. 533, 'when it was now the seventh year of Justinian's reign, about the summer solstice, the emperor commanded the general's ship to anchor off the strand before the imperial palace. There Epiphanius, the arch-priest of the city, after prayers proper to the occasion, embarked on the ship one of the soldiers who had recently been baptized and taken the name of Christian. And thereupon the general Belisarius and his wife Antonina set sail' (III. xii. 1–2). Procopius goes on to relate how he too was with them, and recounts a dream which caused him, though previously he had greatly feared the perils of the expedition, to regain confidence and courage. The whole voyage plainly made a deep impression on him. At Abydos on the Dardanelles Belisarius made a public example of two of his men, Huns by race, who during a drinking bout had killed a comrade. The two offenders were impaled on a hill near by; Belisarius delivered a sermon on drunkenness and violence, and 'the whole army, when they heard his words and looked up and saw the two men impaled, feared exceedingly and resolved to live soberly' (III. xii. 22).

From the Dardanelles the armada sailed across the Aegean and round the Peloponnese past Matapan to Methone. Here they were becalmed and put ashore and a serious epidemic broke out, caused by the rotten half-baked bread with which they had been supplied by the praetorian prefect John of Cappadocia. Belisarius saved the situation by supplying the men with local bread, and reported the scandal to the emperor; but he did not at the time bring any punishment on John (III. xiii. 11–20). On the passage from Zante to Sicily there was another calm, and now the drinking water went bad, all except that on Belisarius' own ship, where his wife Antonina preserved it by storing it in glass jars buried in sand in a dark cabin in the hold of the ship (III. xiii. 23–24).

Our narrative now brings us to Sicily, which was then, as now, of fundamental importance for the command of the Mediterranean. When Belisarius first landed there, it was part of the Ostrogoth kingdom that had recently passed from the great Theoderic to his grandson Athalaric, for whom his mother Amalasuntha was acting as regent. The Vandals were not on the best of terms with the Goths. Amalasuntha had cultivated the friendship of Justinian and had promised him to provide a market for his army, which she now proceeded to do (III. xiv. 6). If we are to believe Procopius, it was only after Belisarius had reached the island that he started drawing up a plan of campaign, a statement which becomes credible and comprehensible if we assume that everything turned on the sincerity of Amalasuntha's professions. Procopius represents his commander as desperately worried by the fact that he knew neither what manner of men the Vandals were, how he ought to fight against them, nor where to make his base. Accordingly he ordered Procopius, as his special adviser, to proceed to Syracuse from

the position under Aetna where the Roman army was
encamped, and try to gather information. In this the
historian, according to his own account, was highly
successful. He unexpectedly met there an old friend
engaged in the shipping business, and learnt from him
that the Vandals were not in the least expecting an
invasion and that Gelimer had detached a large part of
his forces to put down the revolt in Sardinia. This friend
actually produced an employee of his who had come
from Carthage, the Vandal capital, only three days
before. Procopius seized the occasion. 'He took the
servant by the hand and walked on to the harbour of
Arethusa where his vessel lay at anchor ... And embarking with him on the ship he gave orders to hoist sail
and set out at full speed for Caucana. The servant's
master stood on the shore wondering that Procopius was
not restoring the man to him, but when the ship was
already sailing Procopius shouted out to him and begged
him not to be annoyed, for it was essential that the servant should see the general and guide the army to Libya
before he came back to Syracuse, which he would very
shortly, in possession of much money.' The armada set
sail complete with this guide, and after touching at Gozo
and Malta landed in Libya at a place called Caput Vada,
five days' journey from Carthage for an active man
(III. xiv).

The disembarkation took place about three months
after the departure from Byzantium. One of the first
acts of Belisarius after the landing was to inflict corporal
punishment on some of his troops who had gone into the
country and plundered the crops; and once again the
exemplary punishment was followed by a public lecture
from the commanding officer in which he pointed out
how such conduct was throwing into the arms of the
Vandals the native Libyans they had come to liberate
(III. xvi). Justinian indeed claimed to be at war neither
with the Libyans nor with the Vandals, but to be en-
forcing respect for the testament of Gizeric, which had
been violated by the usurper Gelimer. A letter to this
effect had been brought from him by Belisarius to the

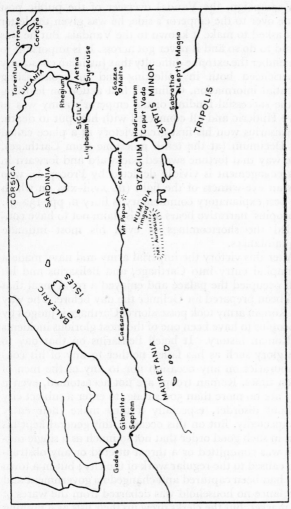

Map to illustrate the Campaign in North Africa

magistrates of the Vandals, and when, at the outset of the campaign, the Vandal overseer of the public post came over to the emperor's side, he was given the letter and asked to make it known to the Vandals. But he was afraid to do so and it never got across. It is important to remember the extreme difficulty that Justinian constantly experienced both in collecting and in broadcasting essential information. Gelimer's first action on learning of the successful landing of the emperor's army was to have Hilderic and all connected with him put to death.

Belisarius won his first great victory at a place called Ad Decimum (at the tenth milestone from Carthage). The way that fortune swayed backward and forward in this engagement is vividly depicted by Procopius, who was an eye-witness of the fight (III. xviii–xix, on which the best explanatory commentary is Bury II. pp. 132–5). Procopius' narrative bears out his claim not to have concealed the shortcomings of even his most intimate acquaintances.

After this victory the imperial army and navy made a triumphal entry into Carthage, and Belisarius and his staff occupied the palace and enjoyed a royal meal that had been prepared for Gelimer the day before. The way the Roman army took possession of Carthage is judged by Procopius to have been one of the most glorious incidents in Roman history. 'It befell Belisarius on that day to win glory such as has fallen neither to any of his contemporaries on any occasion nor to any of the men of olden times. Roman troops are not accustomed, even if they are no more than 500 strong, to enter a subject city without disorder, especially if they make their entry unexpectedly. But on this occasion this general kept his men in such good order that not so much as a single outrage was committed or a threat uttered or any obstruction caused to the regular work of the city; but in a town that had been captured and changed its government and allegiance no household was debarred from the wares of the market, but the clerks drew up their lists as if nothing had happened and quartered the men in the houses, whilst the troops themselves purchased their morning

meal in the market as they severally chose, and went
quietly about their ways' (III. xxi. 8–10).

In spite of Belisarius' efforts to prevent his army ill-
treating the native population, Gelimer secured a
certain amount of sympathy and support. His brother
Tzazon, who had successfully crushed the revolt in
Sardinia, hastened back to his help on hearing of the
disaster of Decimum. Gelimer also succeeded in tampering with the loyalty of a contingent of Huns who were
serving in Belisarius's motley force. A second battle was
fought at a place called Tricamaron, something under
twenty miles from Carthage (IV. ii. f.), about the middle
of December A.D. 533, three months after the Roman
army came to Carthage. Tzazon was killed, Gelimer ran
away, and the Romans gained another great victory and
an immense amount of loot. Discipline was for a time at
an end. The imperial soldiers were extremely poor and
had suddenly become masters of great wealth and of the
persons of many young and exceedingly lovely women,
and as a result forgot all fear of the enemy and respect
for Belisarius (IV. iv). Procopius was convinced that if
the temperamental Gelimer had not been in full flight
they would have been absolutely at his mercy. Gelimer
escaped to Mount Papua, in the heart of Numidia, where
he was ultimately starved into surrender and taken to
Constantinople. We owe Procopius a great debt for the
interesting and convincing study which he has left us of
this degenerate Nordic. He lost the battle of Decimum
because he had a sudden nervous breakdown on discovering the body of Ammatas, another brother, on the
battlefield; and he fled from Tricamaron after the fall
in battle of Tzazon, with whom he had had a most
emotional reunion shortly before. His surrender on
Mount Papua followed a scene that he had witnessed of
two starving children fighting for a scrap of food.
'This distressful incident was too much for Gelimer'
(IV. vii. 6).

The urge to melodramatize himself seems to have
been the most permanent ingredient of Gelimer's
character. Some time before his final surrender on Mount

Papua he had been urged to submit by the Roman officer who had been detailed to maintain the siege of the mountain. This officer himself is an interesting character. His name was Pharas: 'he was a man of vigour and great seriousness and well endowed with virtue in spite of his being a Herule by birth; and for a Herule not to abandon himself to faithlessness and drunkenness but to have some claim to virtue is a hard thing and deserving of much praise' (IV. iv. 29–30). Pharas urged Gelimer to submit and pointed out that he and his fellow Herulians, though of noble birth, were proud to be the servants of an emperor. How absurd to think it the depth of degradation to be a fellow-slave with Belisarius! (IV. vi. 21). When Gelimer had read Pharas' letter he wept bitterly and wrote his famous reply in which he refused to surrender but begged Pharas to send him a lyre, a loaf of bread, and a sponge – the loaf because he had not seen a single baked loaf on Mount Papua, the sponge because one of his eyes was inflamed and swollen from lack of washing, and the lyre because he had composed an ode on his present misfortunes and was impatient to bewail and lament them to the accompaniment of a lyre (IV. vi. 27–33). Gelimer was a good lyre player. The request was made some time before the incident of the two children and the scrap of food.

When, however, Gelimer was finally brought captive before Belisarius (IV. vii. 14f.), he indulged not in tears but in uncontrollable laughter, which made some of the onlookers think that his mind had become unhinged. But his friends argued that he was perfectly sane, and that after the sudden reversal of his fortunes in his old age he realized that the lot of man is only worthy of much laughter. Procopius suspends judgement with a Herodotean aphorism: 'now concerning the laughter of Gelimer let each speak as he thinks, both friend and foe' (IV. vii. 16). The modern reader, with the exceptional opportunities that contemporary history has granted him of studying similar pathological phenomena in high places, will have little doubt that Gelimer's mind was just as sound or as unsound after his surrender as before, and that he was once again indulging his remarkable instinct for the telling melodramatic gesture. It is psychologically in keeping with the rest of his make-up that a streak of effeminacy ran all through his character, and that these copious tears for his own people did not prevent him from treating those whom he feared or hated with the most inhuman cruelty.

The captive king was taken to Constantinople, exhibited in Belisarius' triumph, and brought before the emperor Justinian, on which occasion he very prudently neither wept nor laughed, but merely went on repeating the words of the Hebrew scriptures, 'Vanity of vanities, all is vanity'. Justinian treated him very leniently and granted him estates of no mean value in Galatia, where he was allowed to live with his family. He might have received the signal honour of being enrolled among the patricians, but this would have meant abandoning his Arian faith, which he refused to do (IV. ix. 9–14). We may charitably count this firmness of his for righteousness as well as prudence.

While Pharas had been dealing with Gelimer, Belisarius, from his headquarters at Carthage, had sent various officers with detachments of troops to various parts of the Vandal domains (IV. v). One was sent to secure Sardinia and Corsica, another Caesarea in Mauretania (Cherchel near Algiers, thirty days' journey from Carthage for an active man), another the fort commanding the Straits of Gibraltar, another the Balearic Islands.

With the surrender of Gelimer the Vandalic war was ended (IV. viii. 1) and North Africa apparently reconquered (A.D. 534). But as so often in North African history, this rapid conquest proved very illusory. Immediately on Belisarius' recall to Constantinople the Moors rose in revolt. 'When it was expected that the imperial armada would arrive in Libya, the Moors, fearing that they would receive some harm from it, had resorted to oracles delivered by their women; for that a man should deliver oracles is not lawful in that nation, but women who become possessed as a result of certain holy rites foretell the future as well as any of the ancient

oracles. Now when on this occasion they made inquiry
in the way just stated, the women replied: a host from
the waters, overthrow of the Vandals, destruction and
defeat of the Moors when the Roman general comes
without a beard' (IV. viii. 12–14). The expedition duly
arrived by sea, but as the generals were bearded, the
Moors concluded that it portended ill for the Vandals
but not for themselves. The overthrow of the Vandals
confirmed the first part of their interpretation and encouraged them to attack the conquerors of their conquerors. A revolt broke out, and Belisarius, who was on
the point of embarking for Constantinople, had only
time to hand over the command to Solomon, a very able
young officer from the Eastern frontier, who was a
eunuch. Solomon did much to restore the situation, but
in A.D. 544 he fell in battle as a result of disaffection
among his troops.

The history of the next few years is a most unedifying
welter of perfidy and treachery, in which rival leaders
mismanaged campaigns against disaffected natives and
one another. The two books of Procopius' Vandalic Wars
end with an exciting account of the liquidation of one
of the worst of these chiefs. The net result of all these
senseless struggles was that the land of Libya became for
the most part depopulated (IV. xxiii. 27), but the narrative ends with the record of the appointment as governor
of Libya of John Troglita, who proved an able soldier
and administrator. 'And thus,' to quote the last words
of the Vandalic Wars, 'it came to pass that the survivors
of the Libyans, few in number and utterly impoverished,
found at long last a little hard-won peace' (IV. xxviii. 52).
The exploits of this John are the subject of one of the
least read of the many little read Latin epics, the
Johannid of the contemporary poet Corippus.

CHAPTER III

The Wars – continued

(b) The Gothic Wars and the Recovery of Sicily and Italy

(Procopius, *Wars* V–VIII)

*

THE story of the recovery of Sicily and Italy runs on closely parallel lines to that of North Africa, and the events that led up to it must have confirmed Justinian in his belief that he was divinely pre-ordained to bring back to the one fold and the one true faith all the lost possessions of the empire, Rome itself included. The course of events in Italy from the deposition of Romulus Augustulus in A.D. 476 to the time of Justinian's intervention is vividly described in the first few chapters of the first book of the Gothic wars. Shortly before the reign of Romulus Augustulus the Romans had induced several Gothic nations to form an alliance with them. The results are described by Procopius: 'the more the barbarians flourished among them, the more the Roman troops sank in esteem, and under the specious name of alliance were mastered and oppressed by the newcomers ..., who finally claimed that they should receive a share of all the lands of Italy. ... Now there was among them a certain man, by name Odoacer, belonging to the emperor's bodyguard, who agreed to do what they demanded if they placed him on the throne ... and by giving the barbarians a third part of the land he secured their firm allegiance and maintained his tyranny for ten years' (v. i. 4–8). Odoacer appears to have been a Scirian Goth, in which case he belonged to one of those Gothic nations with whom the Romans had recently formed an alliance.

Odoacer was overthrown by Theoderic, king of the Ostrogoths, who had till recently been settled in Thrace and during the ascendancy of Odoacer in Italy had attacked the Eastern empire and been persuaded by the

Emperor Zeno, 'who always knew how to turn a situation to good account, to proceed to Italy, attack Odoacer, and win the West for himself and the Goths. ... Theoderic was delighted with the suggestion and went to Italy followed by people of the Goths, who placed in their waggons their women and children and all their movables that they could carry' (v. i. 10–12). Odoacer underwent a three-year siege in Ravenna (whose unique position on one of the mouths of the Po, where almost alone in the Mediterranean there is a strong tide, is described in detail by our historian). Then an agreement was made that Odoacer and Theoderic should reign jointly. But after a while Theoderic liquidated his colleague in the fashionable way by inviting him to dinner and there murdering him, 'and having in this manner won over all of his barbarian enemies who happened to survive, he made himself sole ruler of both Goths and Italians' (v. i. 25). Possibly Odoacer may have given Theoderic just cause to suspect him, for after this preliminary act of frightfulness he appears to have ruled well according to his lights. Procopius has high praise for him: 'he was extraordinarily careful to maintain justice and was a firm upholder of the laws; he guarded the land securely from the neighbouring barbarians and reached a very high level of intelligence and courage; he scarcely ever committed any act of injustice against his subjects himself, nor, if anyone else attempted anything of the kind, did he allow it, except that the Goths did share out among themselves the portion of the land which Odoacer had granted to his own partisans. ... He grew to be greatly loved among both Goths and Italians' (v. i. 27–9).

The constitutional position of Theoderic is well defined by Procopius, who says that 'though in name a tyrant, yet in fact he was a genuine emperor, no less so than any who has ever won fame in that office' (v. i. 29). He did not, however, assume the title of emperor, but was called merely king till the end of his life (i. 26). It looks as if he was feeling his way towards a new order in which West Europe and North Africa should form something very like national states as we now know them, while the East was to remain a rather composite and heterogeneous empire. It was perhaps an essential part of his policy to regard the Eastern empire as the senior and most important state of the new order, but as nothing more than *prima inter pares*. He seems to have recognized the distinctive merits both of his own rude Goths and of the Italian heirs of the ancient Roman civilization whom they had conquered. The tedious and time-serving Cassiodorus was one of his secretaries or ministers, and our knowledge of his reign is largely derived from the long-winded and often hardly intelligible pages of Cassiodorus' official correspondence as secretary both to Theoderic himself and to his successors at Ravenna whose struggle with Justinian is our immediate concern.

Another and far greater Roman who served Theoderic was Boethius. On one occasion he had been commissioned by the Gothic king to procure a harper to send to Clovis, king of the Franks. We have the letter composed by the egregious Cassiodorus as Theoderic's secretary, charging him with this task (*Variae* ii. 40). The letter discourses on the nature of music, enumerates the different scales or modes, quotes instances of the power of melody, and concludes: 'be sure to get us that harper who will go forth like another Orpheus to charm the beast-like hearts of the barbarians.' In A.D. 524, however, Boethius fell under suspicion of plotting against Theoderic and was put to death. It was while under sentence of death that he wrote his famous *Consolations of Philosophy*. In the following year his father-in-law Symmachus, who had stood by him, was also executed.

The death of Theoderic himself, according to Procopius (v. i. 32ff.) was the direct result of this, the first and last act of injustice that Theoderic committed. A few days after the execution he was served at dinner with the head of a great fish, and fancying that he saw before him the head of the murdered Symmachus was seized with a violent fit of shivering, rushed to his bed, and shortly after died. After his death (A.D. 526) the government was carried on by his daughter Amalasuntha, acting as regent for her eight-year-old son Athalaric. Her regency, as recorded by Procopius (v. ii f.), shows that the outburst against the two great Romans which clouded the end of Theoderic's reign was not an isolated incident but part of an anti-Roman reaction among certain sections of the Goths in Italy, that was to lead to the intervention of Justinian, who became emperor within a year of Theoderic's death. Amalasuntha at Ravenna, like Hilderic at Carthage, was strongly pro-Roman. Her wisdom and justice are highly praised by Procopius. She wished to give her son the education of a Roman aristocrat and was already making him go to school (v. ii. 4–6). The Goths were by no means pleased. Their leading men complained that their king was not being educated as he should. Letters, they said, were far removed from manliness. Theoderic had never allowed the Goths to send their sons to school and he himself had won a mighty kingdom although he had never even heard of letters (v. ii. 8–16). Amalasuntha had to give way about her son's education. The boy was handed over to the anti-Roman faction and became a particularly repulsive specimen of the vicious Nordic degenerate. His mother continued the struggle, but made preparations for retiring to the protection of Justinian. That she did not do so immediately was due to the fact that she succeeded in murdering her three leading opponents.

The situation was further complicated by the behaviour of another member of Theoderic's family, his nephew Theodatus. Some account of this man is worth giving, not only because of the part he played but also because of the revealing picture of his character which Procopius has left us. 'He was already an elderly man, acquainted with Latin literature and Platonic philosophy, but altogether untrained in war and remote from active life though possessed by an extraordinary passion for money. He had acquired most of the estates in Tuscany and was eager to take the rest by force from their possessors. For to have a neighbour seemed to Theodatus a kind of misfortune' (v. iii. 1–2). He had in fact none of the generous qualities of the not altogether blameless Amalasuntha, with whom he was on such bad terms that he too formed the plan of realizing his riches and going to Constantinople.

It is at this stage that envoys from Justinian first appear in Italy. They were Hypatius the bishop of Ephesus, and Demetrius from Philippi in Macedonia. Their professed object was to discuss some controversial points of Christian theology with their opposite numbers in Italy, but they also had secret meetings with Theodatus, while at the same time another envoy visited Amalasuntha, nominally to complain that she refused to hand over the fortress of Lilybaeum in west Sicily. To this complaint Amalasuntha made answer that Lilybaeum belonged to the Goths from of old and ought to continue theirs. But secretly she agreed to hand over all Italy (and presumably its dependency Sicily) (v. iii. 28). Everything seemed to be going excellently for Justinian when the whole situation was changed by the death of Athalaric (the result of eight years of precocious dissipation) and an ill-judged attempt by Amalasuntha to come to an agreement with Theodatus, with whom she had been violently and very justifiably quarrelling, on the terms that he should succeed Athalaric as nominal king while Amalasuntha retained the real power. Theodatus closed with her offer, but instead of playing the passive part that it assigned to him he at once imprisoned Amalasuntha after putting to death her chief supporters. Once again we hear of the slowness with which news travelled to headquarters at Byzantium. When at last the facts were established, the emperor promptly intervened with the imperial army, once more, as previously in Libya, as champion of the Romanized and more civilized faction of the Nordic barbarians, though before the war started Amalasuntha herself had also been done away with (v. iv. 22–31; and see Chapter X, p. 215f.).

The Gothic war began in the ninth year of Justinian's reign (v. v. 1) with campaigns in Dalmatia and Sicily. The Dalmatian operations were directed by Mundus, general of Illyricum, the Sicilian by Belisarius with a mixed force totalling some 7,500 men. This is the point at which the Franks first appear in our narrative. Justinian asked them as orthodox Christians to help him against the Arian Goths. They at once agreed, though what they actually did we shall see later. Meanwhile Sicily quickly fell to Belisarius. By the end of the year (A.D. 535) the whole island was in his hands. These successes caused Theodatus to offer to abdicate. Justinian had agreed to let him come and live in honourable retirement at Constantinople, when the Romans suffered a temporary setback in Dalmatia. Theodatus at once went back on his word and imprisoned Justinian's envoy. Belisarius now crossed over from Messina into Italy. The first serious opposition was encountered at Naples. The Neapolitans as a whole had been inclined to submit, but the leaders of the war party used an argument that has not been without weight in similar circumstances in more recent times. If they submitted and the Goths won the war their fate would be terrible, 'but should we now show ourselves loyal to the Goths, they will confer great benefits on us if they win, while Belisarius will be forgiving if he proves victor' (v. viii. 37). The city stood a siege of twenty days. Then the Romans found a way in by an old aqueduct. The town was stormed in spite of the desperate resistance of a body of Jews who lived there, and a massacre began which was only with difficulty stopped by Belisarius (v. ix–x).

After this disaster the Goths deposed Theodatus and appointed in his place a certain Vittigis (Wittig), who promptly had Theodatus murdered. Vittigis was faced with that nightmare of central European commanders, the war on two fronts, and made the fatal mistake of dealing with the wrong front first. He left a garrison of four thousand men to hold Rome against Belisarius and himself marched back to Ravenna to face the Franks (v. xi. In the next two chapters Procopius launches into an interesting digression on earlier Frankish history).

Meanwhile the people of Rome, warned by the fate of Naples and strongly urged by Pope Silverius, sent to Belisarius promising to surrender the city without a battle (v. xiv. 4–5). Belisarius accordingly marched on Rome and entered the city by one gate as the Gothic garrison withdrew by another; and thus 'Rome was again brought under the Romans after sixty years' (v. xiv. 14).

There can be little doubt that Procopius felt at this time that he was a witness of momentous happenings, that in

The Campaign in Italy

the words of Virgil 'magnus ab integro saeclorum nascitur ordo'. Like one of his models, Herodotus, he was a master of digression, and his digression at this point in his narrative is significant. Belisarius made his march on Rome along the less famous of the two great south roads, the Via Latina, but our historian seizes the occasion to observe that this runs parallel to the most famous of all Roman roads, the Via Appia, 'made by Appius the consul nine centuries before', and to describe how it had been made and how marvellously it had lasted (v. xiv. 6–11). The Roman roads were, as everyone knows, the foundation of the Roman empire, the arteries that had enabled it to grow into one great living organism, and from this description of the prototype of them all, and its magnificent state of preservation, the reader is surely meant to draw his own conclusion.

Belisarius meanwhile attended strictly to business. He repaired the walls and provisioned the city in preparation for a siege. It was not long before Vittigis, having, as he thought, settled the Frankish question, marched against Rome (v. xvi. 19ff.). The siege lasted over a year and was full of lively incidents which have often an epic ring: not surprisingly, for though the Goths were in some ways degenerate we are in fact back in the heroic age. The Goths and Germans who dismembered the Roman empire in the fifth and sixth centuries A.D. have affinities with Homer's Achaeans who had destroyed the ancient Minoan cities and civilization nearly two millennia earlier. The parallel has been brilliantly worked out by H. M. Chadwick in his *Heroic Age*. Many of Belisarius' own commanders were native Nordic chieftains employed by the empire, and Belisarius himself was an Illyrian or Thracian from a town with the symptomatic name of Germania (III. xi. 21); he went into battle with a large retinue of personal retainers. The siege of Rome by the Goths, like that of Troy by the Achaeans, was by no means a blockade, and Belisarius, whose forces were fewer but far better equipped and more mobile, constantly sent out small bands of exceptionally good warriors who cut up scattered bands of the enemy or

lured larger forces within range of the artillery that he
had set up on the city walls. In one particularly Homeric
encounter Belisarius himself was cut off just outside the
walls and the whole cause of the Romans was thrown
into great danger because the commander-in-chief began
to fight in the front ranks like a private soldier. His horse
happened to be a grey with a conspicuous blaze, and
some deserters in the Gothic ranks recognized it and
raised the cry 'aim at the horse with the blaze'. Belisarius performed prodigies of valour and his faithful
bodyguard, closing round their chief and his gallant grey,
displayed a heroism unmatched in all history. In true
Homeric style 'the whole fight was focussed on the body
of one man' (v. xviii. 13). It is equally typical of the
heroic atmosphere that the hero's wife plays her part in
the struggle: 'and when it was far on in the night,
Belisarius, still fasting, was with difficulty forced by his
wife and friends to taste a very little bread' (v. xviii. 43).
A Homeric hero would have refreshed himself more
generously, but the spirit is the same.

Early on in the siege the Goths put the aqueducts out
of action and thereby inflicted an irremediable injury
on the city. From that day to this they have remained
the imposing ruins that we still see as we approach Rome.
The great baths that were one of the chief amenities of the
city ceased to function, and the townsmen began to
murmur against Belisarius as a result (v. xx. 5). Many
incidents centred round what are still familiar landmarks
and in some cases left their mark on them, as for instance
the assault that was made against the tomb of Hadrian
or Castle of S. Angelo as we now call it, destined to be
the scene, a thousand years later, of the military exploits
of Benvenuto Cellini. A colonnade ran at that time from
St Peter's to the tomb, and this enabled the Goths to
make a surprise attack. The defenders however drove off
their assailants by hurling down on them the statues
that then adorned the tomb (v. xxii. 12ff.).

But successes had their price. Belisarius had to send to
Constantinople to beg urgently for reinforcements for
his garrison, reduced to 5,000 men. The Goths occupied

Portus, the harbour on the north bank of the Tiber that had replaced the earlier Ostia. Nerves were getting frayed and suspicions were rife on both sides. Belisarius thought it expedient to send away to Greece the Pope Silverius, though he had been one of the leading advocates for admitting the imperial forces (v. xxv. 13). Vittigis put to death all the Roman senators who had remained at Ravenna (v. xxvi. 1). Twenty days after the Goths had occupied Portus Belisarius was reinforced by 1,600 horsemen, mostly Huns and Slavs. But this encouraged the Romans to risk a general engagement which ended badly for them (v. xxvii–xxix), after which they no longer dared to face a pitched battle (vi. i. 1).

The main reinforcements from Constantinople had not yet arrived, and 'at the beginning of the summer solstice' (A.D. 538) 'famine and plague simultaneously assailed the inhabitants of the city' (vi. iii. 1). Once more we find the imperial intelligence service somewhat primitive. There were rumours in the city that the relief force had already reached south Italy, so Procopius was sent to Naples to investigate (vi. iv. 1). Antonina was sent with him, nominally 'to await the issue there in safety' (vi. iv. 6), though it is doubtful whether this resourceful lady ever had any such intention. The reinforcements had not arrived, so Procopius raised a force of 500 men, loaded a lot of ships with grain, and waited for further developments. He may have seized the occasion to inspect Vesuvius, which at the time was rumbling more than usual. At any rate he gives us at this point in his narrative an interesting account of the famous volcano (vi. iv. 21 ff.). When, shortly after, the reinforcements did reach Naples, part were sent on to Ostia by sea, the rest made their way by the coast road to Rome. Belisarius, forewarned of their approach, diverted the enemy with his usual skill and Rome was relieved. The vivid account that Procopius has left us of these operations was written eight years after they occurred. This we happen to know because he tells us that one of the Roman commanders was shot through the face with an arrow of which the iron barb completely disappeared inside his head. 'Five years later the tip of it became visible projecting from his face, and this is the third year that it has been gradually coming out. So we may expect that at long last the whole of it will work its way out. But it has not impeded the man in any way' (VI. v. 25–7). Such is the note on which Procopius thinks fit to end his account of the relief of Rome. Thucydides, whom he so often imitates, would have found it childish. But Herodotus, and perhaps Xenophon, would have understood and approved.

The safe arrival of these reinforcements disheartened the Goths. They at once opened negotiations. Meanwhile the Romans reoccupied Portus and received from the Archbishop of Milan an invitation to occupy that city, second only to Rome among the cities of the West in size, wealth and population (VI. vii. 35ff.), and an ominous incident occurred between Belisarius and one of his officers, the Thracian Constantine, who had seized at Perugia two valuable daggers belonging to a distinguished and loyal Roman named Praesidius. Belisarius' attempt to make the Thracian chief restore his plunder led to a scene in which Constantine tried to murder Belisarius. Some time later Belisarius had the refractory officer done away with (VI. viii). In the *Secret History* Procopius expands this account and shows that the intrigues of Belisarius' wife Antonina (see below, Chapter X, p. 213) lay behind Constantine's execution. In any case the scene and its cause are typical of the sort of difficulty that Belisarius had constantly to deal with. It shows how thin was the veneer of civilization of these warriors from the outlying parts of the empire. Once again we are reminded of the quarrels amongst the Achaean chieftains in the Homeric epics.

The siege of Rome was finally raised as the result of Belisarius sending into north Italy a force under John the nephew of Vitalian, which occupied Ariminum (Rimini) only one day's journey south of the Gothic capital Ravenna. John had correctly reasoned (VI. x. 7) that if the Goths learned that a Roman army was close to Ravenna, they would instantly, in anxiety for the safety of that city, abandon the siege of Rome. They did so, and were severely handled by Belisarius as they marched away. The situation would have been still better for the Romans if John had not disobeyed the orders of Belisarius and let himself be shut up in Rimini with a large force of cavalry which would have been far more useful operating from outside. Things were further complicated by the arrival from Constantinople of large fresh forces under an official of very high rank named Narses (VI. xiii. 16f.). Their coming meant further dissensions and divided counsels in the Roman high command (on which see further VI. xviii, xix, xxi. 16f.). Rimini was however relieved (VI. xvii. 12ff.), Narses was recalled (VI. xxii. 4), and Belisarius prepared to attack Ravenna.

In despair of help from his fellow barbarians in the West, Vittigis sent a mission to Chosroes, king of Persia, with whom Justinian had been at peace since the beginning of his war with the Vandals. Chosroes, being by now for other reasons ready to break the 'Endless Peace', declared war again, and Justinian felt obliged to recall Belisarius to deal with this more pressing peril. He ordered Belisarius to offer Vittigis really favourable terms. But Belisarius by this time felt that he had the Goths at his mercy, and now he in his turn disobeyed orders and refused to ratify the generous terms that the emperor had already communicated to the Goths. The next step was with the Goths. They created a most interesting situation by offering to surrender if Belisarius would allow himself to be proclaimed emperor of the West. This proposal was backed by all the best of the Goths. 'They disliked the rule of Vittigis, since he had been so very unlucky; but they shrank from going over to the emperor, since they feared that if they became his slaves they would be forced to migrate from Italy and settle in Byzantium' (VI. xxix. 17). Vittigis himself supported the proposal. But Belisarius had his loyalties. When the envoys came with these proposals, 'he took the other oaths, but touching the kingship he said he would swear only to Vittigis himself and the rulers of the Goths' (VI. xxix. 27). In

short he traded on the Goths' conviction that he would
never refuse so alluring an offer. He refused it only
when he was already in Ravenna and master of the
situation.

Procopius tells us (VI. xxix, 32f.) that while he was watch-
ing the entry of the Romans into Ravenna the thought
struck him that 'it is not by men's intelligence or virtue
that enterprises succeed, but that there is some supernatural power that is always turning their plans awry ...
For though the Goths were far superior in numbers ...
and nothing had happened to break their spirit, still they
were being taken captive by inferior forces and held
it no outrage to be called slaves.' The reaction of the
Gothic women was cruder. They had been told by their
husbands that the Romans were huge men and their
army too numerous to count. When they actually saw
them marching into Ravenna they spat in their husbands'
faces and taunted them with cowardice. Belisarius dealt
gently with the Goths. Not long afterwards 'he set out
for Byzantium; and the winter came to an end and the
fifth year ended of this war of which Procopius wrote
the history' (VI finis, A.D. 540).

The rest of the history of the Gothic wars as recorded
by Procopius covers the reigns of the last two Gothic
kings, Totila and Teias (A.D. 541–52). It is gloomy
reading – a story of perplexity and indecision at headquarters as the conflict spread and fronts multiplied, of
inadequate forces and supplies, of divided commands
and consequent insubordination and lack of co-operation. But apart from the interest such tragedies must
always have, this very disintegration of Roman discipline
brings to the fore the practices of the barbarian chieftains
who formed so large a proportion of the commanders on
both sides. We get glimpses into the manners and customs
of the heroic age which was an outcome of the collapse
of Rome and has left us so fateful a legacy in the
Germanic epics that have done so much to mould the
mind of modern Germany. And from time to time the
forbears of many of the races of modern Europe flit across
the scene: Franks, Lombards, Slavs, Huns all play their

part, a fact which by itself makes the record one of unique interest.

Totila rapidly overran a great part of Italy from Tuscany to Calabria. The imperial commanders shut themselves up in various strong places while Totila collected the public taxes. As a result 'the Roman soldiers did not get their regular pay at the proper time ... which made them inclined still less to obey their officers and glad to remain inside the cities' (vii. vi. 5–7). Like others of these Nordic chieftains Totila could on occasion be generous. He is highly praised by Procopius for two such actions. When he had captured Cumae he treated with the utmost consideration the wives of some Roman senators who had been evacuated there; after he had starved Naples into surrender he took special measures to feed the population, increasing their ration gradually 'fearing that if they suddenly started eating their fill they would probably choke' (vii. viii. 1–4).

The fall of Naples caused Justinian to recall Belisarius from his command against the Persians and send him again to Italy in the summer of A.D. 544. But he was sent with quite inadequate forces and had to leave behind on the Persian front the picked force of personal retainers that he maintained out of his own capacious pocket. He travelled by way of his native Thrace, where he enlisted what troops he could, and finally assembled about 4,000 men at Salones (Spalato, Split) on the East Adriatic, intending to proceed from there to Ravenna (vii. x). Unfortunately, when he got to Pola, Totila discovered how small a force he had brought with him. He did so by a very simple trick. He sent to Belisarius five 'particularly inquisitive' men, who pretended to bring a message from one of the Roman commanders in Italy. The five looked carefully round the camp while waiting for their answer and reported to Totila what they had seen. Belisarius eventually reached Ravenna, but his efforts to win over adherents to the emperor failed.

The situation by now (early summer of 545) was desperate. Belisarius could do nothing but send an urgent appeal to Justinian. Meanwhile Totila went on recovering more cities and began the siege of Rome (VII. xiii). Since the Goths held Naples it was not easy to get supplies into Rome from Sicily, and there was soon a famine. In the hope of hastening relief from Constantinople Belisarius went across to Albania and waited at Epidamnus (Dyrrachium; Durazzo) for reinforcements, where some, but not nearly enough, ultimately reached him. Procopius' criticism of Belisarius' strategy at this point will be discussed in another chapter. It is enough here to note that he was growing very critical of his hero. The fact was that the empire was desperately short of men. This doubtless is why, after the despatch of these meagre reinforcements, 'the emperor sent Narses the eunuch to the Herules to persuade them to invade Italy. Many of them followed him into the regions towards Thrace. They were to winter there and be sent to join Belisarius at the beginning of spring. And it befell them on the way to do a great and unexpected service to the Romans. A horde of barbarian Sclaveni had recently crossed the Ister (Danube), plundered the lands in those parts, and enslaved a great number of Romans. The Herules suddenly encountered these barbarians, defeated and destroyed them, and set free all the prisoners they had enslaved' (VII. xiii. 21–5).

The siege of Rome went on. Belisarius sent reinforcements to the garrison he had left at Portus; but the officer commanding in Rome itself refused to co-operate with the relieving force. Their plans were betrayed to the Goths who ambushed and killed them. Pope Vigilius, at the time in Sicily, sent shiploads of corn to Rome, but they were intercepted near Portus and all on board were killed except a bishop named Valentius who was led alive to Totila. Totila questioned him, accused him of not telling the truth, and cut off both his hands. 'And the winter came to an end and the eleventh year ended of this war of which Procopius wrote the history' (VII. xv. 16). The famine in Rome grew worse. The military commanders disgraced themselves by selling corn and oxen to the rich at fabulous prices while the rest of the population lived or died on nettles. Belisarius, who had at last been reinforced at Dyrrachium, sailed across to south Italy and on from there to the Tiber. Bessas, the commandant in Rome, continued to behave with the same selfishness, and Belisarius' own subordinate at Portus, an officer named Isaac, though loyal, was equally undisciplined. He ruined Belisarius' attempt to get supplies into the city by disobeying instructions, leaving his post to have a hand in a reported victory of his commander and getting killed whilst doing so. The news of Isaac's disaster reached Belisarius while operations were still proceeding, and according to Procopius it so upset him, since he assumed that Portus was lost and his wife Antonina, whom he had left there, either killed or captured, that he broke off what looked like being a successful engagement to hurry back. Antonina and Portus were perfectly safe, but when Belisarius found how needless his alarm had been, he was so distressed that he fell into a fever that endangered his life (VII. xix. 32–3). The hero is not pictured as rising to the occasion. Rome fell to Totila and Bessas fled, leaving behind his ill-gotten gains.

Totila spared the lives of the Romans in the captured city. One of these was Rusticiana, widow of the famous Boethius and daughter of his friend and fellow-martyr Symmachus (VII. xx. 27–31). More remarkable still, he was persuaded to give up his intention of destroying the walls of Rome and turning the city into grazing land. This change of heart Procopius attributes to a letter he received from Belisarius. 'Did Totila,' the letter asked him, 'wish to go down to posterity as the man who destroyed the most glorious city in the world?' Totila read the letter many times, was convinced, and did Rome no further harm (VII. xxii. 17). It would be pleasing to think that this letter was written by Procopius himself. His account of how it impressed Totila is perhaps in favour of so thinking. Unfortunately the general opinion among Byzantinists seems to be that he was not at this time acting as Belisarius' secretary. The capture of Rome left Totila free to overrun south Italy; but this in its

turn enabled Belisarius to reoccupy Rome and rebuild
sketchily the part of the walls that Totila had demolished
before he received Belisarius' letter. Totila came back
and tried to recover Rome, but was not successful. All
these failures seriously undermined his prestige.

The incidents that follow are dreary and have little
significance except in so far as they throw light on conditions in the army of the empire. An imperial general
named Gilacius was captured in the darkness by the
Goths. He could speak no language but Armenian, and
when questioned by his captors the only answer he could
make was 'General Gilacius', for he had heard these
words so often that he had succeeded in learning them by
heart. Unfortunately these words were quite enough.
The Goths were satisfied that he was an enemy and put
him to death (VII. xxvi. 24-7). Whether true or *ben
trovato* the Gilacius story illustrates one of the difficulties
that Belisarius had to contend with in the extremely
motley character of the imperial forces. When, shortly
after, Justinian did send a few quite inadequate reinforcements, Belisarius and his wife joined them in south
Italy. After some minor successes, however, they were
utterly defeated. Belisarius retired to Sicily (VII. xxviii).

The times were indeed out of joint. Sclaveni crossed
the Danube and ravaged as far south as Epidamnus
(Durazzo) in Albania. There were earthquakes in
Constantinople and elsewhere. The lower Nile continued
in flood over seed time so that there was no corn in
Egypt. On the other hand a whale named Porphyry,
which had been sinking boats in the seas round Constantinople and terrifying their passengers for fifty years,
also fell on evil days, got stranded in the mud, and was
finally disposed of. Procopius' reflections on these
prodigies and the way they were interpreted by the
Byzantines (VII. xxix. 17-20) obviously owe much to
similar reflections on similar prodigies that we find in
Herodotus and even in the sceptical Thucydides; but
they serve to remind us of the deep vein of superstition
and craving for the miraculous that is the mark of all
dark ages in the world's history.

At this point an event occurred that had incalculable effects on the whole history of the age. Things were so bad in Italy that Antonina went back to Constantinople to appeal personally to Theodora for help, only to learn on arriving that the empress had fallen sick and died (28 June, 548) after having shared the throne of Justinian for twenty-one years (VII. xxx. I). The state of things in Rome is vividly portrayed by Procopius. 'Then too the troops who had been posted by Belisarius to garrison Rome killed their commander Conon, charging him with having marketed corn and other provisions to their harm. And they sent some of the priests as envoys, affirming that unless the emperor granted them a pardon for this crime and paid up within a fixed period all the arrears of pay owed them by the state, they would without any hesitation go over to Totila. The emperor did as they desired' (VII. xxx. 7–8). It is hardly rash to associate the emperor's compliance with the fact that he no longer had Theodora by his side. Antonina seems to have realized the desperate state of things in Italy and now begged the emperor to recall her husband. Her motive was no doubt a personal concern for her husband's prestige and safety. He did as she asked, 'for already the pressure of the Persian war was urging him to that step' (VII. xxx. 25). In all the history of operations in the west it must be remembered that Justinian was fighting on another front as well.

Between the death of Theodora and the return of Belisarius to Constantinople one of Justinian's leading generals, Artabanes the Armenian, formed a plot to murder the emperor. It was revealed through the loyal members of his household who had been approached by the conspirators. The ringleader was removed from the office he held, and he and his subordinates were kept under honourable guard in the palace (VII. xxxi, xxxii), an extraordinary act of clemency.

It was indeed a black time for Justinian and the cause he represented. 'The barbarians became definitely masters of the whole west', Procopius declares (VII. xxxiii. I), and goes on to give us another glimpse into the outer barbarian world. The Goths had undisputed control of most of Italy, the Franks of most of Gaul. Procopius was particularly distressed that the Frankish king who had occupied Marseilles began striking gold coins with his own image and superscription and that the emperor actually confirmed the Frankish occupation 'to avoid encountering any obstacle from the hostility of these barbarians'. He adds the interesting observation that 'the Franks never felt that they held Gaul securely unless the emperor had ratified their title (VII. xxxiii. 2-4). We need not here follow the movements of the Gepids and Herules, their quarrels when Justinian was far away, their sudden reconciliations when his forces came near them, except to notice how far the northern Balkans were from the shape they have taken in modern times: Herules occupied Belgrade, which still bore the Celtic name of Singidunum. More significant for the shaping of modern Europe was the advance of the Lombards, who at this crisis crossed the Danube on the emperor's invitation to occupy lands in Noricum and Pannonia (Austria-Hungary south and west of the Danube). A force of these Lombards was later employed by Justinian's general Narses for the reconquest of Italy. Narses prudently sent them back to their new home in the Danubian provinces after they had helped him; but less than five years after the emperor's death these same Lombards invaded northern Italy; the rich Po valley became Lombardy, and modern Italy began to take shape. Like the Franks, the Lombards had abandoned paganism for Orthodox Catholic Christianity. The fact that they were not Arians like the Goths and Vandals was a dominating factor in the history of the shaping of the western world.

Belisarius meanwhile had returned to Byzantium. His prestige had been seriously damaged by his five unsuccessful years in Italy, which are very faithfully summarized at this point by Procopius (VII. xxxv. 1); but his personal wealth had increased enormously. Justinian was strongly urged by the Italians resident in Constantinople, and particularly by Pope Vigilius, to make

another effort to recover Italy and Rome, and he promised
to give Italy his personal attention. But the historian is
rather critical of the emperor's way of dealing with the
crisis: 'he was mainly occupied with the dogmas of
the Christians, earnestly intent on arranging a satisfactory settlement of their controversies' (VII. xxxv. 11).

When Belisarius was recalled he had left 3,000 picked
men under a certain Diogenes to garrison Rome. Totila
led his whole army against the city, which was stoutly
defended; but the Goths captured Portus (VII. xxxvi.
1–3), and ultimately Rome itself was betrayed by some
discontented Isaurians among the garrison 'who for
many years had received no pay' (xxxvi. 7). Totila
marched south to Rhegium (Reggio di Calabria), which
withstood him, though a force which he detached from
there captured Tarentum (Taranto), whilst another body
of Goths secured Ariminum (Rimini) far to the north.
Procopius criticizes Justinian severely for his vacillation
and sloth in dealing with the Italian situation, and suggests that 'he was otherwise preoccupied and had lost
interest in it' (xxxvi. 6). The second assertion is highly
questionable, the first was undoubtedly true. The emperor had urgent problems to deal with nearer home.
The Slavs were on the march for New Rome. Justinian
had in fact, after much hesitation, appointed his able
nephew Germanus to the Italian command, when a body
of Sclaveni crossed the Danube and began ravaging
Illyria and Thrace, taking countless prisoners whom they
either impaled or burnt alive (VII. xxxviii). Germanus
had first to deal with this threat to the capital. He raised
a powerful army, largely at his own expense, secured a
promise of support from the Lombards, and took the
remarkable step of marrying a granddaughter of the
great Theoderic, Matasuntha, who had been the reluc-
tant wife and was now the widow of the Gothic king
Vittigis. Germanus himself had, providentially as it seemed, recently been made a widower. But before he could
march into Italy a new and vaster horde of Sclaveni, such
as never was known before, crossed the Danube and
approached Naissus (Nish in Yugoslavia), and prisoners

taken by the Romans reported that their objective was Salonica. Germanus, who was at Serdica (Sofia), was ordered by Justinian to postpone the invasion of Italy and deal with this more immediate peril. The Sclaveni, in fear, turned aside into Dalmatia, and Germanus was at last preparing to invade Italy and attack Totila, when he was taken ill and died.

New commanders were appointed, and the army moved its headquarters to Salones on the Adriatic, near the famous palace of Diocletian at Spalato (Split). But when the Roman army thus moved west, the Sclaveni reappeared in the east (incited, so Procopius suggests, by Totila), won a great victory at Adrianople, and advanced as far as the outer defences of Constantinople itself. 'But not long after, the Roman army overtook part of their force, attacking them suddenly, and routed them. They killed many of the enemy and set free a great crowd of Roman prisoners. ... But the remaining barbarians made their way home with the rest of the booty' (VII. xl. 44–5). This irruption of the Sclaveni was in fact only a raid for loot on the grand scale; but it may remind us that the great city walls that had been built to keep out the Huns in the fifth century were still in Justinian's time, as they continued to be for centuries after, a bastion against the barbarians of the outer world. It is a fact that has to be given its full weight in any estimate of the wisdom or unwisdom of Justinian's wars.

Totila meanwhile had starved Rhegium into surrender after previously overrunning and plundering practically all Sicily (VII. xxxix. 1–5). Like Germanus, he sought to strengthen his position by a political marriage. He sent to the ruler of the Franks asking for his daughter; but the Frankish king thought poorly of his prospects and refused the offer (VII. xxxvii. 1). We at this end of Europe are apt to forget how large the power of the emperor at Constantinople loomed in the minds of our Frankish and Anglo-Saxon ancestors. More than a century later, when Theodore of Tarsus was appointed archbishop of Canterbury and was on the way from Rome to his new see, his chaplain Hadrian was detained in France by the then mayor of the palace on the suspicion that he was on a political mission to the Anglo-Saxon royal house from the emperor Constans II, who was at the time at Syracuse (Bede, *Ecclesiastical History* IV. i). The concentration of the imperial forces at Salones decided Totila to withdraw from the south and prepare to meet an invasion of north Italy.

The events just described are recorded in the last chapters of book VII of the *Wars*. The eighth and last book was published some time after and is composed on a different system, events being recorded in more or less strict chronological order, without separating the material on a geographical basis. There are other differences too between this book and its predecessors. Something had gone out of life as Procopius saw it; a change had happened of which there are already symptoms in the later of the books composed on the geographical system.

The supreme command against Totila was finally entrusted to the aged eunuch Narses. He had played an important part from almost the beginning of Justinian's reign and had been prominent at the time of the Nika riots (below Chap. X, p. 201f.), but there are few generals in all history who began their military career so late in life. Procopius has much to say about the reasons which may have prompted Justinian to appoint this very elderly statesman and pass over Belisarius (VIII. xxi). It is impossible, he maintains, for an emperor's intentions to be ascertained except when he himself so wills; but he inclines to think that Justinian was unwittingly fulfilling a prophecy that one day a eunuch would undo the ruler of Rome. Justinian may have had more consciously in his mind the consideration, also mentioned by Procopius, that the unruly staff of generals that had caused Belisarius such trouble might be more likely to obey this aged statesman than any fellow general. The reason why Belisarius was not sent to Italy may well have been, though Procopius does not say so, that the emperor felt the urgent necessity of keeping his most able general nearer the much threatened capital.

The story of Narses' campaign against Totila and the defeat and death of the Ostrogothic king are told in Procopius (VIII. xxi f.). Before the arrival of Narses' forces in Italy Totila did his utmost to strengthen his position. His men were instructed to do all they could for the preservation and restoration of the antiquities of Rome. A Gothic fleet was sent across the Adriatic to ravage Corcyra (Corfu) and the mainland behind it with a view to impeding Narses' concentration (xxii. 17f.). Sardinia and Corsica were also occupied by the Goths, and an attempt to drive them from the islands was heavily defeated (xxiv. 31f.). Both Goths and Romans tried to secure the support of the Franks who had recently occupied much of north Italy, the Goths by promising to leave them unmolested at least till they had overcome the Roman menace, Justinian by giving them great sums of money, for which they agreed to help him in the coming struggle (xxiv. 13). The Franks, in the true Merovingian tradition, took everything that was offered them and bided their time.

Justinian's preparations against Totila were further delayed by a fresh incursion of the Sclaveni from across the Danube. These Sclaveni found it easy to recross the great river at the end of their raid, thanks to the help they received from their neighbours the Germanic Gepaides, who ferried them back to the north bank at a flat rate of one gold stater per head (xxv. 5). Fortunately for Justinian the Gepaides were at constant strife with their other neighbours the Lombards, and he took advantage of this fact to make an alliance with both to their mutual detriment.

The final battle against Totila was fought in 552 at a place called Busta Gallorum somewhere near the great North Road (Via Flaminia) roughly on a level with Lake Trasimene. Like the battle of Trasimene itself this too was essentially a battle for Rome fought by two armies both coming from the north. For the actual battle and the operations that led up to it the reader must be referred to the account in Procopius (VIII. xxix–xxxii) and the excellent elucidation of that account in Bury (II. pp. 261 f.). Two points, however, may be mentioned here because of the light they throw on the manners and habits of a Gothic army. When the two forces came into contact, Narses sent envoys to the Goths calling on them to surrender; but if Totila insisted on fighting the envoys were to invite him to name a definite day for the battle. In making this proposal Narses was making use of a familiar practice of the northern barbarians. We are reminded of the way that Boiorix, the leader of the Cimbri, appointed a place and day for his battle with Marius on the Raudine Plain in 101 B.C., or of the battle in which Clovis overthrew the remnants of Roman power in Gaul when the Frankish chief, sending to Syagrius the Roman commander, *campum pugnae praeparari deposcit* (Gregory of Tours, *Hist. Franc.* II. 27). Narses knew what he was doing when he made this apparently simple proposal. Totila accepted it, named the eighth day as the day for the battle, and, as Narses had anticipated, proceeded to attack the Roman army on the very day following the interview (xxix. 6–10). The way the fight began was no less typical of the age. A Gothic champion rode in front of his line and challenged a Roman champion to meet him in single combat. The Goth, whose name was Coccas, made the first rush, but Anzalas, the Roman champion, by suddenly making his horse to swerve, frustrated him in his attack and getting on his flank thrust his spear into his left side. He was thrown from his horse to the ground and lay there a corpse (xxxi. 11–16). The incident of Bruce and de Boune at Bannockburn in Scott's *Lord of the Isles* (VI. 15) offers an exact parallel:

> But swerving from the knight's career
> Just as they met, Bruce shunned the spear.

It all sounds like the full age of chivalry. But it was a degenerate chivalry. Narses knew that Totila would not keep his date; and the duel between Coccas and Anzalus is suspected by Bury to have been a delaying device inspired by Totila to gain time for expected reinforcements to reach the field of battle (Bury II. p. 265; cf. Procopius VIII. xxxi. 17). The Goths were decisively defeated. Totila escaped from the fight but died of wounds shortly after. He had ruled the Goths for eleven years.

The struggle was not yet quite ended. The Goths chose a new king, 'a particularly good soldier' named Teias (VIII. xxvi. 21, xxxiii. 6). Teias tried to get the support of the Franks, who, however, 'had no wish to die in aid of either Goths or Romans, but desired rather to win Italy for themselves' (xxxiv. 17–18). He massacred 300 Roman children whom Totila had taken as hostages (xxxiv. 7, 8), and then marched south with the purpose of securing Totila's treasure, which he had deposited at Cumae; but near Vesuvius, on Mons Lactarius, he was met by Narses' forces, defeated and killed, after performing prodigies of personal valour which are most generously recorded by Procopius. The surviving Goths were allowed, at their own request, to quit Italy (xxxv. 33–36). Those equally alarming barbarians the Lombards, who had helped Narses to defeat Totila, had already been sent home, 'presented with a great sum of money ... and escorted up to the Roman frontier so that they might do no damage as they withdrew' (xxxiii. 2).

The Goths had been finally eliminated from Italy. The Lombards began troubling it again only some sixteen years later, when they came back for good. Justinian himself had still thirteen years to live, and it was not till very near the end of his reign that Narses could report that the whole Italian peninsula was under imperial control. The new trouble came from two other races, who took a leading part in shaping medieval and modern Europe, the Franks and Alamanni. From this point on we no longer have Procopius to guide us, but till A.D. 558 the narrative is still full and consecutive, for the work of Procopius was continued by another contemporary historian who is still extant, Agathias (see below, Chap IX (B)). The Franco-Alamannic invasion of Italy was the outcome of an appeal for help that had been made to the Frankish kings by Totila and Teias.

The young Frankish king, Theudibald, had a shrewd
idea of the power and ability of the imperial army and
its commander and was determined not to involve himself. But this did not prevent him from giving a free hand
and a blind eye to the leaders of the Alamanni, two
brothers named Butilinus and Leutharis. The whole
adventure abounds in ironies both for the participants
and for the modern reader. For the participants there
was the well played farce of non-intervention; for the
modern reader there are Agathias' notes on the two
peoples. The Franks, he repeatedly tells us, are also
called Germans; the Alamanni (Allemands) 'if we are to
follow Asinius Quadratus, a man of Italy well read in the
details of German history, are a motley concourse of
men, which indeed is the meaning of their name' (men of
all sorts) (Agathias I. 6, Teubner, p. 149).

The Alamanni began their invasion of Italy in the
spring of A.D. 553, and 'proceeding in a leisurely way
they ravaged and ruined everything they came upon; and
passing by Rome ... when they had come to Samnium
they split in two ... , and Butilinus with the large and
stoutest contingent proceeded along the Etruscan shore,
ravaged most of Campania, occupied Lucania, and then
attacked Bruttium' (the modern Calabria) 'and advanced to the strait which separates the extremity of
Italy from the island of Sicily. Leutharis, at the head of
the rest of the force, was allotted the task of devastating
Apulia and Calabria and marched as far as Hydrus'
(Agathias II. 1, Teubner, pp. 178–9. Calabria means the
heel of Italy; the name was only later transferred to the
toe. Hydrus is Otranto). Agathias observes that such
true-born Franks as chanced to have joined the expedition treated the churches and their furniture with respect,
but that the Alamanni looted everything they could lay
hands on. It was by now full summer and very hot, and
Leutharis decided to go home with his booty; but when
he had got to Fanum, half way between Ancona and
Rimini, he was defeated by an imperial force he fell in
with, and many of his captives escaped, taking with them
much of the loot he had collected. Finally he got back to

Venetia, where a great plague broke out and Leutharis himself was among the victims (Agathias II. 2–3).

The other brother, Butilinus, was not in such a hurry to return. He hoped to succeed to the throne of Theoderic (II. 2). His army too had suffered seriously, particularly through drinking to excess of newly made wine. But he still had about 30,000 men to oppose to about 18,000 Romans (II. 4). Accordingly, when he heard that Narses' forces were gathering near Capua, he marched northwards to meet him. Butilinus was completely outgeneralled by Narses, who knew even how to turn to account a quarrel he had shortly before the battle with the chief of his allies, the Herules. Butilinus himself fell fighting and nearly all of his 30,000 men fell with him (II. 9. We have another contemporary account of Butilinus, there called Buccelinus, which makes his successes greater and his connexion with the Frankish king much closer. This occurs in the *History of the Franks* of Gregory of Tours. It is demonstrably distorted in some of its statements, but has a special interest for English readers, since Gregory lived to be a friend of the Kentish princess to whom we owe the sending of Augustine to Canterbury only two years after Gregory died).

The operations that Narses had to conduct in Italy after the overthrow of the Alamannic chieftains were of minor importance, a matter of reducing individual strongholds in various parts of Italy and conquering the regions north of the Po, which latter task was completed only a year or two before Justinian died. But the work was at long last achieved, and for a brief space at the end of his reign the homelands of Italy were all once again part of the Roman empire.

CHAPTER IV

The Wars – continued

(c) The Persian Wars

(Procopius, *Wars* I–II and parts of VIII)

*

IN planning and executing his grandiose schemes for the recovery of the lost provinces of the empire, Justinian had one constant preoccupation, namely the danger of exposing his eastern frontier to attack from Persia. Much more than their predecessors the Parthians, whose dominion they had overthrown in A.D. 226, the Persian Sassanid dynasty were from the nature of things the rivals and often the enemies of the emperors at Constantinople. The emperor Valerian had been captured by the Persian king Sapor in A.D. 260 and died a Persian captive. Julian the Apostate had met his death campaigning against Persia in A.D. 363. But the Roman and Persian monarchs had the fellow-feeling that naturally united two great autocrats each inevitably lonely in his exalted position, and the two empires often had the common experience of being seriously threatened by outer barbarian tribes. One might and often did attack the other when that other was weakened by wars with these barbarians. But each was aware that the other represented a long tradition of rival culture which placed them both apart from the hosts of uncivilized or half-civilized tribes who formed their other neighbours.

The *Persian Wars* is in some ways the most attractive of Procopius' writings. There is in it something of the charm that pervades those parts of Herodotus in which, nearly 1,000 years earlier, he had described the wonders and the wisdom of the East. The Byzantine historian shows touches of the dramatic sense of his great Hellenic predecessor when he starts his narrative of the Persian wars by relating how the emperor Arcadius just before his death in A.D. 408 prayed the Persian king, Isdigerdes, to act as guardian to his defenceless child, the infant Theodosius, and how nobly Isdigerdes responded to his prayer and continued in peace and amity with the Romans till his death over thirty years afterwards (I. ii. 1–10), and though his successor Vararanes did indeed invade the Roman dominions with a mighty army in A.D. 441, he was so impressed with the courtesy and respect shown him by Theodosius' envoy that he at once wheeled about with his whole army and rode back to Persia, where with the utmost friendliness he granted the terms of peace sought by the Romans, stipulating only that neither party should build any new fortress near their common frontier (I. ii. 11–15). The Black Prince could hardly have behaved more handsomely to the king of France.

Still in the true Herodotean vein our historian takes us straight (I. iii and iv) from Vararanes to 'a later time', when a new Persian king, Perozes, marched against his northern neighbours the Ephthalites or White Huns. Perozes was trapped by the Ephthalites and forced to do obeisance to their king. Not long after, in spite of his oaths, he again attacked the Ephthalites and was again completely defeated. Perozes and all his sons except one perished in the battle, and with the king was lost a priceless pearl, the story of which Procopius thinks worth telling since 'to some perhaps it may not seem altogether incredible' (I. iv. 17). A ferocious shark had fallen in love with this marvellous pearl and constantly followed the oyster in which it was lodged till a fisherman who had seen the strange sight and reported it to the king was persuaded to try to win it for him. The fisherman won the pearl but just failed to escape the shark. He had however his promised reward: the king provided for his family.

Perozes perished in A.D. 484. His only surviving son, Cabades, lived to wage war with Justinian. The record of his earlier adventures leads directly to the period with which we are immediately concerned. When he became king, Persia was tributary to the Ephthalites; it was only

when he had firmly established his power that he was
able to refuse further payments (I. iv. 35). He seems to
have started his reign as a social reformer, not to say a
revolutionary, one of his innovations being a law that
the Persians should have their wives in common (I. v. 1).
This led to his being deposed and shut up in the Castle of
Oblivion, so called because 'if anyone is cast into it,
death is the penalty for even mentioning his name'
(I. v. 7–8). At this point in the narrative we have a charming digression on the one case when this law was broken.
It tells the story of Arsaces, an Armenian prince who had
been detected plotting against the king of Persia and shut
up in the castle. But his faithful squire rendered great
service to the Persian king, who in return promised in
the grand style of the eastern sultan to grant him any
request he made. The faithful squire asked for a day with
his master in the forbidden castle. The request was
granted. The Armenian prince assumed for the last time
his royal robes and was respectfully waited on at a banquet by his squire. 'And then they tell how Arsaces,
declaring that this had been the sweetest day he had ever
spent ... slew himself with a knife he had stolen for the
purpose during the banquet' (I. v. 38–9).

Cabades himself was romantically rescued from the
castle by his wife, who was allowed to visit him and
enabled him to escape disguised in her clothes. He sought
refuge with the king of the Ephthalites, who gave him his
daughter in marriage. (Procopius explains that he can
say nothing about the faithful wife he had left behind in
the castle because the Persian accounts contradict one
another.) Then with the help of an army provided by the
Ephthalites he recovered his kingdom and put out the
eyes of the uncle who had reigned during his deposition
(I. vi). A little later, in A.D. 502, he went to war with
Anastasius because that frugal emperor refused to lend
him money to pay his Ephthalite debts. But in 506 peace
was signed for seven years, mainly because Cabades was
preoccupied with the Huns. Anastasius took advantage
of the situation to fortify very strongly the cities of Daras
or Anastasiopolis (Diarbekr), some twelve miles from the

Persian stronghold of Nisibis in north Mesopotamia, and Theodosiopolis (Erzerum) in Armenia west of the Upper Araxes.

Anastasius died in A.D. 518 and was succeeded by the almost illiterate Justin, uncle and predecessor of Justinian. Cabades lived on till 531. It was the steps he took to secure that his successor should be his youngest and favourite son Chosroes that led to the life-long enmity between the two princes. To secure the succession for Chosroes the old king Cabades had the bright idea of imitating the emperor Arcadius and getting him adopted by the Roman emperor. If this could be arranged the time would soon come when the Roman emperor and the Persian king of kings would be adopted brothers, and the two great empires of the Mediterranean and the Middle East might begin a period of brotherly collaboration. The idea had its obvious attractions. It would have been still more attractive if those who contemplated it could have seen a little way into the future, when the Sassanid monarchy was to be overwhelmed by the Moslems and the Roman empire of the East to begin against them a desperate struggle that was to last for nine centuries. Justin and Justinian were for accepting Cabades' proposals; but their learned counsellor the jurist Proclus opposed it strenuously, and persuaded Justin to answer that he was ready to adopt Chosroes, but only 'in the way fitting for a barbarian'. The negotiations naturally broke down, and Chosroes went home mortally offended (1. xi. 1–30).

The insult made Cabades eager to attack the Romans; but 'an obstacle arose which made him quite powerless to do so'. It was connected with the situation in the Caucasus, the region on which interest mainly centres in the Persian wars. Three nations occupied the lands there between the Caspian and the Black Sea in the valleys of the Phasis and the Cyrus and the southern slopes of the Caucasus, the regions now known as Georgia, Transcaucasia and Azerbaijan. In the west were the Lazi or Colchians, in the centre the Iberians, in the east the Albanians. These peoples formed buffer states on the one hand for Persians and Romans alike against the Huns who occupied the regions to the north as far west as the Sea of Azov, and on the other hand for the Romans against the Persians and vice versa. A particularly fertile source of dispute was a pass called by Procopius the Caspian Gates, situated 'beyond the borders of Iberia', which was the best and most direct way for Huns from north of the Caucasus to invade the dominions of either of the two great monarchs (1. x). In the reign of Anastasius the Caspian Gates had been held by a certain Ambazuces, a Hun by birth but a friend of the Romans. When Ambazuces was old and about to die he had sent to Anastasius and offered to sell him the Caspian Gates and the fortress commanding them. But the cautious Anastasius, calculating that it was impossible for him to maintain troops in a place so barren and remote, had refused the offer with many thanks. Ambazuces died soon after and Cabades seized the Gates by force from his sons (1. x. 9–12).

The obstacle that prevented him from directly invading Roman territory after the adoption fiasco was an incident in Iberia. The Iberians were Christians though subject to Persia. But just at this time Cabades thought fit to try to convert them forcibly to his own religion of Zoroastrianism and compel them to throw their dead to the birds and dogs, as do the modern Parsis, instead of giving them Christian burial. The result of this missionary effort was that the Iberians sought the protection of the Emperor Justin. The Iberian royal family took refuge across the border in Lazica, and Justin sent Roman garrisons to help the Lazi guard their frontier fortresses. But the difficulty of keeping them supplied was too great. They were withdrawn and the forts were seized by the Persians (1. xii. 1–19).

These operations in the Caucasus region are the most interesting of all the operations of the Persian wars. They are the best recorded. The record is one of a real struggle for power, and it has a special interest as taking us into regions that form part of the great Russian empire and those northern confines of modern Persia that border

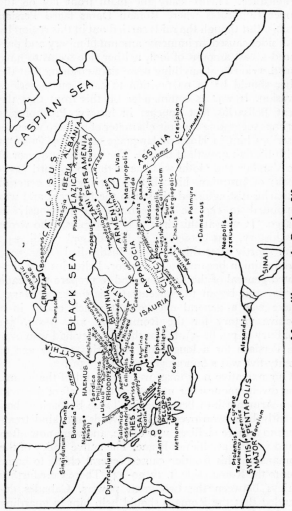

Map to illustrate the Persian Wars

c

on it. The operations in other fields were of less real
significance. Theoretically the main front lay on the
Upper Euphrates where Roman Daras faced Persian
Nisibis. But though the raids carried out in this region by
both sides caused an immense amount of misery and produced a vast amount of loot, neither side seems to have
aimed seriously at anything more than ensuring that the
other should be in no position to carry out a serious
invasion. It was as commander on this front that the
great Belisarius first appears in history. Procopius is
perhaps suggesting the epic character of his hero when he
describes him in Homeric language as πρῶτον ὑπηνήτης
(with his first growth of beard). The future conqueror of
the Vandals and Goths was one of the bodyguard (dory-
phoroi) of Justinian, himself then serving as a general.
Belisarius distinguished himself in the first raid and was
appointed to replace the commander previously in
charge. 'It was at this time that Procopius, who wrote
this history, was chosen to be his adviser' (I. xii. 24).
Very shortly after this the aged Justin died (Aug. 527)
and Justinian became sole emperor. Belisarius was promoted general of the East, ordered to prepare to invade
Persia, and began to concentrate his forces at Daras.
There was a general engagement which ended in a
decisive victory for the Romans (I. xiii. 9–xiv. 55.
Cp. Bury II. pp. 82–5). It was the first they had won over
the Persians for a long time. Belisarius at the age of
twenty-five was a famous general (A.D. 530).

Our narrative now takes us to the land of the Tzani,
who dwelt amongst the mountains to the left of the road
from Armenia into Persarmenia. These barbarians had
recently been won over by kind words and kind treatment to a more civilized way of life, and were now often
found serving as allies of Rome. The active policy of the
Romans on this frontier caused several chiefs to come
over to the Roman side (I. xv. 20–33). There were further
parleys between the two great powers. Cabades demanded that the Romans should help him in guarding
the Caspian Gates and dismantle Daras, but let it be
known that for a payment of money he would be willing

to abandon his claims. The hint was not taken and war went on (xvi). In the early spring of 531 a Persian army, encouraged by a Saracen chief named Alamundaras, planned a large-scale raid on the great city of Antioch in Syria. They defeated the Romans at Callinicum on the Euphrates, but suffered so heavily themselves that they fell back into their own country and the Persian commander was disgraced (xviii).

About this time the Christian king of Aethiopia was trying to impose a Christian ruler on the pagan Homerites of south Arabia. Justinian intervened and sought to ally both these Red Sea states against Persia, and with their aid to get the silk of China, that most essential of court luxuries, without its having to pass through Persia. The attempt failed (I. xix–xx). How at a later time the Romans started their own silk industry with some silkworms' eggs brought from the east by two monks is recorded by Procopius in the last book of the *Wars* (VIII. xvii, A.D. 552).

Meanwhile Belisarius had been recalled to take command against the Vandals in North Africa. There was another Persian invasion of Roman territory, this time into the extreme north of Mesopotamia. The chief operation was a siege of Martyropolis. But at this point the old king Cabades died, and thanks to the arrangements he had made before his death he was succeeded by his favourite son, Chosroes (I. xxi). Peace negotiations now proceeded in earnest, and after an appropriate number of hitches and near breakdowns the so-called 'Endless Peace' was signed between the two monarchs in A.D. 532. Daras was to be demilitarized by the Romans, such conquests as either side had made were to be for the most part restored, and Chosroes was to receive a substantial sum of money (xxii). Both monarchs were in fact anxious for peace. Chosroes' personal position was by no means secure. Shortly after this he had to deal with a plot to make his one-eyed brother Zames regent for Zames' own young son, another Cabades. Chosroes was fully engaged for some little time putting down this plot and liquidating all his relations and their friends. The young Cabades was the only one to escape. The blood bath was completed by the execution of the man who had secured Chosroes his throne. 'That,' Procopius reflects, 'is what he got for his good services to Chosroes' (xxiii. 29).

Justinian too had his domestic troubles at this time and the rest of Book I records them. They centre round the famous disturbance known as the Nika riot and will be described in a later chapter (Chap. X, p. 201f.).

How war again flared up between Byzantium and Persia (A.D. 540–5) is told at the beginning of Book II. There seems to be no doubt that Chosroes was the aggressor. He incited his vassal the Saracen chief Alamundaras to quarrel with Arethas, another Saracen, who sided with Rome, about the sun-baked treeless no-man's land south of Palmyra, and the dispute became, as it was intended to, a question of Roman prestige. The Gothic king Vittigis too, already worsted in his war with the empire, sent an envoy to Chosroes and further incited him to war (II. ii). There were similar incidents leading to similar appeals, equally unspontaneous, on the Armenian border, where Persian and Byzantine interests so often clashed. The situation as it appeared to the enemies of Rome is well stated in a speech which Procopius puts into the mouth of one of these Armenians appealing to Chosroes for aid. Justinian is a menace: witness his interferences in Africa, Italy, the Caucasus and the Red Sea. His forces are at present mainly at the other end of the world. The loyalty of his great general is suspect (see above, Chap III, p. 44). 'When Chosroes heard this he was pleased' and decided to make war on the Romans at the beginning of spring. He could not do so earlier, for it was already late autumn (A.D. 539, II. iii).

At this point two unforeseen events occurred. The first was a great comet. Procopius describes it but leaves his readers to judge what it portended. The second was an invasion of the empire by an unprecedented host of Huns from across the Danube who penetrated as far as the suburbs of Constantinople itself and returned home unopposed with 120,000 captives and much booty. Another wave invaded Greece, by-passed Thermopylae when they found it valiantly defended by the Greeks, and destroyed almost all the Greeks except those of the Peloponnese. This devastating raid may remind us how precarious life was in Justinian's realms and may help us to realize what he was aiming at in his settled policy of trying to restore the ancient frontiers and the ancient military power of the empire. For Chosroes on the other hand the moment seemed marked out more than ever for an attack in full force on the hereditary foe. He proceeded to make it in spite of a dignified and reasonable appeal that Justinian now made him. The 'Endless Peace' of A.D. 532 was ended (II. iv).

Chosroes' objective was Antioch. Marching west and north up the right bank of the Euphrates he reached Sura, some 150 miles east of Antioch, and tried to take it by assault. The people of Sura resisted bravely, but their commander was killed and they sent their bishop to plead for terms. Chosroes received him graciously and sent him back with the impression that all was well. But along with the bishop he sent a guard of his own troops who rushed the city gate and sacked the city. Afterwards, however, whether moved by humanity or greed or to please a woman of Sura for whom he had conceived so great a passion that he made her his wedded wife, he decided to do some good to the people of Sura. So sending to Sergiopolis, a city subject to Rome some sixteen miles south of Sura, he bade Candidus, the bishop there, ransom the 12,000 captives for two centenaria. 'But he, asserting that he had no money, refused outright. Chosroes therefore demanded of him that he should hand over a written undertaking to pay later, and on this condition for a small sum purchase all these many slaves. Candidus did accordingly and promised to pay the sum within a year, swearing the most fearful oaths and declaring that if he did not pay in the time stipulated his punishment should be to pay double and himself be unfrocked as one who had broken his oath. When Candidus had made this written agreement he was handed over all

the Surenians. Only a few of them, however, survived.
The great majority perished soon after, unable to bear up
against the affliction that had befallen them' (II. v. 28–
33). The incident throws an interesting light on the duties
of bishops of frontier cities at this period and also on the
way that rulers of the Chosroes type in all ages can
persuade themselves of their own generosity.

The Roman situation was none too happy. The officers
actually facing Chosroes were unenterprising and inefficient and their forces inadequate. The defences of
Antioch were very vulnerable. Germanus, the emperor's
able nephew (see above, Chap. III, p. 52) was sent to
take over the command, but he brought no reinforcements with him and soon realized, as did also the men of
Antioch, that his presence would only make Chosroes
more eager to take the city complete with so distinguished a captive. So once more the Romans turned for
help to the church. Megas, bishop of the Syrian Beroea,
who happened to be on a visit to Antioch, was sent to
plead with Chosroes. He did so with more than Christian
humility but completely failed to appease him and was
detained with the Persians while they marched on
Hierapolis. The Hierapolitans, 'not wanting to have
their land ravaged', agreed to pay Chosroes 2,000 pounds
of silver. 'Then indeed Megas began pleading with
Chosroes for all the Romans of the East, and did not let
him go till he had agreed to take ten centenaria of gold
and quit all the Roman dominions' (II. vi. 9–25). Megas
hurried back to Antioch, but found the people there unwilling to accept any terms from Chosroes. A high
official (*a secretis*) had arrived from Justinian to negotiate
with Chosroes and was naturally anxious that no step
should be taken to prejudice his negotiations, and
Chosroes meanwhile had put himself out of court by
marching on Beroea and demanding a large ransom of
the unhappy Beroeans, 'since he saw that their walls
were open to attack at many points' (II. vii. 5). They
were finally shut up in their citadel and forced to surrender. By this time Megas was back at the Persian
headquarters with the unwelcome news that Antioch

rejected the Persian terms. Fortunately in a sense for him Chosroes' ill faith had supplied the bishop with something else to talk about and he seems to have been moved to some very bold and plain speaking. Perhaps it was as a result of this that the bishop persuaded him to let the Beroeans go their way unmolested. Most of the troops however who had been garrisoning the city went over to Chosroes, complaining that for a long time past they had not received their pay (II. vii. 36-7). The grievance was only too well founded. One fundamental weakness of the Byzantine government was that it was often not in a position to pay its way.

Chosroes now marched on Antioch, but declared that for ten centenaria of gold he would withdraw, and made it clear that he would take even less (II. viii. 4). Negotiations were started. 'But on the following day the people of Antioch hurled many insults at Chosroes from the battlements, for they are not seriously minded but very prone to be frivolous and disorderly ... and Chosroes, boiling with rage, resolved to storm the walls' (viii. 6-7). The Antiochians, civilians as well as soldiers, fought back bravely, but typically neglected to occupy a rock outside the city that commanded the city walls. Even so they held out till some wooden structures that they had raised to help the defences collapsed. Then there was a panic among the soldiers and they abandoned the city. The young rowdies of the circus factions (see below, Chap. VII (b)) fought on desperately but were overpowered and there was a great and indiscriminate slaughter (II. viii. 34). The regular troops had succeeded in their disgraceful flight because Chosroes had prudently done all he could to help it, but he now claimed that he had done so because 'to trample on the conquered is against the law of God' (ix. 6). After which pious reflection he gave orders to seize as slaves all who were left alive in Antioch, plunder their property and burn the whole city. Once again, however, he showed his eclectic generosity by sparing one particular church from which he had got the richest items in the immense treasure of gold and silver looted from the city (II. ix. 14-18.) The

incident leads Procopius to meditate on the mysterious
ways both of Chosroes and of God (II. ix. 8–13, x. 1–5).

There were further negotiations between the two great
powers, and it was agreed that the Romans should pay
Chosroes fifty centenaria down and an annual contribution of five centenaria to defray the expenses of a Persian
guard at the Caspian Gates (II. x. 24). The agreement was
never ratified. Chosroes is consistently and convincingly
depicted as the megalomaniac autocrat. His capture of
Antioch, which brought him to the Mediterranean, the
mare nostrum of the Roman empire, and put him in
possession of the greatest city of Roman Asia, intensified
his complaint and made him almost impossible to deal
with. He went down to the sea, where he took a solitary
bathe and performed sacrifices to his gods, he visited the
famous grove of Daphnae just outside the city, where he
again made sacrifices, but did no damage beyond burning the sanctuary of the archangel Michael, and he
presided at a race meeting. The charioteers in every
Roman city were of two factions, the blues and the greens,
and as Justinian favoured the blues Chosroes naturally
backed the greens. When the blue charioteer was winning, Chosroes had him stopped so that the Persian
favourite might win the race. But at the same meeting
he showed his royal sense of justice when a Persian was
accused of having violated a young girl of the city. He
ordered the man to be impaled. The victims of the outrage thought the penalty excessive and begged for mercy
for the culprit; so Chosroes promised to let the man go.
But he secretly impaled him not long after (II. xi). The
rest of his conduct was to match. He treated the people
of Antioch as his personal chattels (see below) and on his
way back to Persia he attacked and looted Roman cities
on his line of march with complete disregard of the
armistice agreement. Apamea in Syria, Chalcis near
Beroea and Daras were all plundered or put to ransom,
and Edessa unsuccessfully marched against. It is not
surprising that after all this Justinian was no longer
willing to put the agreement with Persia into effect.

The Antioch campaign thus ended with no ending to

hostilities. But one part of the story remains to be told, that namely which records the fate of the people of Antioch. While negotiations with Justinian were still continuing Chosroes put up all the captives from the city for sale. 'When the people of Edessa learnt this they showed incredible kindness. Everyone without exception brought ransom money for the prisoners according to his means and deposited it in the temple. Some indeed went far beyond their means. The harlots brought their personal ornaments; any farmer who had no tools or money eagerly brought his ass or sheep' (II. xiii. 3–4). Edessa (fifty miles south-east of Samosata), which was itself put to ransom by Chosroes, claimed to possess a letter written by Jesus to a former king of the city. This generosity of its poor and outcasts is perhaps the only piece of evidence that lends the legend any plausibility. It came to nothing, for Justinian's generalissimo, Buzes, happened to be there to put a stop to the proceedings, as any responsible imperial officer was plainly justified in doing at the existing stage of negotiations between the two powers (xiii. 6). Chosroes, prevented from selling his captives, took them back home with him, after which 'he built a city in Assyria on a site a day's journey from the city of Ctesiphon, named it Antioch of Chosroes and settled them all there. He built them a bath and a hippodrome and enabled them to live softly and luxuriously as before. He brought charioteers and musicians from Antioch and the other Roman cities. He fed them permanently at the cost of the state with far more care than is normally bestowed on prisoners, and condescended to have them called "the King's people". They were subject to no authority except the king himself' (II. xiv. 1–3). This remarkable instance of mass deportation throws further light on the workings of the royal Persian's curiously twisted mind.

To meet the very serious situation that resulted from the capture of Antioch Belisarius was recalled from Italy and sent to the East as supreme commander. He took with him as part of the new expeditionary force most of the Gothic prisoners that he had brought from Italy

(II. xiv. 8–13). Chosroes meanwhile was leading an army against Colchis. The Colchians, or Lazi as they were actually called at this period, were subject to Rome, though not as tributaries. They guarded the western Caucasus against the Hun, traded with the Romans, and their successive kings received from the emperor the emblems of royalty. But since the Iberian incident (see above, p. 64) some Roman troops had been quartered in Lazica and had made themselves so unpopular that the Lazi had sent secretly to Chosroes offering to hand themselves over to him (xv. 12–30). It was in answer to this appeal that Chosroes now prepared to occupy Lazica (xv. 31–5). He led an army into the country, received the submission of Gubazes, king of the Lazi, and captured Petra, the stronghold the Romans had built themselves on the Lazic coast. It was, however, neither sacked nor looted, and the garrison joined the Persian army, keeping their own belongings (xvii. fin.). Allegiances were rather fluid in these remote regions. A little kindness could be as great a solvent as the same amount of cruelty.

The main Roman army was not fighting Chosroes in Lazica. It was in Mesopotamia, where Belisarius had recently arrived. It achieved little. An engagement outside Nisibis came near to disaster owing to the insubordination of some of Belisarius' generals, and the situation was only saved by a body of his Italian Goths. The few Persian prisoners that he took were sent to Italy to fight the Goths still resisting there. The chief success of the campaign was won by his Saracen allies under their chief Arethas, whom he sent forward to raid Assyria. Arethas was so successful that fearing he might have to share his plunder with Belisarius he decided to go straight home with it all. He was not punished for this desertion, 'for Belisarius never saw him again' (xix. 26–9, 46). Belisarius' own forces were equally impatient to get back home. One-third of them had fallen sick from the extreme heat, and the Lebanese in particular wanted to get back to Syria because the raiding season was beginning. They became unmanageable and he had to do as they wished. But the news of Arethas' raid caused Chosroes to return to Persia. Belisarius was summoned to Constantinople, where he spent the winter (A.D. 541–2) (II. xix).

In the spring of 542 Chosroes started with a great army to invade Palestine. He marched north-west with the Euphrates on his right, stopping only to attack Sergiopolis. He wanted to punish its priest Candidus, who had failed to pay the ransom for the people of Sura (above, p. 69f.). Candidus came out to meet the king and make a personal appeal to him, but Chosroes tortured him and kept him permanently a prisoner. The city, however, escaped thanks to timely warnings given it by a Christian serving among Chosroes' Saracen allies. Chosroes continued his advance, but at this stage Belisarius was sent back from Constantinople and by a very simple trick caused Chosroes to abandon the whole campaign. Chosroes had announced that he was sending one of his secretaries to Belisarius to lodge a protest about the interruption of negotiations. The envoy found the great general out hunting. The men with him were all exceptionally tall and handsome. Thracians and Illyrians, Goths and Herules, Vandals and Moors were to be seen everywhere, equipped not for war but for the hunt and taking no notice of the envoy. Belisarius received the envoy with great good humour, remarked that the king of Persia was behaving very strangely: 'he first invades us and then makes proposals about peace', and with these brief words dismissed him. According to Procopius the Persian was so impressed that on getting back to his master he urged him to withdraw at once across the Euphrates. Chosroes did so and Belisarius took care that there should be none of his own troops to bar the passage. Envoys from Belisarius now waited on Chosroes and both armies agreed to withdraw. On his way home Chosroes only sacked one Roman city, Callinicum. The people of Callinicum had just taken down a stretch of their town wall which needed reconstruction, and the temptation was too much for the king of kings (II. xxi. 30–2). The whole story of how Belisarius outwitted Chosroes

is reminiscent of Herodotus: of Thrasybulus of Miletus
and the display he made to mislead the envoys of the
king of Lydia, of the Spartans at Thermopylae as observed by Xerxes' scouts, of Themistocles' ruse to get
Xerxes back across the Hellespont. It is Procopius' way
of indicating that his hero had risen to the occasion.
Modern historians, however, are inclined to ascribe
Chosroes' abandonment of his campaign not so much to
the Themistoclean ruses of Belisarius as to the great
plague recorded in the next two chapters (xxii, xxiii)
which 'starting from Egypt came to Palestine ... and
from there fell upon the whole world' (xxii. 6; on the
plague see below, Chap. VII, p. 132f.).

Next year (543) Chosroes turned in the opposite
direction to attack the Romans through Persarmenia.
He made his quarters at Adarbiganon, 'where was the
great fire which the Persians worship above all other
gods' (xxiv. 2) and waited there for envoys from Byzantium, for peace talks were becoming a regular part of
the campaigns. But one of these envoys fell sick on the
way and the plague reached the Persian army. Chosroes
fled from it back to Assyria and Justinian ordered his
generals to invade Persia. The order was carried out by
the various commanders with a lamentable lack of co-
operation. They finally foregathered at Dubios, a great
caravan centre eight days' journey from Theodosiopolis
(Erzerum). Near here a battle was fought and the
Romans were disgracefully beaten. It was a great
disaster, says Procopius (xxv. 33), the like of which had
never been suffered by the Romans. If this was so, it was
a disaster with singularly few repercussions. But the
historian's words are significant. They recall those used
by Darius in the *Persians* of Aeschylus (l. 360) of the
Persian disaster at Salamis. God will forsake Justinian's
Romans as he forsook Xerxes' Persians if they do not
mend their ways.

In 544 Chosroes turned again to Mesopotamia, 'but
this invasion was directed not against Justinian but
exclusively against the God whom the Christians worship.
For after returning unsuccessful from his first march on

Edessa' (II. xii. 31–4, see above, p. 72) both he and the magi had naturally been much depressed at having been vanquished by the Christians' God (II. xxvi. 1–3). The campaign in fact resolved itself into an attempt to capture the divinely protected city. The Persians attacked again and again. The whole population of Edessa, women, children and the aged, joined in repelling them. Finally, after he had been paid a heavy ransom, Chosroes gave up and went back home with all his army (II. xxvii, end). There was indeed a good deal of war weariness on both sides, of which the plague may have been one of the causes. The visit to the great Zoroastrian fire sanctuary when the plague was on its way, and the attack on the holy Christian city of Edessa, both suggest that Chosroes was inclined to believe that the gods were intervening in human affairs; the double failure, first at the holy place of his own god and then at that of his Christian enemies, may have indeed caused him deep dejection. At any rate he now started serious negotiations. After prolonged discussions a five-years' truce was at last signed in A.D. 545 (II. xxviii. 11).

Chosroes may have meant to keep the truce, but he was by now incapable of understanding that his side of a promise was binding on him. The truce soon began to appear to him as a divinely sent opportunity to capture by surprise the great Roman frontier fortress of Daras (xxviii. 15–17). A Persian envoy named Isdigusnas was sent to Constantinople with a retinue of 500 chosen warriors and instructed to ask to be put up at Daras on the first stage of his journey. When once they were inside they were to seize the city. The plan was foiled by a certain George, under whose persuasion only twenty of the 500 were admitted into the city. So the *coup* was not even attempted and 'the barbarian went on to Byzantium, taking with him his wife and two daughters who were the excuse for his huge retinue. When he appeared before the emperor he found nothing whatever to say on any serious topic ... but he presented him with the gifts from Chosroes as custom demands and with a letter in which Chosroes begged Justinian to let him know if he was in the best of health' (II. xxviii. 38–9). The magnificent way that Justinian entertained this ill-intentioned ambassador provoked much very natural annoyance among the emperor's faithful subjects. The record of it here by Procopius prepares us for the violent attack on the whole régime of Justinian that he makes in his *Secret History* (below, Chap. IX).

Daras, on the main frontier, was an isolated incident. But in remote Lazica the truce operated little if at all. Chosroes sent more troops there (II. xxix. 1f.), and when its king Gubazes appealed to the Romans begging forgiveness for past backslidings, Justinian sent 8,000 men to his help, and Lazi and Romans united to besiege Petra. Gubazes asked further for his arrears of salary as a silentiary of the palace and also for three centenaria to pay men of two neighbouring tribes whom he had promised that sum for help against the Persians. 'The emperor intended to do as he asked, but he was preoccupied with some other business and failed to send the money in time' (xxix. 30–2). In the campaign which followed, the Persians held out at Petra with remarkable determination, but the Romans secured various successes against a large relieving force under Mermeroes, and the large contingent which he left behind in the country after relieving Petra was finally forced to withdraw. 'And the fourth year of the truce with Persia ended, with Justinian in the twenty-third year of his reign' (xxx. 48).

The next phases of the Lazic war are recorded in Book VIII (see above, p. 74). This opens by recording how in A.D. 550 a great Persian army invaded Lazica, but it at once digresses into an account of the peoples who dwell round the Black Sea and the lands they live in (VIII. i. 7–v). We cannot do more here than mention those who play a part in the subsequent narrative: the Pontici towards the east end of the south coast with their famous capital Trapezus (Trebizond), Scymni and Suani 'behind' Lazica, the Apsilii opposite Petra, the Sabeiri Huns north of the passes across the Caucasus from Lazica, the Abasgi on the coast north of the Apsilii, then, proceeding north along the east coast, the Zechi

and the Saginae, then Utiger Huns onwards round to the
Maeotic Lake and the Tanais (Sea of Azov and Don),
behind them in the interior the Antae, Tetraxite Goths
by the mouth of the Sea of Azov, Cotrigur Huns from the
Sea of Azov to the Danube. The Tetraxite Goths deserve
a special word. They cherished the Christian way of life,
but whether they were Arians like the rest of the Goths or
held some other doctrine Procopius is unable to say
'since they do not even know themselves, but they
honour the faith in quiet simplicity' (iv. 9–11).

This whole excursus is of interest from more than one
point of view. It shows the extent and limitations of the
historian's geographical knowledge; it gives a useful
conspectus of the various peoples who play their various
parts in this theatre of the war; and it deals with a region
from which issued many peoples who helped in the shaping of modern Europe and which itself, though it lies off
the main highways of the world, has always had its own
importance. In the art of digression Procopius is a pupil
of the great Herodotus, and there can be no doubt that
he has chosen this point in his history for his Black Sea
excursus because he realized (see particularly II. xxviii.
23) that on these Lazic campaigns hung the issue whether
the Persians were to challenge the Romans on the Black
Sea. This explains the persistence of Chosroes' efforts in
Lazica. Apart from other possibilities they offered the
attractive prospect of attacking Constantinople by the
land route along the north coast of the Black Sea (VIII.
vii. 12–13).

In the campaigns recorded after this excursus the Lazi,
Abasgi and Apsilii play the chief role. The Lazi, once
more allies of Rome, attacked the Persians single-handed
and were only saved from disaster by timely help from
the Roman forces. The Abasgi and Apsilii both revolted
from Rome and called in the Persians, but were both
finally brought back to the Roman allegiance. These
buffer states were the chief sufferers. Constantinople was
never even remotely threatened.

At this point in the *Wars* we have another of Procopius' illuminating digressions. 'Chosroes fell seriously

ill; it was even said that he had departed this life, for he was of a sickly constitution' (x. 10). When his eldest son Anasozadus learnt of his father's illness, he started a revolt in the city to which he had been banished for previous misdeeds. The revolt was suppressed, the rebel captured, and his eyes disfigured with hot needles. This ensured that he would never succeed his father. For the laws do not allow a man suffering from a disfigurement to be crowned king of Persia (x. 10–22). This illness of Chosroes leads Procopius to mention a famous doctor about whom there had been a special clause in the earlier truce of A.D. 545, when Chosroes had stipulated that he should be allowed to retain him for a specified time (a year in fact) as his personal physician (II. xxviii. 8–10). The man in question was Tribunus, a Palestinian by birth, second to none in medical skill, godfearing and endowed with a singular wisdom and goodness (VIII. x. 12). When asked by Chosroes how he would like to be rewarded for his services, he had asked for nothing except that Chosroes should release for him some of the Roman captives. Chosroes had responded by releasing 3,000. We may very possibly owe to Tribunus some of the vivid details in Procopius' convincing study of the royal patient, just as we owe some of the details in Herodotus' Persian pictures to Greek physicians who attended Persian monarchs a thousand years earlier. We have already seen how Chosroes loved to have his occasional moments of cheap self-satisfying generosity, and it is not by accident that Procopius mentions this particular instance in close connexion with the account of the inhuman cruelty that Chosroes displayed to his own son. The wise and good Jewish doctor knew his patient. We may even conjecture that, when choosing to be remunerated in the way that he did, he was not unaware that he was at the same time prescribing for his patient's unhappy and incurable condition. However that may be, we may feel sure that Procopius has intentionally introduced this account of Chosroes' domestic troubles immediately before the discussions for a new truce that are recorded in the following chapter (VIII. xi).

To negotiate the truce Chosroes again sent Isdigusnas, attended as before by wife, daughters, brother, and an army of retainers. And once more Procopius notes how irritated the people of Byzantium were by the excessive respect with which Justinian received the ambassador, 'a supercilious fellow, indescribably pretentious, whose inflated vanity the Romans found intolerable' (xi. 4). Isdigusnas began his mission by making charges against the Romans which Procopius regards as frivolous and made only to protract the negotiations (xi. 10). They did indeed drag on, and our narrative reverts to the operations that were still proceeding in Lazica.

Each side wanted to improve its position for bargaining by strengthening its hold on the disputed province. The Roman commander Bessas made a desperate attempt to recover Petra; and it was desperately defended. Bessas himself, though 'fat and extremely old' (xi. 48) was the first to mount a scaling ladder and, when wounded and hurled down at the first attempt, continued to direct operations and again mounted the ladder directly he had been set again upon his feet. The Persians resisted with equal courage, using burning naphtha against their assailants. But a sudden change of wind caused the naphtha to set fire to their own defences. Many were burnt to death, and many more made prisoners. Even then some 500 made their way to the citadel and fought on there. Bessas offered them good terms, but when these were rejected he set fire to the citadel. 'But even so they all refused to yield and perished in the flames. Then indeed it was revealed how seriously Chosroes regarded Lazica: he had picked his most famous troops and stationed them in the fortress of Petra' (xii. 17).

The Romans found provisions for five years in the city and abundant water. The Persians had built three pipe lines, one above the other; the top line ran above ground and was cut by the Romans at the beginning of the siege; the second ran underground below the first and was discovered and cut by them after they had learnt from prisoners that the town still had abundant water; the third ran below the second and was not discovered till after the city had been stormed. Procopius has some ground for his comment that 'they were led into error by the slackness with which they worked' (xii. 23). Bessas sent all the prisoners to the emperor, razed the walls of Petra to the ground, and recovered his reputation (xii. 28–30). His appointment by Justinian to the Lazic command after his failure to save Rome had been bitterly criticized, and Procopius concludes this chapter (VIII. xii) with some reflections on the theme that God moves in a mysterious way. These reflections are an oblique criticism of the emperor. They are one of many indications that Procopius was undergoing a process of gradual disillusionment and are symptomatic of the extreme revulsion for Justinian and all his works that we shall find in the *Secret History* (below, Chap. IX).

When Petra fell, Mermeroes was on the march to relieve it. It was easy for him to move his troops, including cavalry and elephants, thanks to the admirable roads that had been built through even the most impassable districts by the Persian engineers (xiii. 5). The fall of the city seems to have left him without a plan, and he was further handicapped by fear of his Hun allies (xiii. 6–7). Eventually he fell back on Mocheresis, the best land in Colchis, producing wine and crops in general of good quality (xiv. 46).

Bessas meanwhile had withdrawn among the Pontici and Armenians and was spending his time collecting the local revenues. Procopius criticizes him severely for not having followed up his success at Petra, and declares that, if he had, he could have cleared Lazica for ever of the Persians. He blames Justinian too for Bessas' negligence, 'for the emperor was generally inclined to pardon his commanders when they went wrong, with the result that they were constantly found misconducting themselves both in their private and their public life' (xiii. 11–14). This is a charge that has been brought against great statesmen in all ages. It is often the reverse side of an element of real greatness.

Each side having thus failed to oust the other from

Lazica, serious negotiations were at last begun in Constantinople. It was agreed there should be another five
years' truce, during which a permanent peace should be
negotiated after the points of disagreement about both
Lazica and the Saracens had been settled, and further
that the Romans should pay the Persians twenty centenaria of gold. Justinian wished to pay four centenaria
yearly, that he might have some surety that Chosroes
would not violate the agreement. Isdigusnas on the other
hand demanded the whole sum on the spot, and to this
the Romans eventually agreed, 'to avoid the appearance
of paying an annual tribute. For it is disgraceful names,
not facts, that men are most ashamed of' (xv. 1–7). But
in spite of this face-saving 'most of the Romans were considerably annoyed with the treaty, though whether their
censure was at all fair, or, like most popular outcries,
quite unreasonable, I cannot say' (xv. 13). Once more
Procopius complains of the extraordinary privileges that
were granted to Isdigusnas and his exceedingly numerous
staff, who all the time they were in Constantinople 'were
at full liberty to consort with whom they would, take
their walks in every quarter of the city, and buy and sell
whatever they pleased ... with no Roman escort to keep
them under observation as is usually done' (xv. 19–20).
Diplomatic immunity had normally a restricted connotation in Justinian's Constantinople. The exceptional
freedom and favour granted to Isdigusnas is explained
by Procopius himself when he tells us that the ambassador had promised the emperor to persuade Chosroes to
remove the Persian army from Lazica (xv. 11). But his
whole account of Isdigusnas implies also that the emperor had mistaken his man.

Before the truce was finally ratified Mermeroes had
strengthened his hold on the rich district of Mocheresis,
taken by treachery the fortress of Uthimereos, and
brought Scymnia and Suania under Persian sway. Many
Lazi in the districts under Roman occupation went over
to Persia. King Gubazes, his family and all his loyal
subjects took to the mountains (viii. xvi).

Such was the state of things when after the winter

season (A.D. 552–3) Isdigusnas arrived back at the court of Chosroes with the terms of the truce and the 'tribute' money. 'Chosroes, upon receiving the money, set his seal to the armistice without delay ... but used the money to win over as allies a lot of Sabeiri Huns, whom he at once sent with some Persians to Mermeroes. ... He also sent him many elephants.' Mermeroes thereupon moved against the Romans and their Lazi allies. But he achieved very little. The chief of the Huns was killed and the Persians had to retire to Mocheresis (VIII. xvii. 9–19).

CHAPTER V

The Peace With Persia

*

WITH the events of A.D. 552–3 Procopius' narrative ends. The armistice was not followed by a peace treaty till nearly ten years later (A.D. 562). Fighting ceased on the other frontiers, but it went on in Lazica, as Chosroes' behaviour immediately after the armistice shows him resolved that it should. The record of this fighting for the years 553–8 may be read in Agathias (on whom see below, Chap IX, pp. 184ff.); but Agathias, though in many ways a not incompetent historian, was no soldier, and he had no personal knowledge of Lazica. We will therefore pass over the details of these military operations and devote most of this chapter to one illuminating incident that occurred in Lazica – the murder of King Gubazes and the public trial of the officers who did away with him – and to the actual peace treaty with the negotiations that led up to it. In the Gubazes incident Agathias, as a trained lawyer, is dealing with matters that he really understood. For the peace negotiations and treaty our authority is Menander Protector (see below, pp. 92–101 and Chap IX, pp. 187–190) whose account is based on the memoirs of the chief negotiator on the Roman side.

Agathias[1] fully understood the significance of the struggle for Lazica. He begins by recalling the recent armistice, the limitations which made it not apply to Lazica (II. 18) and the importance of the country for both parties. 'Chosroes had already annexed many important districts of the country and ... planned to reduce the rest, while to Justinian it seemed intolerable and wicked to betray Gubazes and his people, who had always been his

---

[1] The references to Agathias in this chapter state the book, chapter and where necessary the page and lines of the Greek text in the Teubner edition (*Historici Graeci Minores* vol. II, ed. Dindorf).

loyal subjects and confessed the same faith ... He reflected with alarm that if the Persians won the war and
controlled the whole country, there would be nothing to
prevent them sailing the Black Sea and penetrating to the
innermost parts of the Roman empire' (II. 18, p. 201,
14–27).

In the first campaign after the armistice Mermeroes,
the old Persian commander, died. His body was exposed
to be devoured by dogs and vultures according to the
Persian practice, and Agathias seizes the occasion for a
learned excursus on Persian burial customs and Zoro-
aster (II. 22–3). It was shortly after Mermeroes had been
succeeded as Persian commander in Lazica by Nachoragan (III. 2) that the series of events occurred that led
to the murder of Gubazes and the subsequent trial of his
murderers. Gubazes had written to Justinian complaining of their mismanagement of the war. 'He complained
most of Bessas and after him of Martin and Rusticus.'
Martin was the general who had been responsible for a
recent Persian break through the Roman lines; Rusticus
was a Graeco-Galatian, not a soldier but a confidential
finance officer with the special task of remunerating
those who distinguished themselves in the war. Justinian
removed Bessas from his command and sent him to
Abasgia to await his further pleasure, but though very
angry with Martin too, placed him in supreme command
with Justin and Buzes under him (III. 2, p. 238). Relations
between these officers and Gubazes were naturally of the
worst, and they sent John, the brother of Rusticus, to
Justinian to tell him secretly that Gubazes was a traitor.
Justinian, in great perplexity, told John to instruct Martin and Rusticus to send Gubazes to Constantinople.
'And what,' asked John, 'if he refuses to come and
resists us?' 'Then,' said the emperor, 'he shall meet the
fate of tyrants and perish miserably.' 'And will his killers
have no cause for alarm?' 'Not if he show fight and be
destroyed for his disobedience.' These instructions were
put into writing and carried back by John (III. 3). The
unfortunate Gubazes was summoned to meet the generals,
asked to go, not to Constantinople, but with the generals

themselves to attack a strong enemy fortress, and was easily led on to recriminations in the course of which he said that the Roman officers had let the Persians in and it was their business to drive them out again. Thereupon John struck him down and one of Rusticus' bodyguard finished off the murder. Justin and Buzes were distressed but kept silence, imagining that the others must be carrying out the emperor's definite instructions (III. 4).

The murder of their king had a depressing effect on the Lazi. For the time they took no further part in the war and avoided all contact with the Romans (III. 4, p. 242. 16–21), whose prestige was further shaken by a disgraceful defeat in battle (III. 5–8, p. 249. 10). Eventually they held a secret conference in a gorge of the Caucasus to discuss their whole future policy, whether to go over to the Persians or in spite of all to remain loyal to the empire (III. 8, p. 249. 10–250. 9). What finally decided them to adhere to the emperor was the fear lest, if they changed sides, they would have to give up their Christian faith (III. 14, p. 261. 29–32). A messenger was sent to Justinian reporting their decision and asking that the wicked officials should be punished and that Gubazes' younger brother Tzathes should be sent from Constantinople to be their king. Justinian agreed and sent to Lazica a distinguished civilian named Athanasius, who immediately arrested Rusticus and John (III. 14). Tzathes too was sent back to Lazica complete with the insignia that the emperor always bestowed on the Lazic kings (III. 15, p. 263). Tzathes made his entry into Lazica in full regal majesty and was given an impressive reception by the whole Roman army. The Lazi were restored to cheerfulness and became once more the loyal supporters of the empire.

Their cheerfulness was justified. The Constantinople government seems to have realized the seriousness of the situation in Lazica. Its reaction to it was not unworthy of the best traditions of imperial Rome, with diplomacy and pageantry lending their support to the might of Roman arms and the majesty of Roman law. The military display at Tzathes' return to Lazica restored the confidence of the demoralized Roman army both in itself and in its Lazic allies. Shortly after this its able if sometimes lax and unscrupulous commander Martin won a crushing victory over the Persians. Their commander Nachoragan retired to Iberia (A.D. 555. III. 20–8).

'When the war had reached this victorious stage and there was a momentary lull in operations, the investigation was opened into the outrage on Gubazes. Athanasius' (Justinian's special legate) 'took his seat on a high tribunal ... attended by men who were trained reporters and skilled in the rapid reading of records. There were other majestic functionaries learned in the niceties of court procedure, loud-voiced criers and masters of the whips, all selected from public offices in Byzantium. The proper officials were there with collars of iron and other instruments of torture. And I think,' our historian continues, 'that this was no accidental piece of routine. The Emperor Justinian had ordered the trial to proceed with all this pomp and circumstance from a shrewd idea of what was fitting, in order that an impressive exhibition of Roman practice might be made to the barbarians of those parts ..., and if Gubazes were proved to have supported the Persians he might be shown to have been justly removed and the Colchians no longer feel aggrieved ... while if his slayers were convicted of having fabricated the whole charge and committing a foul crime, and were led forth before the whole multitude and beheaded with the sword of vengeance in the sight of all, the final verdict might be the more impressive. For he knew that if he merely ordered Rusticus and John to be done away with secretly in the barbarian way, the Colchians would not feel that the outrage had been adequately written off ... He rightly recognized that when the court had been established and pleas had been lodged on either side and officials were darting about and arranging that each of the parties should stand and answer in his proper place, the majesty and solemn language of the court and the awful doom impending would all enhance the overwhelming effect. ... Even the citizens of Byzantium are cowed, and there is no spirit left in them after such proceedings, often as they take place there. Still more so would barbarians be who were not accustomed to them. This was the reason why a Roman or rather a completely Attic court of justice was assembled under the Caucasus' (IV. 1).

'Rusticus and John were now brought into court from their prison and took their places as the defendants on the judge's left. On the other side, to conduct the prosecution, stood those of the Colchians who were most intelligent and had been longest acquainted with the Greek language. These latter begged that the letter of instructions that had been brought by John from the emperor should be read aloud' (IV. 2). It was. Next the Colchians pleaded their cause. It was, they argued, a test case for Roman justice. The loyalty of all the provinces depended on a just decision, the crime being so flagrant that no assertions by the defendants as to their motives ought to have any weight. Even if Gubazes had been at all to blame, which they denied, 'what law,' they asked, 'either in your empire or in foreign lands, would approve of the accusation being made after the sentence? If that were allowed, why should we not have taken the law into our own hands against the murderers instead of appealing to Roman justice? Permit this sort of thing and we shall all mutually exterminate one another. "Make an example of one traitor," the defendants say, "and it will have a sobering effect on all your allies." Our reply is: "Allow one crime like this of Rusticus and John to go unpunished, and the loyalty of the whole empire is undermined." Gubazes had been remarkably loyal to the empire under the most trying circumstances. It was a time when it was imperative to make such loyalty attractive not only to the subjects of Rome but also to the races beyond the Roman borders' (IV. 3–6).

Rusticus took the line of defence habitual to his kind. He was the man who had done the dirty work and saved the empire. A Persian court would have far better reason to condemn him. The one indisputable fact was that the Romans were still in Colchis, and that fact was due to the way that he and John had suppressed Gubazes. 'In many places in our cities we see itinerant swindlers and robbers and other malefactors now deprived of their heads, now with their feet severed. We do not in such cases blame the government as inhuman ... but reflect that the criminals are paying the price of their misdeeds, and we rejoice at their savage punishment. It would be equally absurd to blame us for the fate that Gubazes brought upon himself. Every barbarian race, even if subject to Rome, has a profoundly alien outlook which puts a wide gulf between it and the Romans. It hates our ways and if it could have a free choice it would live completely independent. Failing that it turns naturally to those whose ways and outlook are like its own. Gubazes had this alien outlook. Like all his race he was by nature untrustworthy and disloyal. His whole history shows it and particularly his behaviour in the matter of Onoguris and Justinian's letter. Our action against him was right and just and it was carried out not without the approval of Martin' (IV. 7–10).

Athanasius was at first influenced by these pleas, but after further examination and reflection found the facts to be as recorded above. The case of Martin he decided to refer to the emperor, but Rusticus and John were condemned to death, and the verdict recorded in writing. They were set on mules, paraded round the city accompanied by a loud-voiced herald bidding men fear the law and refrain from murder, and were then beheaded. The execution put an end to the indignation against them and restored the old good feeling of the Colchians for the Romans (IV. 11).

The lull in military operations that had been used by the Romans to stage this spectacular trial proved to be in fact the beginning of the end of hostilities with Persia. It was only disturbed in the following year (A.D. 556–7) by trouble with the Misimians, a people vassal to the vassal state of Lazica, who had murdered, not without provocation, a Roman official quartered in their country.

When the Misimians had been punished, Justinian removed the able and popular Martin, the one remaining officer who had been implicated in the Gubazes affair, from his command, and in his place appointed Justin son of Germanus as general plenipotentiary (στρατηγὸς αὐτοκράτωρ) of the Roman forces in Colchis (Lazica) and Armenia. The drive against corruption and dishonesty had run its course. Justin was a competent officer, but he got involved in a financial scandal which recalls those of the days when Cicero was a provincial governor. He brought with him a certain John the Libyan, a man of humble origin and entirely unscrupulous. This John asked the general for a specified sum of gold and promised, if he got it, to provision Justin's whole establishment, including servants and bodyguard, and to make him an annual payment as well. Justin accepted the offer and John carried out his engagement (IV. 21). His method was simple. He would go to a district where oxen were scarce, demand an impossible number of oxen at a reasonable price, and then force his victims to pay an enormous sum for not providing them. In another district, where camels had not so much as ever been heard of, the same result was attained by a similar demand for camels. In corn-growing districts he bought up the harvest at a nominal price. In ship-building centres he commandeered the ships. The corn was loaded on to the ships and sold abroad at a high price whilst the Colchians were left to starve. The victims appealed again and again to Justin, but he kept his wicked bargain with John (IV. 22).

After Justin's appointment to the Lazic command hostilities with Persia came practically to an end. Chosroes recalled Nachoragan to Persia, where he was punished for his cowardice 'according to the custom of the country' by being flayed alive (p. 330). Chosroes realized that with Justinian controlling the Black Sea he could never gain full control of Lazica. A high official with the Persian title of Zich, which Agathias, for all his claims to inside information about Persia, states to have been his personal name (and indeed it now appears that he may have made a similar mistake in the case of Nachoragan), was sent to Constantinople, and terms were agreed on by which each side was to keep what it held. 'When this was reported to the generals, their forces remained for a long time entirely inactive, and the state of things that had in fact been already long established was now ratified by treaty' (iv. 30, end).

This ends Agathias' account of events in Lazica. He does not tell us that the provisional arrangements for ending the war made on the Zich's visit to Constantinople in A.D. 557 were not followed up by the formal signature of a peace treaty at a peace conference till A.D. 562. For an account of that conference and the terms of the actual treaty we have to turn to Menander Protector, the writer who continued Agathias' history as Agathias had continued that of Procopius. The work of Menander (see below, Chap. IX, pp. 187–190) has unfortunately come down to us only in fragments, but one of these (frag. 11, *Hist. Graec. Minores* ii. pp. 10–32) deals with the peace finally ratified between Rome and Persia in A.D. 562 and the negotiations that led up to it. It is based on the detailed records of the principal Roman delegate. As Bury well observes (ii. 123), it is rarely that we get a glimpse like this into the formal diplomatic procedure of ancient times. An abridgement of Menander's version will form the final section of this chapter and conclude our study of Justinian's wars. It is given at some length and in part verbatim, as no English translation of this author has yet appeared.

'In Lazica there was an armistice between the Romans and Persians. So since the peace question was as it were half solved ... Justinian sent Peter, master of offices, to negotiate with Chosroes about a definite treaty. When he reached the frontier at Daras ... , a Persian ambassador was also sent to that place, one who held the office of Zich, by name Iesdegusnaph. He was a gentleman of the bedchamber to his sovereign. The ambassadors met, and when the provincial governors were assembled, Peter, the Roman ambassador, a man of wide culture and special legal training, spoke as follows ...'

The wide culture and special legal training sound rather ominous qualifications, and the fear expressed by

Peter that his opponents might find him pompous and wordy were not unfounded. He argues that peace is a blessing and that victory in war is a misfortune second only to defeat. Justinian is suing for peace solely to prevent the Persians from gaining the glory that this step would bring to those who led the way in taking it. True, the Persians gained a great success when they sacked Antioch (A.D. 540, see above, Chap. IV. pp. 69f.); 'but this reverse was decreed by God for the special benefit of the Romans, to remind them that even they are as other men. The purpose has been achieved and there is no further need for God to use the Persians to teach the Romans this lesson. So let us both do what the land of Persia and Rome herself, if they could speak, would beg of us, and let us not be ashamed to lay down the burden of war and stop the bitter complaints of our subjects, who are now accusing the governing classes of bringing ruin on them by their blunders.' In reply to Peter the Zich said simply that all Peter's fine words scarcely disguised the fact that the Romans were a beaten people praying like cowards for peace. The Persians were not elated by the capture of Antioch: 'we do not bestow our admiration on the obviously easy. But it is a mark of nobility to regulate conduct by what is right. We are men who hold peace in the greatest esteem, and so we accept your message.'

The boastfulness of both speeches may antagonize the modern reader. It is doubtful whether they so affected the participants at the conference, for Menander tells us that the interpreters on either side, in translating the speeches of the other party, expounded the gist of them; and we may fairly suppose that these experienced functionaries used much discretion in their translations and expositions. Both sides in fact were eager for peace. The Persians were ready to surrender Lazica – for a price; the Romans were ready to pay – up to a limit. The real question was how much they were to pay and when the payment, or payments, should be made. What indeed gives this long fragment of Menander its unique interest is the fact, already noticed, that it seems to embody an authentic account of how at this period peace negotiations were conducted and peace treaties drawn up. If at times the account seems tortuous and long-winded it will only be reproducing the atmosphere of the Greek original and also, we may feel fairly sure, of the actual proceedings.

The Persians wanted a perpetual peace and perpetual payments. The Romans wanted to make as few payments as possible and these to be of the smallest possible amount. 'A heated dispute took place on this point, and the speeches made were by no means brief'; but in the end it was decided that a peace valid on all fronts should be made for fifty years, the Persians to evacuate Lazica and the Romans to pay them 30,000 pieces of gold annually, starting with two block sums, the first seven years' payments to be made down on the spot, those for three years more to be paid in a single sum at the end of the first seven years (p. 15).

'The agreement of the Roman emperor about the peace contained the usual preface and is perfectly familiar to us. That of the Persian king was written in Persian, but may be translated in about these words: "The divine, good, ancient Chosroes, father of peace, king of kings, fortunate, pious, beneficent, to whom the gods have given great fortune and great dominion, giant of giants, who bears the stamp of the gods, to Justinian Caesar, our brother. We are grateful to our brother the Emperor for his request for peace between our two states and we gave orders and authority to Iesdegusnaph the divine chamberlain, while our brother the Emperor gave orders and authority to Peter, the Master of the Romans, and to Eusebius to confer and treat. And the Zich and the Roman official called the Master and Eusebius conferred and treated together on the question of peace, and they agreed to a peace of fifty years and all of them signed. We therefore, in accordance with the proceedings of the Zich and the Master of the Romans and Eusebius, are firmly maintaining the peace and abiding by it." These were the precise words. And the agreement of the Roman Emperor was similarly couched, but with-

out the preface which the Persian royal document contained, and thereupon the conference broke up' (pp.
16–17).

The detailed clauses of the treaty promised by
Menander are not given at this point. The continuation
of his narrative explains why. There were still some
points to settle, notably the position of the Saracen chiefs
who owed a loose allegiance to one or other of the two
great monarchs and the status of the petty Caucasus
kingdom of Suania, which had long been dependent on
its southern neighbour Lazica but had recently been
occupied by the Persians. A second meeting was accordingly called. The way that these two thorny subjects were
raised, talked round, dropped and raised again, well
illustrates the methods of Byzantine-Persian diplomacy.
We must of course constantly remember that our account
comes from a Byzantine, not a Persian historian.

The Zich opened proceedings 'by talking big and indulging in boasts about King Chosroes' (p. 17. 8–9). To
this Peter replied with a moral tale about the old
Pharaoh Sesostris, who used to drive about in a chariot
drawn by captive kings until one of these captives, point-
ing to the chariot wheels, taught Sesostris the lesson of
Fortune and her wheel and thereby induced him to
release his captive team and set them up again in their
kingdoms. 'They then resumed the discussion of the
agenda. Only the question of Suania remained in sus-
pense ... So Peter spoke thus: "... It is not idly that I just
now told my tale. ... I should like to be a little more
explicit. Suania belonged to the Romans and the
Romans ruled the Suani. Very well. When Tzathius was
chief of the Suani, a certain Deitatus, a Roman gentleman, chanced to be in command of the Roman forces in
those parts. Certain others of the Romans were living
in Suania. But when a quarrel arose between the King
of the Lazi and Martin the Roman, who was then general
in that region, the Colchians as a consequence did not
send the Suani their usual allowance of corn. ... The
Suani, annoyed at being deprived of their customary
supplies, informed the Persians that if they came there

they would hand over Suania to them. ... And the
Persians speedily arriving took Suania. So you must
gather from this that it belonged of old to the Romans
and the Romans have a right to it to-day. For if we have
with the fullest right established our power in Lazica, as
indeed you have proclaimed, we shall not be wrong in
claiming Suania, which is subject to Lazica." But
Surena said "The fact is rather, Romans, that you are
annoyed because a nation has of its own choosing and
free will come over to us". Here the Zich interposed and
said "The Suani have been independent and never
bowed to the rule of the Colchians". Then again Peter
addressed the Zich: "If, O Zich, you do not want to
insert the name of Suania in the peace terms, indicate that
you restore to me Lazica with the nations subject to it."
Said the Zich, "If I do this, an opening will be given you
to dispute about Iberia as well, and you might say, if you
liked, that it too had been subject to the Lazi". "You
have been discovered, O Zich," said Peter, "not to want
to restore to us all Lazica, but only a part of it." Much
else the Romans and Persians said and heard about
Suania, but they failed to come to terms. They resolved
therefore on this point to consult the King of the
Persians. And the Zich pledged himself, in the way it is
customary for Persians to swear, that he would support
Peter when he came to Chosroes in the matter of Suania'
(p. 17. 20–20. 13).

At this point in Menander's narrative the Zich reverts
to the question of the Saracen chief Ambros, and claims
that he should receive a regular subsidy from Justinian,
a sort of blackmail or Danegeld to buy off this chieftain
from raiding Roman territory and incidentally to bind
him to the King of Persia as the power that ensured him
the blackmail. Peter replied that Justinian and Ambros'
predecessor had indeed exchanged presents on various
occasions, and that the emperor would not object to their
continuing this practice; but that if he hoped to become
a regular pensioner of the emperor he was indulging in
idle fancies and would get nothing whatever (p. 20. 13–
32). In other words Justinian was ready to buy Ambros

off only when that chieftain was in a position to make himself a nuisance.

'When these and other points had been discussed, the fifty years' truce was written out in Persian and in Greek, and the Greek version translated into Persian, and the Persian into Greek ... And when the agreements on either side had been put into writing, they were compared with one another to make them correspond in sense and language. All that the terms of peace specified is stated below' (p. 20. 32–21. 11).

(*i*) 'Through the pass called Chorutzon and the Caspian Gates the Persians shall not allow either Huns or Alans or other barbarians to penetrate into the realms of the Romans; and the Romans shall neither in that land nor on other parts of the Persian frontier send any army against the Persians' (p. 21. 12–18).

(*ii*) 'The Saracen allies of either state shall on their part too abide by the terms, and neither shall those of the Persians take arms against the Romans nor those of the Romans against the Persians' (p. 21. 18–22).

(*iii*) 'Merchants, Roman or Persian, of whatever kind of goods ... shall, according to the practice that originally prevailed, conduct their trade through the specified customs houses' (p. 21. 22–6).

(*iv*) 'Ambassadors and persons employing public post horses to bear messages, alike those arriving in Roman territory and those arriving in Persian, shall be honoured as their rank demands and as is fitting in each case, and shall receive all necessary attention. They are to depart again without delay, but may traffic the merchandise they bring without hindrance and exempt from any dues' (p. 21. 26–22. 2).

(*v*) 'Saracens and barbarian merchants of any kind belonging to either state are not to travel by strange routes, but only by Nisibis and Daras, nor may they proceed without an official order into foreign territory. If, contrary to order, they venture on any such course or, in vulgar parlance, engage in smuggling, they shall be tracked down by the frontier officials with the goods they are conveying, whether these be Assyrian or Roman, and handed over to receive punishment' (p. 22. 2–11).

(*vi*) 'If any persons deserted during the period of the war, either from the Romans to the Persians or from the Persians to the Romans, they shall not be prevented or hindered from returning home if they so wish. Those however who in time of peace desert or escape from one side to the other are not to be received but by every possible means are to be handed over, even against their will, to those from whom they escaped' (p. 22. 11–20).

(*vii*) 'Those who complain that nationals of the other state are doing them some harm shall settle the dispute by arbitration, action being taken either on their own part by the men who have suffered the harm or by special persons meeting on the frontiers at the quarters of the officials of either state; whereafter the person who has inflicted the damage shall make the loss good' (p. 22. 20–7).

(*viii*) 'Neither state shall henceforth fortify against the other nor strengthen with any circuit wall any of the positions on the frontier, in order that there may be no ensuing pretext for disturbances and the truce be consequently broken' (p. 22. 27–23. 1).

(*ix*) 'The members of one nation shall not make attacks or war against any subject race or any place belonging to the other, but rather, without inflicting damage or harm in any way, remain where they are, that these too may enjoy peace' (p. 23. 1–5).

(*x*) 'No large force shall be stationed at Daras, but only one adequate to garrison the city. The general of the East shall not make his headquarters there, to prevent inroads being made into Persian territory and damage being done to the Persians. But if any such should occur it was laid down that the governor of Daras should deal with the offence' (p. 23. 5–11).

(*xi*) 'If one city inflicts loss on another ... not in accordance with the laws of war nor by military force but in some other way by guile or theft (for there are certain such ungodly men, who do such deeds that there may be a pretext for war), it is hereby agreed that such proceedings shall be carefully investigated and punished by the judges stationed on the frontier of either state. And if they prove incapable of putting a stop to the losses so inflicted ... the case shall be referred to the general of the East, on the understanding that if within six months the dispute is not settled and the sufferer has not recovered his losses, the offender shall thereupon be liable to the injured party for double the penalty. If even so the case shall not be settled, it is enjoined that the injured party shall send a deputation to the sovereign of the offender. Then, if he fails to secure satisfaction even from the sovereign and to recover the doubled compensation according to the agreement within a year, as far as that clause goes the peace will be regarded as broken' (p. 23. 11 – 24. 1).

(*xii*) 'As the twelfth clause of the truce you will find supplications to God and also imprecations: e.g. that if a man observes the peace God may be gracious to him ..., but if a man uses guile and seeks to alter any of the terms, God may be his adversary and enemy' (p. 24. 1–7).

(*xiii*) 'The truce shall be for fifty years, and the terms of the peace shall be valid for fifty years, the year being reckoned in the ancient style, each year terminating on the 365th day. ... Documents shall be taken away by either side indicating that both parties agree to the terms as settled by the envoys' (p. 24. 7–15).

'When all had been decided on and put into force, separate consideration was given to the question of the Christians in Persia, and it was agreed that they should build churches and hold services freely ... and further that they should neither be compelled to attend Magian services nor to invoke against their will the gods in whom the Medes believe. And the Christians on their part agreed that they would by no means venture to convert Magians to our belief. And it was further enacted that in the matter of the dead the Christians should have permission to bury them in graves as is customary among us' (p. 24. 16–28).

'When this agreement had been arrived at and reduced to an orderly arrangement and the officials appointed for

this purpose had received the drafts of the two documents and rendered the meaning more precise by finding
words that had the same force and significance, they at
once executed other copies. And the originals were rolled
up and secured with seals of wax and others such as the
Persians are accustomed to use and with impressions of
their signet rings by the envoys and twelve interpreters,
six Roman and as many Persian; and thereupon they
interchanged the documents with the terms of peace.
The one written in Persian was handed to Peter by the
Zich, that in Greek to the Zich by Peter.' And then again
when the Zich had received a counterpart of the Greek
version but written in Persian and not secured by the
seals, to be kept for consultation, Peter likewise was given
a Greek translation of the Persian original and the exchange of documents was completed (p. 24. 28–p. 25. 14).

The rest of the proceedings must be merely summarized. The Zich immediately returned to Persia
while Peter stayed behind to celebrate Christmas and
Epiphany. Meanwhile 'certain Persians arrived at Dara
along with certain interpreters and the controllers of the
scales, and there were paid over to the Zich's officials the
payments due for seven years according to the terms on
which the agreement had been ratified' (p. 25. 22–7).

Peter now proceeded to Persia to be received by Chosroes himself, and the question of Suania, that 'spark of
trouble', as Peter calls it, was once more raised. Peter's
speech (as recorded by himself) mingles appeals to
Chosroes' generosity with references to documents showing that Suania had always been an appendage of Lazica.
Chosroes in his reply claimed that the Suani had voluntarily come over to Persia, and expressed astonishment
that the Romans could make a claim so remote from
justice. The discussion then shifted to the question of the
Saracen chiefs, with both parties repeating what they
had said at the previous conference. Then the Suanian
discussion was resumed and the arguments were all gone
over again, and Peter produced a document showing
which of the kings of Lazica had nominated rulers of
Suania. Chosroes accepted this as far as it went, but

pointed out that it did not make the status of the existing Suanian kinglet any less ambiguous. 'However, if the Suanian wants to be subject to Rome, I shall take no steps to prevent him. Further than that I cannot go.' At this Peter suggested that the Suanians themselves might be consulted. 'Will you not enquire, Sire, from the Suanian, on which side he wishes to be? For he is his own master up to that point.' 'Understand,' said the king, 'that I am not prepared to make any enquiry of the Suanians concerning Suania, since it is neither holy nor in any way right that the question of the land itself should depend on the decision of a slave' (p. 31. 26–32. 5).

With this forthright declaration by the king of kings on the 'unholiness' of the doctrine of self-determination[1] the fragment of Menander ends and the curtain drops on this valuable if sometimes tedious picture of a sixth-century Byzantine peace conference. It forms a fitting conclusion to the long story of Justinian's wars.

[1] Bury (II p. 123) regards Chosroes as making the proposal of self-determination, which may be a matter of opinion, but there is no justification for his statement that Peter turned it down.

CHAPTER VI

The Bureaucracy[1]

*

THE administrative organization that governed and controlled the empire of Justinian was the direct descendant of that which had grown up with the growth of the Roman empire itself. Consuls had been replaced by emperors, and the power and position of the emperor had undergone successive changes from the disguised autocracy of the 'princeps' Augustus to the ritualistic absolutism of the pagan Diocletian and his Christian successors. The senate had changed from being at one time the virtual master and director of the chief magistrates to something much nearer to the Hitlerian Reichstag. The army had usurped the power originally exercised by the sovereign people. Armies could and often did appoint the supreme head of the state, the imperator or commander-in-chief. The provincial system, originally improvised when Rome first made conquests in Sicily and Spain, was still the basis of imperial administration in the outer parts of the empire, though with the growth of absolutism the provinces and their governors had got more and more to be directly controlled from the centre.

In the early days of the empire this had undoubtedly been a good thing for the provincials. A provincial governorship was no longer, as in the days of Verres and Catullus, a means for the governor to repair his private fortune and accumulate priceless collections of works of art. Agricola in Britain, as pictured in the pages of Tacitus, or the younger Pliny in Bithynia, as we see him in his correspondence with the emperor Trajan, are plainly honest and well-meaning officials with the interests of the provincials whom they are governing very

[1] For the facts embodied in the first part of this chapter see further Bury's *Later Roman Empire* (A.D. 395–565) chapters ii and xxi ('The Administrative Machinery' and 'Administrative Reforms and Finance').

close to their hearts. But with the increase of control from the centre there had inevitably been a loss of initiative. Witness the ridiculously trivial questions on such matters as the personnel of the local fire brigade that Pliny thinks it necessary to submit to his emperor. But when we find Pliny's questions rather absurd we should remember that, if once we concede the imperial position, we have also to grant that the danger above all to be avoided was the sort of thing that had followed the death of Nero, when three rivals for the throne of the Caesars, Galba, Otho and Vitellius, plunged the empire into civil war. The same thing was to occur again in the time of Severus, Niger and Albinus, and of Constantine and his rivals. Consequently a provincial governor who showed independence could only be regarded with suspicion at headquarters. This danger had been in the forefront of Diocletian's mind when he reorganized the provincial system by increasing the number of provinces, making the governors purely civilian, forming these new and smaller provinces into groups, each called a diocese, and grouping these dioceses into four prefectures, two in the West (the one embracing Italy and North-West Africa, the other Gaul, Spain and Britain) and two in the East (the one taking in Macedonia, Greece and Dacia, the other Thrace, the Asiatic provinces and Egypt). Governors of provinces were known variously as *consulares*, *correctores* or *praesides*, of dioceses as vicars, of prefectures as prefects. The emperor could deal with these officials either through their superiors (if any) or directly; which meant that the ways of any official who aspired to make himself independent and seize the throne were rendered extremely difficult. It will be noticed that some of these titles are still in common use among the hierarchy of the church. The reason of course is that the church borrowed its organization from the state, as indeed it did also the form of its churches (cf. such words as *basilica* and *chancel*).

The population of the various provinces consisted, as have all populations of all civilized communities, of townsmen and country folk; but those of us who live in a

country like England, which has enjoyed an exceptionally peaceful development for centuries, are apt to forget
an essential difference between our market towns and
those of the Roman empire in the days of Justinian, when
the general insecurity meant that the towns were the
only places of comparative safety for the well-to-do.
From the fourth century onwards, with the increasing
peril from raiders and the crushing cost of meeting these
perils, the provincial governors had become more and
more absorbed in the pressing need of raising more and
more taxes, and these unhappy towns had been increasingly called on to play their part in paying them.
Each town had a body of councillors called decurions
or *curiales*, and the position became so burdensome that
laws had to be passed to prevent citizens from evading
this office. The desperate financial position must often
have been decisive with the emperor in making appointments of high officials. There was no room for squeam-
ishness. This fact must be constantly borne in mind when
we find, as we shall later in this study, serious criticisms
of Justinian's methods and appointments.

Administration at the centre was entrusted to a group
of high ministers of state. The first in rank of these at
Constantinople was the Prefect of the East (i.e. of the
provinces in Thrace, Asia and Egypt); his colleague the
Prefect of Illyricum (i.e. the provinces that embraced
Dacia, Macedonia and Greece) had his headquarters at
Salonica. The prefect, as has already been implied, had
the general responsibility for the appointment of provincial governors and provincial administration. The
administration of Constantinople itself was in the hands
of a separate official, the Prefect of the City. The chief
legal officer and head of the Privy Council was the
Quaestor of the Sacred Palace. Finances were administered by two high officials, the Count of the Sacred
Largesses (*Comes Sacrarum Largitionum*) and the Count of
the Private Estates, or, as we should call it, Privy Purse
(*Comes Rerum Privatarum*). Lastly there was an official
of the highest standing whose pre-eminent position in
the time of Justinian was of comparatively recent growth,

he Master of Offices (*Magister Officiorum*). He was so
alled, to quote the words of Bury (Vol. 1, p. 29), 'from
he authority which he exercised over the civil service,
ut especially over the secretarial departments in the
'alace', *officium* being the word for the body of civil ser-
ants (*officiales*). He also controlled the public post (*cursus
ublicus*), the secret service (*agentes in rebus*), and the state
rms-factories, and was responsible for the conduct of
ourt ceremonies, including the reception of foreign am-
assadors. The possibilities of a post which gave its
older all these powers need not be amplified.

A whole army of clerks and assistants was employed by
nese high officers of state. These subordinate permanent
ivil servants belonged to one or other of a group of
ureaux (*scrinia*, whence Fr. *écrin*), notably the *a memoria*,
b epistulis and *a libellis*, each under a magister (*magister
emoriae*, etc.) and trained respectively to draft or make
inutes of imperial answers to petitions, to deal similarly
ith correspondence with foreign or provincial authori-
es, and with legal appeals.

Besides this elaborate civil service organization there
as also a hierarchy of rank; officials of the very highest
ank bore the title *illustris*, those of the second rank were
ectabiles, of the third rank *clarissimi*. These honorific
bels were as much sought after and appreciated as are
tles and decorations in this country at the present
ay.

Our chief sources for the very considerable knowledge
nat has come down to us of this complex organization
nclude various enactments dealing with them in the
odes of Theodosius and of Justinian himself; the corres-
ondence of the Roman Cassiodorus (published by their
uthor in A.D. 537 under the title *Variae* (sc. *Epistulae*),
c. Miscellaneous Correspondence) who was master of
ie offices and praetorian prefect to the Gothic king
heoderic and his immediate successors; the *Notitia
ignitatum*, a handbook of imperial officials and their
affs, of which our extant copy belongs to the year A.D.
28; and an interesting but by no means lucid work
lled *de Magistratibus Populi Romani* written by John

Lydus, a civil servant who served most of his long period under Justinian. Procopius too has much to say about the activities of the most notable praetorian prefect of his own days.

The rest of this chapter will be devoted to illustrating the activities of particular officials, high and low, from these various works, in the hope of giving the reader some notion of the kind of information that we have and perhaps also incidentally of the kind of men to whom we owe it.

The *Variae* of Cassiodorus are mainly actual letters composed on various state occasions; but those of Books VI and VII are what he calls Formulae, i.e. model letters suitable for announcing appointments to the various offices of state. He claims that in these 'Formulae' he says nothing about the qualities of the individual office holders but has made such explanations as seemed suitable concerning the office. They are of course all designed for officials in the western half of the empire, but in essentials they hold good for the corresponding officials in New Rome. The author's unrivalled gift for irrelevant digression and verbosity makes it necessary for us to content ourselves with extracts only from the already abbreviated version of Hodgkin.

Cass. *Variae* VI. 3: formula of the praetorian prefecture: The prefect's position was foreshadowed by that of Joseph under Pharaoh king of Egypt, which shows how it is stamped by the Divine approval. He inflicts heavy fines on offenders, he distributes the public revenues as he thinks fit, he has a like power in bestowing rights of free conveyance (i.e. free passes by the *cursus publicus*) ..., he punishes the offences of the provincial judges, he pronounces sentence by word of mouth (whereas all other judges had to read their decisions). He may almost be said to have the power of making laws, since the reverence due to him enables him to settle law suits without appeal. On his entrance into the palace he, like ourselves, is adored by the assembled throng, a practice which in other cases would be considered a matter for accusation. No soldier marks out the imits of his jurisdiction ... His staff is composed of men of the highest education, energetic, strong-minded, intent on prompt obedience to the orders of their head and not tolerating obstruction from others ... His forethought nourishes the Palace, procures the daily rations of our servants, and provides the salaries even of the judges themselves. By his arrangements he satiates the hungry appetites of the ambassadors of the nations. And though other dignities have their specially defined prerogatives, by him everything that comes within the scope of our wisely-tempered sway is governed.

Cass. *Variae* VI. 4: formula of the prefecture of the City: You judge on appeal causes brought from certain provinces defined by law. You ride in your state coach through a populace of nobles (the sovereign people). ... How will you deserve their favour? By seeing that merchandise is sold without venality (interpreted by Hodgkin as meaning 'that you are not bribed by monopolists'); that the fires kindled to heat the wholesome baths are not chilled by corruption (the Roman baths were one of the great amenities of the cities of the empire, cf. the remains in Rome, to which Cassiodorus is here specially referring, and in our own Bath. The 'Turkish' bath is a direct descendant of these institutions); that the games which are meant for the pleasure of the people are not by partisanship made the cause of strife (on the games see below, Chap. VII).

Cass. *Variae* VI. 5: formula for the quaestorship: You must have knowledge of the law, wariness in speech, firmness of purpose. To you the provinces transmit their prayers; from you the senate seeks the aid of law. You are expected to suffice for the needs of all who seek from us the remedies of the law. Let your learning be such that you may set forth every subject on which you have to treat with suitable embellishments.

The 'suitable embellishments' thus stressed by Cassiodorus are ominous. They mean the antiquarian preciosity that is to us so distressful a part of the outlook and outfit of the average conscientious civil servant of the period. We shall have occasion to quote illustrations of this weakness later in this chapter from one of Justinian's own civil servants.

Cass. *Variae* VI. 6: of the magisterial dignity and its excellence (i.e. of the master of offices) : The master's is a name of dignity. To him belongs the discipline of the Palace; he calms the stormy ranks of the insolent *scholares* (household troops). He introduces the senators to our presence, cheers them when they tremble, calms them when they are speaking, sometimes inserts a word or two of his own, that all may be laid in an orderly manner before us. It rests with him to fix a day for the admission of a suitor to our Aulicum Consistorium and to fulfil his promise. The opportune velocity of the post horses (i.e. the care of the *cursus publicus*) is diligently watched over by him. The ambassadors of foreign powers are introduced by him, and their *evectiones* (free passes by the postal service) are received from his hands. ... The members of his staff, when they have served their full time, are adorned with the title of *princeps* and take precedence of the Praetorian cohorts and those of the Urban Prefecture (i.e. of the officials serving in the bureaux of these two prefects), a mark of favour which almost amounts to an injustice, since he who serves in one office (the Master's) is thereby given precedence over all those who have been serving in another (the Prefect's).

It will be noticed that the duties here assigned to the master of offices sometimes overlap those of the praetorian prefect. This is no accident. It is part of the system of checks and counterchecks designed to prevent either from acquiring a power that might challenge that of the emperor.

The Formulae of Cassiodorus deal with the various offices comprehensively but vaguely. The quotations in the *Digest* (for an account of which see below, Chap VIII, pp. 141ff.) suffer, from our immediate point of view, from a quite different limitation. They are nearly all of them pronouncements made by eminent jurists on some special occasion to meet some special and concrete point. It is for this reason hard to give effective illustrations. But one or two are here chosen in the conviction that any con-

crete example gives the reader a better idea of the
material we have at our disposal than even the most
lucid and learned general statement about its nature.
The extracts which follow are taken from pronouncements about the duties of the city prefect and those of the
provincial governor. They are quotations from eminent
jurists who were already ancient classics in Justinian's
age; but the fact that they are incorporated in the *Digest*
shows that they were regarded by Justinian and his
ministers as being still relevant. The translation is that of
C. H. Munro.

Digest I. xii (Ulpian, d. A.D. 228): on the office of the
Prefect of the City: The jurisdiction of this magistrate
embraces all criminal offences of every kind ... committed within the city. Where slaves flee to statues for
refuge, the prefect will hear their complaints against
their owners. He will also hear applications by impe-
cunious patrons who complain of their freedmen,
especially where they allege that they are in ill health
and desire that their freedmen should support them.
He has power of deportation into any island which the
Emperor may prescribe. ... If a man's complaint is that
his slave has committed adultery with his wife, the case
may be brought before the prefect. ... Guardians are
brought before the Prefect of the City where they act
corruptly in respect of their guardianship. ... With regard
to the above statement, we must not understand this
to mean that slaves may bring criminal charges against
their owners; ... what is supposed is that a slave makes a
respectful representation. ... The prefect will be bound
to take measures that moneychangers conduct themselves
honestly in all branches of their business. ... The duties
attached to the prefect's office comprise the supervision
of the whole of the meat trade; accordingly the pig-
market is under this officer's care. ... It is held to be part
of the duty of the prefect to see that the public are unmolested and to maintain order at public exhibitions. ...
The Divine Severus laid down a rescript that persons
who are alleged to have formed an illicit association
should be prosecuted in the court of the prefect.

The above extract is rather exceptional in that it covers
the same sort of ground as would a Formula of Cassiodorus; and it need hardly be pointed out how much
more competently it does so. The following extracts on
provincial governors are much more typical.

Digest I. xvi. 7 (Ulpian): If the proconsul arrives at
some populous city or at the chief town of the province,
he ... must show no impatience at receiving a com-
plimentary address.

Digest I. xviii. 13 (Ulpian): It may be expected from
any *praeses* of character and conduct that he should take
care that the province which he governs shall be settled
and orderly. This he will have no difficulty in bringing
about, if he studiously aims at securing that the province
shall be clear of bad characters; he is bound to seek out
persons guilty of sacrilege, highway robbers, manstealers
and thieves. ... In the case of lunatics whom their friends
cannot keep under control, the *praeses* ought to apply a
remedy, viz. that of confining them in prison. This was
laid down by the Divine Pius.

We may get some notion of how much Roman law,
like our own, was case law, by collating the last enactment of the quotation just given with that which follows.

Digest I. xviii. 14 (Macer, early third century A.D.):
the Divine Marcus and Commodus issued a rescript to
Scapula Tertullus in these words: 'If you have clearly
ascertained that Aelius Priscus is in such a state of insanity that he is permanently out of his mind and thus
entirely incapable of reasoning, and no suspicion is left
that he was simulating insanity when he killed his mother,
you need not be concerned with the question how he
should be punished, as his insanity is punishment enough.
At the same time he must be closely confined and, if you
think it advisable, even kept in chains ... If however he
has intervals of sounder mind, you must carefully investigate the question whether he may not have committed the crime on one of these occasions, and so have
no claim to mercy on the ground of mental infirmity. ...
The object of providing keepers for lunatics is to keep
them not only from doing harm to themselves but from

bringing destruction on others; and if this last-mentioned mischief should come to pass, it may well be set down to the negligence of any who were not sufficiently assiduous in the discharge of their office.'

As a sample of Justinian's own enactments we may take two novels (new laws issued after the publication of the code) dealing with the decuriones of the provincial cities which have been alluded to above. Each novel has an explanatory preface which states the reasons and occasion for the detailed enactment that follows. For those who are not specialists in legal or constitutional history the preface is often the most interesting part of the novel.

Novel xxxviii (A.D. 535). Justinian to John, the most glorious Praetorian Prefect of the East: Those who of old established our form of government thought right that following the precedent of the capital city they should form in each city an assembly of the well born and give it a senate through which public business should be conducted and everything be done in its proper order. The scheme so prospered and gained such reputation that the greatest and most numerous families had members in the senates, the senators forming a large body, and what were regarded as the burdens of the service being by no means unsupportable to any of them. For through being distributed amongst a large number the burden was almost imperceptible to those who shouldered it. But when gradually certain individuals began to get their names removed from the senatorial lists and to discover pretexts why they should be exempt, then little by little the senates shrank, since countless pretexts were devised the result of which was that private interests were likely to prosper but the general weal of the community to suffer. The public services devolved on a small body of men, and this state of things undermined their fortunes and did such injury to the cities that they fell into the clutches of those pernicious hirelings who are known as *vindices* (apparently tax farmers, see Bury I. p. 442). The state system has become a sink of all iniquity. This condition of things we have been constantly investigating and we have decided that we must apply a remedy. But the more we laboured at this problem the more the senators (i.e. the decurions) devised every trick to thwart our right and just enactments and the public interest. When they saw that they were being forced by every possible means to reserve a fourth part of their estate for the senate and that this provision had with great difficulty been entered among our laws, they started dissipating their property so as to die in poverty and to leave the senate not the quarter due to it but a property completely bankrupt; next, having decided to deprive the senate even of their persons, they formed the most impious plot of all, abstaining from lawful marriage and choosing rather to die childless from the legal point of view than to prove themselves useful to their race and to their senate.

The rest of the preface and the enactments that follow are all designed to prevent every form of evasion; the preface mentions the ominous fact that Justinian had already decreed that nobody should be allowed to withdraw from the senate on which he was serving except to take up one of the very highest offices of state, namely the prefecture or the still more exalted dignity of consul or patrician.

The novel to be quoted next deals with a special problem connected with the general question of the decurions:

Novel xlv (A.D. 537). Justinian to John, praetorian prefect, ex-consul and patrician: (Preface) Your eminence recently sent us a memorandum stating that certain amongst the senators are Jews or Samaritans or Montanists or men of some other detestable sort who are not even now illumined by the true faith ... And since we hate heretics they think that they are for that reason exempt from service in the senate, and you submit that a decision should be pronounced on these questions. We were astonished that your intelligence and acumen could listen to such arguments and did not straightway tear in pieces those who talked like this. If there are certain men who think that their extreme perversity constitutes a claim to privileges which we have reserved for the highest dignities, who will not detest their miserable folly? Let such men serve on the senates and let them be sorry that they have to; let them be liable to perform senatorial services ... and let no form of religion exempt them from such a lot; ... but let them be deemed unworthy of every senatorial honour. And whereas the laws grant many privileges to senators, such as that of not being flogged or publicly exposed or being deported to another country, let them not enjoy any of these ... but let them persist in the degraded condition in which they have chosen that their souls should be.

Such is the emperor's answer to John's question about Jews, infidels and heretics. Detailed instructions were hardly called for, and the novel contains only one short chapter which enacts that heretics may give evidence in favour of orthodox defendants but not against them.

There remains the *de Magistratibus* of Johannes Lydus, a work devoted to the study of the Byzantine civil service and written by a civil servant in Constantinople during Justinian's reign. He was a praetorian. The praetorian service had two branches. In one the highest position attainable was that of *cornicularius*, or chief secretary, the position which Lydus himself ultimately reached. In the other the summit of the career was the post of *primiscrinius*, an official who appears to have been a sort of accountant. Within each of these branches there was a rigidly fixed *cursus honorum*, the various steps in which need not detain us. Promotion was by seniority, and as the service was overcrowded a man was too old for serious work by the time he reached the headship of a department. So at least Lydus assures us. Everyone began as a *tachygraphos*, or simple clerk, and the clerks, he tells us, 'need many years to reach the top of the service, for they are many in number. And if by chance time brings them to the full term of their toils, they are afflicted with old age which makes hard work impossible. Naturally therefore, being unequal to the demands of these high positions, which prove almost too much for those who are upheld by youthful vigour as well as practical experience, they need assistants'. Hence arose a system of nominally temporary assistants (*adjutores*, *boethoi*), clerks of special ability, told off to do the work of their senile chiefs. The office of the *cornicularius* was staffed entirely by ex-*adjutores* (III. 9).

These details are enough to illustrate the character of the Byzantine civil service of the sixth century; but by themselves they are dry bones. Our great debt to Lydus is that he has made these dry bones live: not indeed by the lucidity of his description, for nothing could be more muddle-headed and obscure, but by the amount of personal feeling and reminiscence that he puts into his narrative, which at one point digresses into a brief consecutive account of his own career (III. 25–30).

It begins sadly, with a dropping of warm Euripidean tears:

> ' What follows I could not describe in words
> Without a flood of tears

to quote the *Peleus* of Euripides; for when all these had already been ruined like the rest, I too had my share of the ill fortune of the time, attaining to the highest of the grades in the service, but getting nothing for it beyond the title ... and all too late I repent when I reflect as I ought and ask myself what I got attending the court so long a time. But I deserve to have had this experience for entering such a service.'

As Lydus had served for forty years it would appear that his stipend was forty years in arrears. It is not surprising under the circumstances if he felt a certain discontent and seized this opportunity to ventilate it as he does in the autobiography which follows.

'When I was in my twenty-first year, in the consulship of Secundian, I came from my native Philadelphia, which lies under Mt Tmolus in Lydia, to this blessed city; and after much consideration I decided to join the *memoriales* of the court and don the uniform with them.'

Secundian was consul in A.D. 511. The *memoriales* were clerks or secretaries in the bureau of the *magister memoriae*, one of the emperor's chief secretaries.

'To avoid seeming to waste the intervening time, I

resolved to attend the classes of a philosopher. Agapius
was flourishing at that time, about whom Christodorus
the poet, in his volume about the pupils of the great
Proclus' (Neoplatonic philosopher, b. A.D. 410, d. 485)
'speaks thus:

Agapius last but foremost of them all.

Under him it was my fortune to study the first part of the
Aristotelian doctrine and to attend some lectures on the
Platonic philosophy. But fortune, having it in view rather
to thrust me aside into this service, advanced Zoticus, a
fellow citizen of mine who took an extreme delight in me,
to the prefecture of the praetorians under the mildest of
all monarchs, the emperor Anastasius; and having it in
his power not only to persuade but also to compel me,
he enrolled me among the clerks of his office, in which
it so happened that the most equitable Ammianus also,
a nephew of my father's, occupied a distinguished
position.'

'Equitable' is a well-chosen adjective to dispel any
suspicion of family jobbery. But to appreciate it fully we
must read further: 'And to prevent my growing slack by
any chance, the prefect pointed out to me every road to
gain, so that all through his period of office – it was not
long, only just over a year – I gained no less than 1,000
pieces of gold through my prudent behaviour. So naturally, being grateful – how could I have been otherwise? –
I composed a brief eulogy on him. He was delighted and
told me to take from the bank a gold piece for each line.
And those who are summoned to act as *adjutores* by the
official called "ab actis" invited and accepted me – a
thing that had happened never before – to be first
chartularius. There were only two others, both old men
who had been appointed only after first agreeing to make
a present of money; and not this only, but they further
appointed me a yearly stipend of twenty-four gold pieces.'
The 'ab actis' mentioned in the last sentence was the
head of one important branch of the prefect's office, that
namely which dealt with appeals in non-criminal cases.

The *adjutores* are the clerks already mentioned as chosen for special ability to help the normally senile heads of departments. Each *adjutor* chose from the ranks of the clerks an assistant who was called a *chartularius*. Note that all these special clerkships were generally bought. The purchaser refunded himself from the fees (*sportulae*) received by those who held these special positions. The system in short was much like that which still prevails in some restaurants and hotels.

This is not the end of the official activities of Lydus at this time. The court of the 'ab actis', being much concerned with questions of property and finance, kept elaborate minutes and précis of all its proceedings. It was in fact a regular record office, and Lydus grows almost lyrical in his description of the way these minutes were kept and indexed. He found the praetorian service in these early days stimulating and agreeable. And the climax of his good fortune, the event no doubt that enabled him to bear up while decade by decade his pay fell more hopelessly into arrears, remains to be told:

'And Zoticus, at the suggestion of the altogether excellent and reasonable Ammianus, who all his life was devoted to learning and philosophy, secured for me a wife who brought me a dowry of one hundred pounds of gold, and, moreover, excelled all women who at any time have won a reputation for sobriety'.

But after this there comes a change in his attitude. Our author himself ascribes it to 'the development in public affairs of which I have given an account and the fact that Fortune no longer looked with disfavour upon learning'. He is vague as usual not only about the cause but also about the date. Apparently he had lost his high-placed friends or they had lost their high places. Justinian had come to power and was applying a much needed economy axe to the civil service. It was Justinian too who finally closed the ancient university at Athens, the one remaining centre of purely pagan learning. Men of combined learning and orthodoxy like Lydus – his orthodoxy is established by the religious test imposed on applicants to the civil service – were perhaps being encouraged to turn to teaching and literature as part of the same anti-pagan policy.

Anyhow, to resume our author's narrative: 'I took a dislike to the service and gave myself over entirely to my books. And the emperor, recognizing my devotion to literature, first condescended to bid me compose a panegyric on him, at a time when, as it happened, the élite of greater Rome were present, who are always interested, even in times of trouble, in the pursuit of literature. As a result of this he commanded me to write the history of the war that he had auspiciously undertaken against the Persians, when from the afflicted city of Daras they withdrew with no small loss, never again to return.' The war in question was probably that of A.D. 527–32 (see above, Chap. IV). It would have been interesting to compare Procopius' account of it with that of Lydus, but the latter has not survived.

Meanwhile, to return to the career of Lydus, not only did he thus become a sort of historian royal; he was further made a professor in the imperial and orthodox university of Constantinople. Finally, after forty years of service, he retired with the title of *clarissimus*, the rank of a count of the second class, and a testimonial from his chief. This last he quotes in full:

'John the great writer – for this is the title that pleases him rather than the distinctions conferred on him by virtue of his office – has already before now so distinguished himself in the most honourable of all spheres – we refer to learning and literature – that not only is he admired but so also are many others who are the product of his teaching. And thinking it apparently a small thing if he should be adorned only with the verbal arts – and yet what could anyone think greater than these? – he took part too in affairs of state. And serving in our courts of law he preserved all through a certain sort of uniformity, in all cases following the appropriate precedent and teaching by his actual career that good natural parts are able to produce the best results no matter what path of life they take.'

And so he proceeds, with more simplicity and dignity

than is normal with him, to describe his final withdrawal from the public service.

'This honour I got from the court in place of much money, and then proceeded to the palace escorted by my sweetest comrades, and having received the distinction that is customarily bestowed by the Emperor on those who have completed their service, I went back to my books.'

The date of this retirement was A.D. 551. The three treatises of Lydus that have come down to us were written after that event: the *de Mensibus* first, the *de Ostentis* second, and the *de Magistratibus* last.

Lydus was not in any sense a great man. Everything he tells us about himself proves the opposite. What really appealed to him was pomp and ceremony and the externals of learning and culture. He tells us, for instance, that he could not refrain from tears when he thought of the vanished freedom and glory of ancient days. But what are the departed glories that he so lamented? They are all items in an elaborate system of legal formalism and ritual. Even the mere multitude of the officials who in earlier days had thronged the praetorian prefect's court profoundly impressed Lydus as in itself an admirable thing, and he had a veritable passion for copper-plate writing on the very best paper: 'The lost signs of ancient grandeur are many and beyond count. The members of the order actually stoop to ask paper of those who bring them business, whereas previously it was the custom not only not to engage in such meanness but further to employ only the very finest paper in transactions, while the clerks were as resplendent as the paper they wrote on. But now both are gone, and they exact a most mean and miserable fee and issue leaves of grass instead of leaves of paper (χόρτον ἀντὶ χάρτου) with cheap writing that smells of poverty. All this has perished and departed never to return' (III. 14).

Pomp and circumstance and documents beautifully written on the very best paper are well enough in their way. But it seems never to have occurred to Lydus that they might on occasion have to be sacrificed for higher

and more urgent things. Justinian was no enemy to
ritual, but in sanctioning the reforms that Lydus so
laments he was making a serious attempt to simplify the
law courts as he simplified the laws. His motives were no
doubt mixed. He may have economized in the civil
service to enable himself to be extravagant with his
Byzantine churches and his Gothic wars. But there can
be little doubt that he was also genuinely anxious to make
it easier for the poor to enjoy the protection of the law,
and that could hardly be when legal documents were all
drawn up on the most expensive and resplendent paper
by officials equally resplendent and expensive. But such
a broad and reforming outlook seems to have been altogether beyond our author's comprehension.

Or we may take another reform, started indeed long
before Justinian's reign but carried further during it,
that namely of conducting legal business in the Greek
which was the language of the Eastern empire instead of
the Latin which was spoken only by educated officials.
This eminently sensible change was regarded by Lydus
not merely with disapproval but with superstitious
alarm: 'And if anyone should consent to take account of
the prophetic guesses which some call oracles, the saying
of Fonteius the Roman has received its accomplishment.
That writer says, and quotes certain verses that were
once, he actually declares, delivered to Romulus written
in the native tongue, that Fortune would desert the
Romans when they forgot their native speech. The above-
mentioned oracle I have inserted in my writings about
the months. This is how such oracles found fulfilment: a
certain Cyrus of Egypt, who is still to this day admired as
a poet, held both the city prefecture and also at the same
time the office of praetorian prefect, though he knew
nothing of anything except poetry. Thereupon he dared
transgress the ancient practice and issue his decrees in
the Greek language, and along with the Roman language the empire lost its fortune also' (III. 42).

In other words, this dropping of one artificial variety
of compulsory Latin (in A.D. 441) seemed to Lydus
sufficient explanation of all the disasters that were

overtaking or ever likely to overtake the state. His attitude on this question deserves notice if only because it so excellently illustrates the truth that the greatest enemies of a cause are nearly always its die-hard supporters.

These personal outpourings of Lydus are indeed all very deplorable. But for an understanding of Byzantine bureaucracy they are invaluable. For our honest Lydian is typical of his age. He is indeed too utterly lacking in imagination to be anything else. Hence his little autobiography helps us to realize how, if ever some emperor or prefect did make an effort to improve or reform things within the rigid framework of the imperial system, whatever other obstacles he might surmount he was bound to come up ultimately against the solid barrier of a civil service which honestly disbelieved in the possibility of progress and was convinced that change and decay were practically synonymous. No emperor surmounted it. It is always rash to ascribe any phenomenon to one single cause. The decline and fall of the Graeco-Roman civilization has been attributed to a number of factors ranging from the abandonment by the empire of the worship of the old gods to the invasion of the empire by the malarial mosquito. But if we accept the high authority who told us that corruption can come only from within, then amongst those to whom we might with reason ascribe the gradual decline and ultimate end of the imperial system Johannes Lydus and his like must be given a high place.

CHAPTER VII

Church and Circus

*

(a) The Church

In spite of the shortcomings in the Byzantine system that have already been indicated, it is doubtful if the people who lived under it felt particularly sorry for themselves. No doubt friends of worthy men like Lydus complained of the way they had been treated by an ungrateful country, whilst their enemies might mutter that it was not everyone who had a friend in high place like the 'equitable' Ammianus. People with friends in the service could tell scandalous stories like that of the half-baked bread that brought deadly sickness to so many of the troops and filled the pockets of the wicked prefect John the Cappadocian; but even the services, as we have already seen, had their excitements and their rewards for the lucky ones, and when off duty there were amusements that the masses found as absorbing as their modern counterparts do the films and the football ground.

But above all the Byzantine had his church and his theology. The emperor, his generals, his prefects, his bishops and all their numerous subordinates might be criticized and even cursed in detail; but the ideal of one Christian empire with one law and one church was probably as generally accepted, and with the same sort of complacency, as were the ideals that centred round the Victorian Sunday in the England of Queen Victoria. We know much more, of course, of what Justinian thought on this question than we do about the views of the man in the Constantinople street, and if only for that reason it will be best to begin with the imperial attitude. It could not be better stated than it is in one of the emperor's own edicts (Novel cxxxii), entitled 'edict to the people of Constantinople concerning the faith'. It is dated A.D. 554 and runs:

'We believe that the first and greatest blessing for all mankind is the confession of the Christian faith, true and beyond reproach, to the end that it may be universally established and that all the most holy priests of the whole globe may be joined together in unity and with one voice may confess and preach the orthodox Christian faith, and that every plea devised by heretics may be rendered null and void. This our policy is illustrated by statements and edicts drawn up by us on various occasions. But forasmuch as the heretics, neither having any sense of the fear of God nor taking any thought of the penalties with which men of this sort are threatened by the rigours of the law, persist in the accomplishment of the work of the devil and, deceiving certain of the more simple-minded folk, continue secretly to hold unlawful gatherings contrary to God's holy catholic and apostolic church and to perform unlawful baptisms, we have deemed it our sacred duty by this present edict of ours to admonish such offenders, that hereby they may desist from their heretical madness and furthermore may not by guile cause the souls of others to perish, but rather may rally to God's holy church, wherein true dogmas are respected and all heresies with their champions are counted anathema. For we would have all know that if hereafter any are found either convening unlawful assemblies or assembling with those who convene them, we will by no means longer endure it, but will confirm holy church in the possession of the houses in which offences of this kind are committed; and we give orders that against those who convene such unlawful assemblies or who foregather with the conveners the penalties prescribed in our laws are to be applied in every possible way.'

The English reader will find nothing new in this edict even if he knows nothing of Byzantine history. It is an earlier version of our own seventeenth century acts of uniformity. The one unpardonable sin in a clergyman is not that he should disregard the teaching of the ten commandments or of the Sermon on the Mount, but that he should have what Justinian regarded as wrong views (unorthodox is the Greek word) on certain theological subtleties. In the sixth century A.D. the chief problems that exercised the would-be orthodox concerned the nature of the Second Person of the Trinity. The Word made Flesh was both human and divine, and theologians were exercised, as they had every right to be, with the problem of understanding and defining this double nature. The chief heretical sects of the period were pronounced to be heretical on the ground that they failed to do full justice to this double nature. They were thus all more or less the spiritual descendants of Arius, the opponent of Athanasius in the time of Constantine, whose doctrine, as we have seen already, still persisted amongst the Goths and Vandals. The most important of these sects was that of the monophysites, 'believers in a single nature', whose name sufficiently explains their doctrine. Another group of some importance were the Nestorians, whose name was derived from the founder of the sect. Nestorius held that the Virgin Mary was not the mother of the Word, and since St John tells us that the Word was God, it was wrong to give her the title of Theotokos (Mother of God). Yet another sect often heard of at this time is that of the Aphthartodocetists, whose heresy consisted in believing that the Flesh of the Word Incarnate was not as other flesh but incorruptible (*aphthartos*).

Justinian's attitude towards these monophysite heretics may be illustrated from a law (Novel xlii) which he issued in A.D. 536 entitled 'against Anthimus, Severus, Peter and Zoaras'. By way of preface it will be useful to state briefly what is known of these four heretics. Severus, the most important of them, was a monophysite monk who first appears in Constantinople in the time of the Emperor Anastasius with two hundred other monks of the same way of thinking. Anastasius himself had monophysite leanings. He received Severus with honour. Encouraged by the presence of these stalwarts the new patriarch of Constantinople, Timothy, also something of a monophysite, introduced a monophysite formula into the liturgy in the great cathedral of Sancta Sophia (Nov. A.D. 512). The innovation led to a riot in the cathedral. The police had to be called in, there were numerous casualties, and the outcome was a revolt against the emperor, who offered to abdicate. This offer by 'the mildest of monarchs' appeased the rioters and seems to have eventually strengthened the emperor's position. He became openly monophysite. Severus was made patriarch of Antioch and proceeded to anathematize his orthodox opponents. All this however was changed when Justin became emperor and his nephew Justinian began to control policy. Severus was deprived of his see and expelled from Antioch, but allowed to live at Alexandria. The deposed monophysite was not given to compromise. He attacked the aphthartodocetists as fiercely as he did the orthodox; and when in A.D. 529 Justinian tried to organize a conference to reach some understanding, he refused to attend. The conference was held in 531 but effected nothing.

The other three heretics are less important. Peter of Apamea is known only as one of fifty monophysite bishops who lost their sees in the purge that drove Severus from Antioch. Zoaras was a monophysite monk who came to Constantinople about A.D. 536, secured an interview with Justinian and openly upbraided him for not accepting the truth as expounded by the monophysites. Anthimus was a crypto-monophysite who had been made bishop of Trapezus (Trebizond); in A.D. 535, at the suggestion of the empress Theodora, who herself had monophysite leanings, he was made patriarch of Constantinople. This was the time when Justinian was trying to come to terms with the monophysites, who were extremely numerous and influential in many parts of the Eastern empire. Anthimus sent to Severus a letter in which he confessed the monophysite faith. This letter caused Ephraim, the new and staunchly orthodox patriarch of Antioch, to appeal to the Pope (Agapetus). The Pope came in person to Constantinople and got Anthimus deposed (Mar. 12, A.D. 536). The deposed patriarch was sheltered by Theodora.

Such was the situation when Justinian issued Novel xlii, denouncing the four heretics. It is too long to quote in full, but its many repetitions make it the easier to abbreviate:

'Justinian to the most holy and blessed Menas, archbishop and ecumenical patriarch: (preface) In proceeding to the present law we are taking a course not
unfamiliar to the imperial power. For every time that the
clerical vote has promoted to the episcopal throne any
persons unworthy of the sacred office, such as Nestorius
... and Arius and others not their inferiors in wickedness,
the imperial power has always come to the support of
the priesthood, to the end that through our right judge-
ments things divine and human may blend to form a
single harmony. Something of this sort has, we know,
been recently done in the case of Anthimus, who was
driven from the episcopal throne of this imperial city by
Agapetus of sacred and renowned memory, who was
then prelate of the most holy church in old Rome, on the
ground that Anthimus, in violation of all the sacred
canons, had usurped the throne which in no wise
belonged to him, though he had been condemned and
deposed alike by the decree of the aforesaid man of
sacred memory and by the holy synod held in this place,
because he had departed from the true doctrine and
abandoned the tenets which he appeared to accept,
making many pretences that he conformed to the four
sacred councils (Nicaea, Constantinople, Ephesus, Chalcedon) though he did not in fact accept their findings nor
take advantage of our kindness and condescension which
we had displayed for the furtherance of his own salvation. ...

1. For all these reasons therefore our imperial power
ratifies the decree of deposition pronounced against him
by the holy synod ... Nor in the matter of the decree
rightly pronounced against Severus by practically all the
archiepiscopal and patriarchal thrones with the approval
of the monasteries, sentencing him to be anathematized,
do we withhold our imperial ratification; who previously
in violation of our sacred ordinances, seized the throne of
the most holy church of Theopolis (Antioch: so renamed
after it had been destroyed by earthquake and rebuilt by
Justinian) and threw all things into such confusion as to
bring the most holy churches into a state of undeclared

war with one another, since he adhered only to the foul
and unholy doctrines of the two misguided arch-
heretics ... Accordingly let him also fall under the aforesaid anathema ... And we further forbid anyone to
possess any of his writings; and even as no one is allowed
to copy or possess the writings of Nestorius ... , so also
let not the words or writings of Severus be kept in the
home of any Christian, but let them be counted profane
and alien from the catholic church, and let them be
burnt by their possessors unless those who have them wish
to imperil themselves. And let them not be copied hereafter by any copyist, whether one who makes fine or one
who makes rough copies, nor by anyone else whosoever;
for the penalty for anyone who makes a copy of his works
is the cutting off of his hand. And likewise we absolutely
forbid this man too to approach the imperial city or its
neighbourhood or any other of our more important
cities, but command him to settle in some desert spot and
not corrupt others or lead them into blasphemy or be
always devising something new against the true faith
whereby he might strive once more to bring confusion on
our most holy churches.'

The chapters passing sentence on the other two
heretics are on the same lines. A few new points are introduced, e.g. the pronouncement 'and if hereafter any of
them be found doing anything contrary to our decrees,
let him be assured that he will have to answer for it under
our secular laws, which inflict severer pains on those who
disregard milder penalties'. But for the modern reader
their chief value lies in the way that they reiterate and
emphasize the outlook of the whole novel. The emperor
is indeed the defender of the faith, always ready to come
to the help of the orthodox hierarchy when attacked by
wicked heretics and always solicitous for the weaklings
of the bishops' flocks, who are also the emperor's flock
and must be protected by every weapon, ecclesiastical
and secular, from the malignant wiles of false teachers.
'This we enact on behalf of the peace of our most holy
churches, that the whole hieratical order may henceforth abide in peace and quiet. For if it is kept in peace,

the state at large will flourish, possessed of the peace from on high which our great God and Saviour Jesus Christ, one person of the Trinity, the only-begotten Word of God, proclaims and bestows on those found worthy to glorify and adore Him in sincerity and truth.'

Unity, peace and concord are imperishable ideals, but for Justinian unity meant uniformity. Universal uniformity brings universal peace, but it is the peace of death. The first task of Justinian's benevolent faith-defending despotism was to make sure that the children of the church never grew up to have minds of their own. Socrates, whose faith in the Word never faltered, would have been horrified; but the aged Plato, who lived to lose his faith and write the *Laws*, would have been not unsympathetic.

No one can read the evidence and yet doubt that Justinian, however misguided, was entirely honest in his desire to secure theological uniformity for its own sake. But the passage last quoted from Novel xlii may remind us that theological considerations were in his mind inextricably bound up with purely political ideals. In the important provinces of Egypt and Syria the monophysites were a power that had to be reckoned with; if Justinian was to secure a permanent hold on Italy, the imperial theology must be acceptable to the Pope; in the Frankish realms also the catholic faith was generally accepted. From the point of view of realistic politics the emperor was stating a simple fact when he declared that if (and only if) the church was at peace with itself undisturbed by heresies, could the restored empire that he unswervingly aimed at really flourish. The only question was whether this peace could be secured by an appeasing compromise like Zeno's 'Henotikon' or only by the rigorous suppression of all heresies and the heretics who maintained them. Most unfortunately, the latter solution had far the stronger appeal. Indeed, on this point the heretics themselves were of the same way of thinking as their orthodox opponents. The only point on which they differed was on the question of who were the orthodox.

Contrast with these intolerant dogmatics, which show

such a lamentable insensibility alike to the limitations of human intellect and the greatness of the subject with which they profess to deal, the words of Socrates in the *Phaedo*, after he has been offering to his friends just before his execution his own speculations on a future life. They are based, like those of the theologians of Justinian's age, on an acceptance of the religious beliefs current in his own age and country. 'Now to insist that all this is precisely as I have described is not fitting for a man of sense; but to insist that either this or something like it is the fact about our souls and their habitations, seeing that the soul is manifestly something immortal, that I do think fitting. And it is well worth while taking the risk of holding this belief, for the risk is an honourable one. Indeed we must go on as it were chanting something like this to ourselves. Which is why I have told my tale at such great length' (*Phaedo* 114 d).

It is interesting to note, and makes the above observations immediately relevant, that something very similar was felt by some minds even in Justinian's own days, and notably by the historian to whom we owe our clearest and most intimate knowledge of the period. Here is what Procopius has to say on the subject. He is dealing with the year 534. 'After Theodatus had thus resolved, there came as envoys from Byzantium to the chief priest of Rome Hypatius priest of Ephesus and Demetrius from Philippi in Macedonia to discuss a question of dogma on which Christians are divided and engaged in controversy. The point of the controversy I shall not mention though I am thoroughly acquainted with it. For I hold it a sort of mad folly to research into the nature of God. Even human nature cannot, I think, be precisely understood by man; still less so can the things which appertain to the nature of God. So let me shun this peril and pass these questions by in silence, if only to avoid casting doubt on things revered. For I personally will say nothing whatever about God, save that He is altogether good and holds all things in His power. But let each man speak about this according to the knowledge that he thinks he has, both priest and layman' (*Wars* v. iii. 5–9).

These words were published during the lifetime of Justinian, yet there is no reason to believe that their author got into any trouble for publishing them or that any copyist of his work had his hand cut off in consequence. It seems a curious departure from the paternal censorship so well formulated in the forty-second Novel. As to how it came about, some suggestions will be offered when we come to consider the literary activities of the period as a whole (below, Chap. IX).

The religious peace which Justinian so consistently sought was not achieved by Novel xlii. The beaten monophysites found a champion in the Empress Theodora, who contrived that the orthodox Pope Silverius should be deposed and his place taken by a certain Vigilius who had been papal nuncio (*apocrisiarius*) at Constantinople. Vigilius had succeeded in making Theodora believe that he favoured the monophysite cause. But when once enthroned as Pope at Rome Vigilius became much less monophysite; and so the struggle went on. A new crisis occurred when Justinian was persuaded by Theodora to issue an edict in three chapters against three great churchmen, Theodore of Mopsuestia, Theodoret, and Ibas, whose writings were alleged to savour of the Nestorian heresy detested by the monophysites. There was a particular piquancy about this controversy of the Three Chapters, as it is generally called, because the theologians attacked had all been approved by the orthodox council of Chalcedon. The unhappy Vigilius was summoned to Constantinople to help settle it, and arrived in the city in A.D. 547. The council that was eventually held in A.D. 553 raised more problems than it solved. Finally, in the last years of his reign, Justinian himself, to quote the words of Evagrius, a younger contemporary of the emperor, 'turning aside from the high road of true doctrine and taking the path untrod by the apostles and fathers, fell among thorns and briars ... He drafted an edict in which he described the body of the Lord as incorruptible' (Evagrius, *Ecclesiastical History*, IV, 39). In

E

other words he lapsed into the deadly heresy of aphtharto-docetism.

Heretics could and did rouse the deepest passions in the whole empire. As compared with these heretical controversies the interest stirred by Jews and infidels was a very tame affair. All the same the emperor was not unconcerned for their spiritual welfare, and on occasion made paternal enactments in what he conceived to be their interest. We must content ourselves here with one illustration, taken from Novel cxlvi (A.D. 553), entitled 'Concerning the Hebrews':

Novel cxlvi: Preface: 'In listening to the Holy Scriptures the Hebrews should not have fixed their attention on the bare words but should have had eyes for the prophecies enshrined therein, whereby they proclaim Jesus Christ the great God and Saviour of the human race. And even if hitherto, giving themselves over to senseless interpretations, they have strayed from the true faith, yet, since we have learned that they are disputing with one another, we have not endured to leave them in unsettled confusion. For from actual information that has come to us we have learnt that some of them adhere to the Hebrew tongue alone and wish to use it only in the reading of the Holy Scriptures, whilst others demand the adoption of the Greek ... We therefore, learning about this dispute, have decided that they are the better men who are willing to accept for the reading of the Holy Scriptures either the Greek tongue or, in a word, any tongue which the locality renders more suitable and more familiar to the congregation.

'Chap. 1: We therefore decree that any Hebrews who like are at liberty in their synagogues, where the people are entirely Hebrew, to read the Holy Scriptures to the congregations either in the Greek tongue or may be in our native tongue (we mean the Latin language) or, in a word, any other, adapting the language and the reading therein to the locality, provided only that what is read is clear to the congregation and that they live and publicly behave in accordance with the same; and those who expound the scriptures to them are not to be allowed to admit the Hebrew only and then pervert it as they choose, using the ignorance of the multitude to conceal their own malignity. ...

'Chap. II: But if any among them seek to introduce impious inanities, denying that there is a resurrection or judgement or the existence of God's creation the angels, we would have these driven from every place ... For if they attempt to utter any such wickedness, we subject them to the extremest penalties, purging thereby the Hebrew race from the error they are introducing.

'Chap. III: And our wish is that they should listen to the Holy Scriptures in this or that tongue, but whilst so doing should be on their guard against the wickedness of those who expound them.'

These examples are perhaps enough to show the intense importance that the sixth-century Byzantines attached to orthodoxy and the range of speculation within which it was assumed that absolutely right opinion could be irrefutably established. When every possible allowance has been made, many students of the period will be driven to the conclusion that the whole religious outlook of these Byzantines was inspired far more by fear and hatred of their enemies than by love for their neighbours.

And there was another fundamentally unchristian conception that pervaded the religious conceptions of the age. Justinian's subjects lived in a devil-ridden world. Hosts of evil spirits were always lying in wait for the Byzantine, as many and as hard to evade as the deadly germs that prowl around the human pilgrim in this scientific age, and ready at any moment, like the modern germ, to become openly and actively malignant. In A.D. 542 for instance the empire was visited by one of the worst recorded outbreaks of bubonic plague. Procopius has left us (II. xxii, xxiii) a long account of it which is of great value from many points of view. But along with good descriptions of the way it spread, its symptoms and character and its effect on the morale of the sufferers and of the population generally, we have passages like the

[*Text continued on page* 133]

The Plates

Plates 1–13 are intended mainly to illustrate Chapter XI (*The Buildings*). Plates 14–16 have been added with a triple purpose. In the first place they provide, with the mosaics of Plates 12 and 13, a contemporary portrait gallery of some of the leading personages whose characters have been drawn in words by Procopius and other writers of the age. In the second place they form a useful supplement to *The Buildings* by showing us specimens of the craftsmanship of the period as applied to one of the most important of the minor arts. In the third they introduce us to the vital subject of coinage and finance. In a book like the present, which attempts to present the Age of Justinian as his contemporaries saw and described it, coinage and finance could hardly form the subject of a special chapter. Allusions to it in our authors are made only incidentally, but the coins often serve as valuable commentaries on these incidental allusions.

1. Constantinople seen from Scutari, the Asiatic suburb, across the Sea of Marmora, which is seen spreading out to the South on the left of the picture.

2. Constantinople. A closer view across the small narrow reach of the Sea of Marmora. In the centre rises S. Sophía, to the right of it S. Irene.

3. Constantinople. The Golden Horn.

4. Constantinople. Santa Sophia. On the right the narrow northern extremity of the Sea of Marmora and the beginning of the Bosporus stretching away to the right beyond Leander's Tower, which can be seen just off the Asiatic shore. On the left the Golden Horn with Galata beyond it.

5. Constantinople. S. Sophia, the interior.

6a. Constantinople. Exterior of church of SS. Sergius and Bacchus
(Little S. Sophia)

6b. Architectural details from the interior of the above church.

7. Constantinople. The reservoir Bin-bir-Direk.

8. Constantinople. The reservoir Yera Batan.

9a. Ravenna. Exterior of the church of S. Apollinare in Classe.

9b. Ravenna. Exterior of the church of S. Vitale.

10. Ravenna, S. Apollinare in Classe, Interior.

11. Ravenna. S. Vitale. Interior. On the extreme right is part of the
mosaic reproduced in pl. 12.

12. Ravenna. S. Vitale. Mosaic portraits of Justinian and his court.

13. Ravenna. S. Vitale. Mosaic portraits of Theodora and her ladies

14. Coins of Justin and Justinian.

15. Coins of kings of the Vandals, the Ostrogoths, and of Persia.

16. Gold medallion of Justinian.

The Coin Plates

Plates 14–16 illustrate coins of Justin and Justinian, of Vandal and Gothic kings whose history is recorded above in Chapters II and III, and of the Persian Chosroes (above Chapters IV and V). All except the last have been published by Wroth in the *Catalogue of the Imperial Byzantine Coins in the British Museum* Vol. I (1908) and *Catalogue of the Coins of the Vandals, Ostrogoths and Lombards* (1911).

PLATE 14

1. *Imp. Byz. Coins*, pl. IV, 6. Gold coin (solidus) of the last months of Justin's reign when Justinian was associated with him as Emperor. *Obv.*: Justin and Justinian enthroned; inscribed DNIUSTINETIUSTINIPPAUG (our lords Justin and Justinian ever august) and in the exergue CONOB indicating the place of minting (CON for Constantinople) and metal (OB for obryzum, refined gold). *Rev.*: Winged Victory; inscribed VICTORIAAUGGG (Victory of the Augusti) and in the exergue CONOB.

2 a, b. *Ibid.*, pl. V, 5. Bronze follis of Justinian struck in Constantinople in A.D. 550–1. *Obv.*: Bust of Justinian; inscribed DNIUSTINIANUSPPAUG. *Rev.*: M, the numerical sign for 40 (nummia) and cross; inscribed ANNOXXIIII, i.e. the twenty-fourth year of Justinian's reign, and in the exergue the mint mark CON (Constantinople).

3 a, b. *Ibid.*, pl. X, 12. Bronze follis of Justinian struck at Ravenna in A.D. 560–1. Type as No. 2 but thirty-fourth year and mint Ravenna.

4. *Ibid.*, pl. VIII, 4. Bronze follis of Justinian struck at Antioch in A.D. 539–40. Type as No. 2 but thirteenth year and mint mark (in Greek) ΘΥΠΟ, i.e. Theoupolis, the official name for Antioch.

5. *Ibid.*, pl. X, 2. Bronze follis of Justinian struck at Carthage in A.D. 540–1. Type as No. 2 but fourteenth year and mint mark CAR.

PLATE 15

1. *Coins of the Vandals, Ostrogoths and Lombards*, pl. II, 14. Silver coin of Hilderic. *Obv.*: Bust of Hilderic; inscribed DNHILDERIX-REX (our lord King Hilderic). *Rev.*: Standing woman personifying Carthage; inscribed FELIXKARTG.

2. *Ibid.*, pl. II, 19. Silver coin of Gelimer. *Obv.*: Bust of Gelimer; inscribed DNREXGEILAMIR (our lord King Gelimer). *Rev.*: The letters D N with a cross above them and the letter L (= 50 denarii) below.

3. *Ibid.*, frontispiece, pp. xxxi and 54. Gold coin (triple solidus) of Theoderic, king of the Ostrogoths, struck probably in Rome. *Obv.*: Bust of Theoderic; inscribed REXTHEODERICUSPIUS-PRINCIS (King Theoderic pious prince). *Rev.*: Winged Victory; inscribed REXTHEODERICUSVICTORGENTIUM (King Theoderic conqueror of nations); in the exergue COMOB (Comes Obryzi-acus, the officer in charge of gold coinage).

4. *Ibid.*, pl. VIII, 19. Bronze coin of Athalaric. *Obv.*: Bust of Rome: inscribed INVICTAROMA (Rome the unconquered). *Rev.*: Within a wreath the inscription DNATHALARICUSREX (our lord King Athalaricus).

5. *Ibid.*, pl. IX, 15. Bronze coin of Theodatus. *Obv.*: Bust of Theodatus; inscribed DNTHEODAHATUSREX (our lord King Theodatus). *Rev.*: Winged Victory; inscribed VICTORIAPRINCIPUM (Victory of the princes) and S C (=senatus consulto, by decree of the senate).

6. *Ibid.*, pl. X, 1. Silver coin of Vittigis. *Obv.*: Bust of Justinian; inscribed DNIUSTINIANUSPPAU (our lord Justinian ever august). *Rev.*: Within a wreath the inscription DNVVITIGESREX (our lord King Vittigis.

7. *Ibid.*, pl. XI, 4. Silver coin of Totila. *Obv.*: Bust of Anastasius; inscribed DNANASTASIUSPPAUG (our lord Anastasius ever august). *Rev.*: Within a wreath the inscription DNBADUILAREX (our lord King Baduila, i.e. Totila).

8. *Ibid.*, pl. XVI, 6. Bronze follis of Justinian struck at Rome. *Obv.*: Bust of Justinian; inscribed DNIUSTINIANUSPPAUG (our lord Justinian ever august). *Rev.*: Within a wreath M (=40), surmounted by a cross and framed by the letters R O M A; below it a star.

9. Silver drachm of the Persian king Chosroes. *Obv.*: Bust of Chosroes with title around. *Rev.*: Zoroastrian fire altar with two attendant priests.

PLATE 16

Imp. Byz. Coins, frontispiece. Large gold medallion of Justinian. *Obv.*: Bust of Justinian; inscribed DNIUSTINIANUSPPAUG (our lord Justinian ever august). *Rev.*: Justinian in full armour on a war horse preceded by a winged Victory; inscribed SALUSET-GLORIAROMANORUM (the salvation and glory of the Romans), and in the exergue CONOB (struck at Constantinople, of refined gold). The medallion weighs the equivalent of 36 solidi or half a Roman pound (cf. the gold payments recorded above in Chapters IV and V). On the history of the piece see *Imp. Byz. Coins*, p. 25, where it is tentatively dated about A.D. 534. The portrait may be compared with that of the S. Vitale mosaic, pl. 12, and Procopius' description of the emperor, Chapter X.

following: 'And in the second year in mid-spring it reached Byzantium, where I too happened to be living at the time. This is how it attacked. Apparitions of demons in every human shape were seen by many people, and all who encountered them thought that they were being struck somewhere on their body by him whom they encountered. And directly they saw this apparition they were seized by the plague. Now at first those who met them sought to avert them by repeating the most divine of names and using other adjurations as they were variously able. But it was absolutely without effect, since even if they sought refuge in the churches, as most of them did, they perished.' (II. xxii. 9–11)

It was not only breakdowns in the physical world that brought the devils out into the open. The Byzantine who felt himself in the presence of moral evil was equally liable to see before him a devil in bodily form. Procopius himself became a victim of this same obsession. For the moment one illustration must suffice. It is taken from the *Secret History*. 'They say also that a certain monk specially beloved of God, induced by those who dwelt with him in the desert, journeyed to Byzantium to seek aid for their nearest neighbours, who were suffering intolerable violence and wrong, and that when he arrived there he immediately secured permission to enter the royal presence. But when he was on the point of entering the presence chamber and had already crossed the threshold with one foot, he suddenly stepped back and sought to withdraw. The eunuch who was ushering him in and all who were there implored the man repeatedly to go forward, but he answered them not a word but like one out of his senses rushed off to the room where he was lodging. And when those who escorted him asked him why he was behaving in this way, they say that he replied that he had seen the prince of the devils seated on the throne in the palace, and that he would not stoop to consort with him or beg anything of him' (*H.A.*, xii. 24–6).

The devil has come into his own in various ways and at various periods of history. Sometimes he has been called in by the ill-treated and oppressed who saw no prospect of getting their own back in this world and consoled themselves with picturing the retribution that would overtake their oppressors in the next. Sometimes, as with our own William Cobbett when he declared that the devil is the sheet anchor of the Christian system, he seems to be mainly an embodiment of the evil that the Christian will defy and discomfit, possibly in the other world but certainly in this. Sometimes he has merely helped men to gratify an innate streak of cruelty, as seems to have been largely the case with all the devil-haunted infernos that trace their origin to the Etruscan hell as pictured for instance in the Tomba dell' Orco. The Byzantine devil seems to have been mainly of the first class, the product of defeatism and frustration, but with a certain element of the third, for one cannot cultivate the *odium theologicum* and not regard the devil as in some ways a friend and ally.

In the romantic picture of the age that Mr. Graves has given us in his *Count Belisarius* there is much that is hard to reconcile with our original sources. But he does seem to have suggested a fundamental fact when he makes the old pagan eunuch who is supposed to write the whole story say of Justinian that he seemed to have been genuinely trying to champion the Christian religion but that somehow he never managed to get the hang of it. What makes Justinian so interesting and significant is that he so largely embodied the spirit of his age.

(b) The Circus

In the famous tenth satire of Juvenal, which was the model closely followed by Dr Johnson in his *Vanity of Human Wishes*, the Roman satirist, writing about 400 years before Justinian became emperor of New Rome, bewails the fact that the Roman people, who in the great days of old bestowed on whom it chose supreme power, armies, everything, has now shed all its responsibilities and longs anxiously for two things only, the bread dole and the races in the circus, *panem et circenses*. He dates the catastrophic change to the time when the people ceased to have votes to sell.

> . . . . ex quo suffragia nulli
> vendimus, effudit curas.

The story of these highly organized and commercialized races, mainly chariot races, will be familiar to most readers if only from modern novels with Roman settings. The charioteers belonged to one or other of a group of rival factions, each with its own colour and each colour with its mass of supporters who must have much resembled the football crowds of the modern proletariat. In another satire (xi. 193f.), where the setting is the day of one of these great race meetings, Juvenal pictures the whole population of Rome (himself excepted) as crowded in the circus and hears a deafening shout from which he infers the victory of the popular 'green' charioteer. If the favourite side had lost you would have seen the city as downcast as when the consuls were vanquished at the disaster of Cannae.

It is a striking illustration of Byzantine conservatism that the same passion for the circus and indeed the same organization into factions that championed one or other of the rival colours is found inspiring the same passionate interest and indeed securing the same outlet for mass expressions of partisanship in the Constantinople of Justinian as in Juvenal's Rome. It is in fact doubtful whether the passion and partisanship ever reached such intensity at any other time. The 'Nika' riot that broke out amongst the blues and greens in A.D. 532 (below, Chap. X, pp. 201ff.) nearly cost Justinian his life and did cause the destruction of many of the most notable buildings in the city. The great church of Sancta Sophia as it stands to-day is the masterpiece that Justinian built to replace the cathedral destroyed in this riot. And it is to this same riot that we owe Procopius' description of the perverted activities of the factions of the rival colours. 'The common people in each city have from ancient times been divided into blues and greens, but it is only recently that for the sake of these names and of the seats they occupy at the shows and races they have taken to

F

lavishing their money and exposing themselves to the most painful tortures and thought it well worth their while to die by a most disgraceful death, fighting their rivals without knowing what they are risking their lives for but well aware that even if they get the better of their enemies all that will be left them will be to be taken off at once to prison and there to perish in extreme agony' (I. xxiv. 2–3).

The practice of ending any serious football match with a free fight between the supporters of the rival sides is said to be not unknown in some parts of these islands. But if we are to believe Procopius the matter went much further than that amongst the blues and greens of Justinian's cities (I. xxiv). His account of their feuds and fights recalls Thucydides' famous description of the excesses of the political factions in Corcyra (Thuc. III. 70–85) and it is very possible that Procopius made this description his model. The more rowdy elements of the two factions seem to have developed a systematic sort of gangsterdom: 'They formed organized bands which after nightfall robbed respectable people both in the market place and in side streets, taking their victims' clothes and girdles and brooches of gold and anything else they had on them. Sometimes they dared to follow up robbery with murder to prevent these victims reporting what had happened to them' (*Secret History*, vii. 15–16). This was felt to be going too far even by what Procopius calls the 'non-militant partisans' of the dominant faction of the blues; but as against this we hear that many young men who had not previously been members joined just because they were attracted by the opportunities for violence and outrage (*ibid*. vii. 17, 23).

As seems to be so often the case with parties organized for absurd acts of lawless violence, the blues and greens of this period wore a special kind of shirt. Procopius has left us a description of these extraordinary shirts or tunics and of the general appearance and bearing of faction members in their full war paint. 'The members of the two factions had adopted a new and strange way of wearing their hair, and used to cut it in a way quite different from the rest of the Romans. The moustache and beard they did not touch, but always let them grow to the greatest possible length like the Persians. As to their heads, they shaved the front as far as the temples, but let the back hair grow full length in an absurd way like the Huns ... Secondly, in the matter of clothes they all thought fit to be finely dressed, wearing garments far too showy for their various stations in life ... The sleeves of their shirts were as tight as possible at the wrists, but from there to the shoulders they expanded to an enormous breadth; and as often as they waved their hands in the theatres and hippodromes while shouting and cheering in their usual way, this part literally rose up on high, giving foolish people the impression that their frames were so fine and strong that they had to be clothed in garments of this shape' (*Secret History*, vii. 8–13).

The whole picture of these uniformed gangs of hooligans is not without its resemblances to that of the organized crowds who used to gather from time to time in the Sportpalast at Berlin. There is however one fact that to some extent explains and excuses the conduct of the Byzantine 'factions'. They seem to have afforded the only outlet for the deep instinct for party groupings that is the essence of democracy. Perverted though this outlet was, it is still perhaps not without significance that the Nika riot developed into an unmistakable political demonstration and that at the siege of Antioch (see above, Chap. IV) it was members of the factions that put up a really desperate resistance to Chosroes when he captured the city.

Note

The account of the blue and green 'factions' given above follows strictly what is said about them by Procopius. English readers familiar with Saturday afternoon football crowds may find it sufficiently convincing as it stands. But a memoir written in Serbo-Croat by G. Manojlović in 1904, but which attracted little attention till it was translated into French by the eminent Byzantinologist H. Grégoire (*Byzantion*, Vol. XI, 1936), suggests

that these 'factions' may have been something more than
mere partisans of rival colours at the races. Manojlović
points out that the word in *Wars* i. xxiv. 2 translated
above (p. 135) 'the common people' and by Dewing in
the Loeb edition 'the population' is οἱ δῆμοι (plural)
though in the previous sentence, where Procopius says
that the riot brought great trouble on the people, he uses
the singular (τῷ δήμῳ). In the classical idiom which our
author follows so closely the word *demos* is used in a
double sense – for the people in general, whence our
word democracy, and for a ward or parish of a city or
district. This at once suggests that the greens and blues
came from different quarters of the city, and Manojlović
argues that the greens came from the poorer quarters.
But the most interesting part of his thesis is that in which
he collects evidence that the demes were the basis of an
organized militia, and that these local units were also
responsible for keeping in repair their particular sections
of the city walls and further that all three activities were
maintained by taxes raised from and largely administered
by the 'demes' themselves. This armed militia, with
duties to the state and with the opportunities that the
races offered of expressing its opinion on public matters
which affected it, had to some limited extent, according
to Manojlović, revived the democratic tradition of the
Greek city state. Hence the turbulence of its meetings,
but hence too in no small measure the vitality of the
Eastern empire. Manojlović draws his evidence from all
periods between the fifth century and the tenth and no
item of it is decisive. But his conclusions have at least the
merit of making much that we are told about the circus
'factions' more comprehensible and significant.

CHAPTER VIII

The Laws

*

THE rule of law was from first to last one of the fundamental conceptions of the Roman empire. It is indeed
rightly claimed as the outstanding contribution of Rome
to the development of civilization, and Justinian's
codifying of the laws is admitted on all sides to be the
main achievement which establishes his claim to a
notable place in world history. The fact has not helped
towards an intimate appreciation of his work. The law,
or at any rate Roman law, has always tended to be the
preserve of professional lawyers or, at the widest, of
people who have studied in a faculty of law; and the
continued existence of such faculties has tended to
frighten away from the subject those who are not so
qualified. The army and the church are regarded, perhaps rightly, as legitimate subjects of study and criticism
for all the historically minded, whatever their attitude
towards war and religion; for the average citizen has
probably some acquaintance with the armed forces, and
churchmen, or even anti-clericals, with the church. But
the law-abiding citizen tends to show his law-abidingness
by keeping very clear of the law. The present writer has
his full share of this inhibition, and his treatment of this
side of Justinian's work is emphatically not that of a
specialist. It owes much to Bury and his predecessors in
the nineteenth century, who in their turn owe an
immense debt to the famous forty-fourth chapter of
Gibbon's *Decline and Fall*.

The outcome of Justinian's codification of Roman law
was his great *Corpus Juris Civilis*. It fills three quarto
volumes which together contain well over 2,200 closely
printed pages in the Berlin edition of Mommsen, Krueger,
Schoell and Kroll which began publication in the
seventies of the last century and has been frequently

reprinted. Even allowing for the fact that much of the work is printed in two versions, Greek and Latin, and that sometimes we have two Latin versions as well as the Greek, still the bulk of this massive work makes the Mosaic law look slight as set forth in the books of Leviticus, Numbers and Deuteronomy. To appreciate the task that Justinian and his jurists had set themselves, we must remember that when they started on their work the Roman state had already been constantly making laws for about a thousand years. From the publication of the famous Twelve Tables, of which we still have fragments, in 451 B.C. to the completion of Justinian's codification in A.D. 534 is 985 years. The Romans were a nation of legislators and litigants. They were also pre-eminently a nation that sought precedents for everything they did. *Moribus antiquis stat res Romana.* Laws centuries old were still valid in Justinian's days; and something not altogether unlike our judge-made or case-made law (i.e. interpretations of legal enactments, made in some test case, that were regarded as binding on subsequent judges) had become an essential part of the civil law of Rome. A succession of famous jurists (*juris consulti, juris prudentes*) from republican days onwards had devoted all their ingenuity to this business of legal interpretation. It was an occupation that had a special attraction for lovers of legalism, and immense ingenuity was displayed in the process, with the natural result that these interpretations often contradicted one another.

All this meant that to equip himself to act as a judge in a court of law, or even to plead in one, the Roman of the early sixth century A.D. had to master not only a vast mass of legal enactments, some of them almost inaccessible, but also a huge and often self-contradictory literature of legal interpretations. The *res Romana* was in danger of being buried under the mass of *mores antiqui* that had once been its foundation.

It was to reduce this overwhelming accumulation of material to manageable proportions and to eliminate the contradictions in which it abounded that Justinian commissioned the most distinguished lawyers of his realm, headed by the celebrated Tribonian. The results of their labours in this work of codification were issued in two great works: (*i*) the *Code* and (*ii*) the *Digest* or *Pandects*. The first to be published was the *Code* (A.D. 529), but this was later revised after the publication of the *Digest* (A.D. 533), and it is only this second edition (A.D. 534) that has come down to us. That is why, in our printed editions of the *Corpus*, the *Digest* comes before the *Code*. It is a reversal of the natural order, for it is the *Code* that contains the actual enactments that constitute the laws. These laws are set forth in twelve books. Each book is divided into a number of 'titles' or subjects, and the legislation on each subject is set out in clauses prefixed by the name of the emperor who enacted it and ending with the precise date on which it was enacted. A single 'title' may contain enactments of various dates promulgated by various emperors. The earliest go back to the reign of Hadrian (A.D. 117–38), the latest belong to the earliest years of Justinian himself. The *Digest* is in fifty books, and each book, like those of the *Code*, is divided under a number of 'titles', each dealing with a separate and specific legal point. But the items of these 'titles' are pronouncements of the great Roman jurists. According to the tables published in Roby's *Introduction to Justinian's Digest*, pp. 272–3, there are 2,464 extracts from Ulpian, 2,081 from Paulus, 601 from Papinian, 578 from Pomponius, 535 from Gaius and a further total of 2,883 extracts from thirty-three other jurists. Of the five named above Pomponius, who died in A.D. 138, is the earliest, Ulpian, who died in A.D. 228, the latest. Of other authorities frequently quoted some are as late as the early part of the fourth century A.D., some go back to the first half of the second century A.D. Still earlier jurists, some of them of the Ciceronian period, are also occasionally quoted, but generally in extracts from jurists of a later period. The great mass of the extracts are from the jurists of the second and third centuries A.D., i.e. from the period before Christianity became the official religion of the empire.

The twelve books of the *Code* and the fifty of the *Digest* were intended to be the legal library of the magistrates of the empire. The law of Rome and the authoritative interpretation of it was thereby made accessible in a form which enabled every magistrate to have the complete work, and that work was of manageable dimensions and free from contradictions. But what of the students beginning their studies in the great schools of law at Constantinople and Berytus (Beirut)? For their benefit Justinian commissioned Tribonian and his colleagues to produce a handbook expounding the law on those subjects which were of main importance in the courts of the period. This work is known as the *Institutes*. It was published like the *Digest* in A.D. 533. It is a comparatively short work, occupying only fifty-six pages of the Berlin edition of the *Corpus*, and is divided into four books.

They are introduced by a preface which explains the emperor's object in publishing the treatise and incidentally makes illuminating references to the *Code* and *Digest*.

'In the name of Our Lord Jesus Christ ... to the youth desirous of studying the law. ... Having removed every inconsistency from the sacred constitutions' (i.e. imperial laws) 'hitherto inharmonious and confused, we extended our care to the immense volumes of the older jurisprudence, and, like sailors crossing the mid-ocean, by the favour of Heaven, have now completed a work' (the publication of the *Digest*) 'of which we once despaired. When this, with God's blessing, had been done, we called together Tribonian, master and ex-quaestor of our sacred palace, and the illustrious Theophilus and Dorotheus, professors of law, ... and specially commissioned them to compose by our authority and advice a book of *Institutes*, whereby you may be enabled to learn your first lesson in law no longer from ancient fables, but grasp them by the brilliant light of imperial learning ... After the completion therefore of the fifty books of the *Digest* or *Pandects*, in which all the earlier law has been collected by the aid of the said distinguished Tribonian and other illustrious and most able men, we directed the division of these same

Institutes into four books, comprising the first elements of the whole science of law. In these the law previously obtaining has been briefly stated, as well as that which after becoming disused has been again brought to light by our imperial aid. Compiled from all the *Institutes* of the ancient jurists, and in particular from the commentaries of our Gaius on both the *Institutes* and the common cases and from many other legal works, these *Institutes* were submitted to us by the three learned men aforesaid, and after reading and examining them we have given them the fullest force of our constitutions.

'Receive then these laws with your best powers and with the eagerness of study, and show yourselves so learned as to be encouraged to hope that when you have compassed the whole field of law you may have ability to govern such portions of the state as may be entrusted to you.

'Given at Constantinople, the 21st day of November in the third consulate of the Emperor Justinian, ever August.'[1]

When the young Queen Victoria asked her mentor Lord Melbourne whether she ought to read the works of Horace, his answer was that it was sufficient for her to be acquainted with the existence of that author. There must be thousands of people whose knowledge of Justinian's *Corpus Juris Civilis* is of just this extent. For anyone in this position who probes further it will be something of a shock to discover how entirely unoriginal that work is. It is not only that it is all codification and summarization; it is codification and summarization that had been done before. The laws had already been codified three times: those from the time of Hadrian (the earliest emperor whose laws appear in Justinian's code) to A.D. 294 by Gregorius, those of A.D. 296–324 by Hermogenian, those from Constantine (d. A.D. 337) to Theodosius II by Theodosius' own jurists in A.D. 438. The *Digest* is a compilation of extracts from similar earlier compilers. The *Institutes* acknowledges its debt to 'our Gaius'.

[1] The version quoted above is that of J. B. Moyle, *Imp. Just. Institutiones* vol. II, 1883, pp. 1–2.

But the student who experiences this preliminary shock would be completely misunderstanding Justinian and his age if he imagined that either the emperor or any of his contemporaries would have thought this lack of originality was a reflection on their achievement. On the contrary, they gloried in the unquestionable absence of all innovation. When the disillusioned Procopius turned against the emperor and wrote his *Secret History* (below, Chap IX, p. 174f.), innovation is precisely the word that he uses in his blackest mood with which to reproach him. The historian's only fear is that he will not be able to substantiate the charge. In a very real sense the conservative antiquarianism of the *Corpus* is one of its outstanding merits. The Roman ideal has many limitations, some of which to some minds seem truly deplorable. To take a single but all-pervading example: anyone who turns from the Sermon on the Mount, with its precepts 'lay not up for yourselves treasure on earth' and 'take no thought for the morrow', will notice how very much of the *Corpus* is devoted to questions of private property, its safeguarding, preservation and transmission. If we omit the large sections devoted to ecclesiastical and administrative matters (and much of the former is concerned with the property rights of ecclesiastical bodies), the titles concerned with the safeguarding and transmission of private property are overwhelmingly preponderant. This concern with the maintenance of a propertied economic order has given the world that adheres to the Roman tradition an intensely conservative attitude towards this whole question which is the more influential because it is largely based not on the selfish interests of a moneyed clique but on the long unbroken tradition of a great profession exercising its ingenuity in perfecting one particular system.

But this conservative traditionalism has another side whose merits cannot be sufficiently emphasized, especially in a time of change like the present. The code of Justinian was drawn up for an empire that was unequivocally and even aggressively Christian according to its lights. The first 'title' of the first book runs 'De Summa Trinitate et Fide Catholica et ut nemo de ea publice contendere audeat' (Of the Most High Trinity and the Catholic Faith, and that no one dare publicly to dispute it). Yet if we turn at the end of Krueger's edition to the chronological list of constitutions (as the laws are called), we find that of the twenty-one pages that the list occupies the first nine are taken up with laws enacted by the successive emperors from Hadrian to Diocletian (A.D. 117–304), all of whom were pagan and some of whom, notably Decius and Diocletian, were notorious persecutors of the church. The second part of the list too contains constitutions of the apostate Emperor Julian.

Decius, Diocletian and Julian seem strange figures to be found legislating for a great Christian state which certainly was not remarkable for religious tolerance. But the state was Roman as well as Catholic, and then as always the problem of reconciling the two was no easy one. The solution arrived at in the *Code* is perhaps the most happy and successful example of a solution reached so far in history. Doctrinal inflexibility might show its head here and there in particular titles, and even where the secular Roman ideal was allowed full play, it was cramped by a geographical limitation which caused all its thoughts to be turned inward to Rome. What gives the *Corpus* its unique value is its singular freedom from the delusion that all Roman wisdom was to be found in any one age or period. The result of this enlightened traditionalism is that the *Code* and *Digest* embody the accumulated experience and wisdom of centuries. Its merits are those of the British constitution as contrasted with the American. The rule of law was a fundamental conception of the Christian Roman empire, but it is not a conception confined to Christianity. Many of the ideas implied in it are common to every form of civilization, and there was no reason why the Christian empire should have rejected the legacy of its pagan predecessor. But it might well have succumbed to the temptation to do so. It is to its eternal credit that it did not, and the good effects of this great refusal have been more wide-reaching than any of the men who made it could

have possibly foreseen. Few of the laws that it took over
from the pre-Christian régime go back earlier than the
time of the Antonines (Antoninus Pius, A.D. 138–61,
Marcus Aurelius, 161–80); but this is precisely the period
when the empire was at its best and greatest and the
Roman tradition was being consolidated and interpreted in the benevolent light of the stoicism of Marcus
Aurelius.

In all histories of the later Roman empire from
Gibbon to Bury the laws of Rome are dealt with under
the reign of Justinian, and as a result they have come to
be associated in a very particular way with his particular
reign. But enough has been said already to remind us
that we are dealing with an uninterrupted growth that
had started in the earliest days of the city. The *Code*,
Digest and *Institutes* are of course in a sense one of the
main facts of Justinian's reign; but in another and truer
sense they embody the history of the empire and the
republic that preceded it from at least the time of the
Twelve Tables (451 B.C.) onwards. In a monograph like
this it would be as misleading to dwell on them in detail
as it would be in a study of Queen Victoria to go in
detail into the history of all the great cathedrals which
were restored during her reign or of all the poems incorporated in Palgrave's *Golden Treasury*.

It is different with the Novels which form the fourth
section of the *Corpus* and fill the third volume of the
Berlin edition. These Novels are the new laws issued
by Justinian subsequent to the publication of the *Code*.
There are 160 of them. They deal with matters on which
the *Code* was not found adequate, and are thus in the true
spirit of Roman law, regarded as a natural growth based
on the constant new problems which must always be
presenting themselves even in the most conservative
state. Naturally they give no comprehensive picture of
any side of life under Justinian, but they do give us
glimpses into some aspects of it. They are very little
known in this country to any except professional lawyers
and are not easily accessible to English readers. There is

no English translation of them nor any work dealing with them in the way that for instance the letters of Cassiodorus are treated by Hodgkin in his 'condensed' translation of the *Variae*. There are of course constant references to them in such accounts of Justinian's legal activities as we find in Gibbon or Bury. But these accounts, masterly in their way, are highly compressed synopses of a great legal system, and from their nature cannot convey to the reader the atmosphere in which the various enactments were issued and the circumstances that gave rise to them. I propose therefore to devote the rest of this chapter to summarizing a certain number of these Novels with occasional quotations at greater length. By collating them with the historical narratives of Procopius and Agathias and such works as that of Lydus on the administrative system we can form a truer and more vivid picture of life in the realm of Justinian than is attainable in any other way.

Most of the enactments deal with one or other of three main themes: (I) the civil and military administration of the empire, (II) ecclesiastical and theological matters, and (III) the family and private property. It will be convenient to group them under these three heads. The bracketed numbers give the date.

I. *Secular Administration*:

8 (535) prohibits candidates for magistracies from canvassing and from offering payments to secure office.

13 (535) institutes a new office, the praetor of the demes, to replace the prefect of the watch (Bury II. 337–8, connects the change with an attempt to deal more effectively with an outbreak of thieving and robbery in the capital).

15 (535) institutes 'defensores civitatis' to replace the officials called 'curatores'. (These officials dealt with financial suits involving sums not exceeding 300 nomismata; the reform seems to have aimed at getting these minor cases, so important to the humble litigants concerned, out of the hands of corrupt magistrates.)

35 (535) gives special clerks in the office of the *quaestor*

(the chief legal officer) the right to sell their posts to suitable successors. (Cf. Chap. VI, p. 116.)

69 (538). Provincials are to have their cases, whether civil or criminal, tried in their own provinces, unless otherwise allowed by special imperial permission.

80 (539) establishes another new official named 'quaesitor', to deal with provincials visiting the capital, whether men or women, monks or nuns, farmers or provincial lawyers, or people of any other position or rank whatsoever, to keep watch over them, get them quickly out of the difficulty that had brought them to the capital, and send them back home with all possible speed (Bury II, p. 337).

95 (539). Every high official is to remain in his province for fifty days after the expiry of his period of office, whether it be civil or military, and to show himself in public in the district he has been governing, in order to make it clear whether or no he can stand by his actions. Any such official leaving before this period is liable to a charge of *lèse-majesté* and to be sent back to the province he has prematurely left.

134 (556). (*i*) High officials are not to appoint substitutes or unlicensed subordinates except in special cases with the emperor's express permission; they are not to travel in their districts, and if they do so, except at the emperor's express instructions, they will have to bear the expenses; they are on no account to extract them from the people of their province or district.

(*iii*) We hear that certain officials, with a view to making improper gains, put difficulties in the way of our subjects making wills or marriage settlements or burying their dead or registering their property. All who commit or abet such acts are to be dismissed, fined and banished. Our right reverend bishops are to do everything possible to prevent such proceedings.

(*iv*) Officials are to punish the actual perpetrators of serious crimes such as adultery, rape and murder, and not to make a profit by arresting a succession of innocent persons and fining the community in which the crime was perpetrated.

(*v*) If a criminal escapes to another province and the officials of that province, when duly warned, fail to seize him and send him back for trial, they are to be heavily fined and in extreme cases dismissed.

145 (553). Complaints have reached us that the Duke or *Biocolytes* whom we specially appointed to deal with disorders in Phrygia, Pisidia, Lycaonia and Lydia, is now the cause of much oppression there, as his agents threaten and blackmail the innocent. We therefore hereby terminate his authority in those provinces.

152 (534). No instructions to local governors are valid unless they have received the approval of the Praetorian Prefect.

The laws listed above are addressed in the first place mainly to officials and deal with administration generally. Those which follow immediately below are concerned with legal proceedings, and are addressed rather to litigants, though the magistrates are of course also concerned.

53 (537) seeks to prevent defendants summoned to a distant court from having to attend and await trial while their accusers stay comfortably at home.

86 (539) seeks to save citizens from being forced to absent themselves from their native city or village on legal business: if they cannot get satisfaction from the civil authorities they are to appeal to their bishop; if anyone comes to the capital to pursue a case without a recommendation from a local authority, he will be punished, as will also any bishop or magistrate who does not conform to these instructions.

96 (539) makes provisions to prevent collusion between the plaintiff and the officer who executes the judgement of the court and also to prevent the plaintiff entering his case in one court and the defendant filing a rival petition in another.

115 (542). Cases must be tried and decided in accordance with the laws that hold at the time of the trial. ...
(*ii*) If one of the parties is content with the way the case

has been pleaded but the other is not, the judge may postpone his decision for a period not longer than three months.

124 (545). We are issuing this law to establish the integrity of our judges and to prevent litigants from being able to circumvent the law by bribery. (*i*) All litigants are to swear on the gospels that they have not made or promised and will not hereafter make any presents either to the judges to secure their favour, or to anyone else except their own advocate and any officials to whom payments are prescribed by law. (*ii*) Any litigant truly confessing that he has bribed anyone in the court is to be pardoned, but the recipient shall, if the case is pecuniary, be fined and deprived of his office, if criminal, be exiled and have his property confiscated; but if the charge of bribery is not proved, the litigant who has made it is to be punished. (*iii*) Judges, if they find the executors of a sentence to have exacted more than the legal penalties, must make the offender pay fourfold, one fourth going to the wronged litigant, the other three-quarters to the public treasury. (*iv*) *Referendarii* (the emperor's legal secretaries) are specially warned against tampering with or exceeding their instructions.

125 (543). To expedite justice judges are warned against constantly referring difficulties to the emperor in the course of a trial; they are to proceed to a decision and leave it to dissatisfied parties to appeal if they think fit.

II. *The Church:*

16 (535). Clergy may be transferred from one church to another to maintain the statutory number or reduce the existing staff of any church to that number, but never when such transference would lead to that number being exceeded.

37 (535). Churches in Africa and their belongings are to be taken from Arians and pagans and restored to the orthodox faith.

43 (537). Only 1,100 workshops (*officinae*), the property of the great church, are to be exempted from

paying taxes; these 1,100 are to be devoted to the funeral rites of the dead.

55 (537). Previous laws forbidding the alienation of church property and only in certain cases allowing the exchange of such properties are being circumvented; therefore we now further enact that the only such alienations permissible are from the church to the imperial house, and that facilities be given for reversing even these; the same restrictions are to apply in the case of lands held on cultivation tenure.

56 (537). No fee is to be exacted from a clergyman for installing him in a benefice except in the case of the great church at Constantinople.

57 (537). Many clergy serving various houses of prayer draw the customary stipends and then for reasons best known to themselves absent themselves completely from the most holy church to which they have been appointed. We therefore decree that the bishops shall appoint others to take their duties and stipends and that the delinquents shall on no account have either their places or their stipends restored to them. Those who build churches are not to have the right to appoint whom they like as clergy.

65 (538) gives special permission to the church in Mysia (Moesia) to alienate church property for the ransom of prisoners and the support of the poor.

79 (539). Trials of monks and nuns are to be held by their bishops and conducted according to the imperial laws and sacred canons; civil magistrates violating these instructions are to be fined ten pounds of gold and deprived of their offices.

83 (539). Clergy are to be tried by their bishops; if their offences are serious they are to be first unfrocked and then tried by the civil courts.

123 (546): 'On various ecclesiastical topics.' (*i–iv*) Instructions as to elections of church dignitaries (bishops, etc.): who may be elected and how; bribery to secure election is strictly forbidden; if a *curialis* or *officialis* is elected, he is to be sent back to his curial or official post. (*v*) Bishops are not to act as *curatores* or *tutores*. (*vi–viii*)

The clergy are not to take financial posts; bishops are not to be summoned to court as witnesses; judges must send to them and take their evidence at the bishop's own house. (*ix*) Bishops may leave their dioceses only with the permission of the metropolitan, patriarch or emperor. (*x*) The clergy are not to indulge in gaming or theatre-going; no bishop may be compelled against his will to dismiss any of his clergy. (*xi*) A bishop may not exclude anyone from holy communion without showing just cause, nor strike anyone with his own hands. (*xii*) No one may be ordained who is illiterate or unorthodox or has lived an immoral life. (*xiii*) Priests must be 35 years old, deacons 25, readers 18; deaconesses must be 40 and not have contracted a second marriage. (*xiv*) If a candidate for orders is unmarried he is not to be accepted unless he declares that he can live in chastity without a lawful wife; an unmarried priest or deacon who takes a wife after ordination is to be expelled from holy church and sent back to the curia he came from, and a bishop who allows such a marriage is to be expelled from his bishopric.

131 (545): 'Of ecclesiastical canons and privileges.' (*i*) The findings of the four great councils of the church have the force of laws. Accordingly we decree (*ii*) the Pope of Rome is the first of all priests, the archbishop of Constantinople is second, with precedence over all the rest; (*iii*) the archbishop of Justiniana Prima is primate of Illyricum: (*iv*) defines the status of African bishops, including the bishop of Carthage. (*v*) Church estates are to be free of the baser duties but to undertake the repair of roads and bridges like other owners of property; any legacies they receive from the estates of *curiales* are to be exempt from legacy duties. (*vii*) No one is to start building a church till it has been blessed and consecrated by the bishop; once started, the founder or his heirs must complete it. (*viii*) If anyone presumes to celebrate church services in his private house or on his private estate, such property is to be confiscated to the church; if the offence is committed without the owner's knowledge by an employee, the owner is not to be punished but the subordinate is to

be banished and his property confiscated to the church.
(*ix*) Legacies to the church made with no qualification
are to go to the church of the testator's home; legacies to
a particular saint with no reference to a particular
church are to go to the poorest church in the neighbourhood dedicated to that saint. (*x*) If money is willed to
build a church, the church must be completed within
five years; if a hostel or alms house, it must be completed
within one year; heirs failing in this duty are liable to
penalties; the testator may nominate the head of the proposed hostel or alms house subject to the approval of the
bishop, who may make another appointment if the person proposed by the testator is not satisfactory. (*xi*) Legacies for ransoming prisoners or feeding the poor, if no details are specified as to recipients and administrators, are
to be devoted to the distressed of the testator's home city
and administered by the local bishop; if the testator's
heirs are given the task and fail to fulfil it, it is to be taken
over by the bishop and the heirs are to be deprived of
their personal inheritance; if the bishop neglects the task,
it is to be taken over by the metropolitan; (*xii*) if the
estate proves inadequate to meet both the bequests to the
heirs and these pious bequests the latter are to have the
first claim on it. (*xiii*) Any property that comes to bishops
or other ecclesiastical dignitaries in their official capacity, whether this property be mobile, immobile or auto-
mobile, we forbid them to transfer to their own relations;
it must be devoted to the ransoming of captives, the relief of the poor or the maintenance of the church; they
can bequeath to their relations only their private family
possessions. (*xiv*) No heretic is to acquire church property;
if this law is violated, the heretic is to be deprived of what
he has acquired and the properties are to go back to the
church, while the director of church property who has
allowed the transaction is to be banished to a monastery
and excluded for a year from holy communion for be-
traying Christians to heretics; if any heretic, amongst
whom we include Nestorians, Acephali and Eutychian-
ists, shall dare to build a cave of his particular infidelity,
or any Jew to build a new synagogue, the building shall

be confiscated and given to holy church; if the heretical cave or synagogue is built on land purchased for that purpose, the church may claim from the vendor the revenues of the property for the time concerned, unless he can prove that he acted in ignorance. (*xv*) deals with the legal and financial position of the heads of orphanages.

133 (539) prescribes rules of life for monks and 'sanctimonials'; 'the monastic life and the contemplation associated with it is a holy thing which of itself leads souls to God; it not only benefits those who pass into it, but further, through its purity and its prayers to God, brings needed aid to all others also: hence previous emperors have given much thought to the question, and we ourselves have enacted no inconsiderable laws concerning their sanctity and seemliness; for there is no question that is beyond the scope of our majesty, which has had assigned to it from God the common protection of all mankind.' Of the rules which follow this preface it will be enough to quote here two only. (*iii*) No woman shall in any case enter a monastery for men nor any man a nunnery, whether it be on the plea of remembering any man who died and is buried there or on any other pretext, and least of all on the pretext that such a person has a brother or sister or any other relation in the monastery; for monks and nuns who have espoused the heavenly life have no earthly relations. (*vi*) This rule too we desire to be observed absolutely, that if any of the reverend monks be found frequenting any tavern, he be immediately handed over to the *defensores* of the city, and that if convicted he be chastened and his conduct reported to the abbot, that the later may expel him from the monastery as having abandoned this angelic state for the life of shame.

137 (565): ... 'We have received various complaints against clerics and monks and certain bishops to the effect that they are not living in accordance with the divine canon; indeed it has been found that some do not even know the prayers of the holy oblation and holy baptism.' (Six chapters of enactments follow this preface.)

III. *Private Property, the Family, Wills, Debts etc.*:

22 (536): 'Of those who contract second marriages.'
'Antiquity was not particular about either first or second
marriages, but allowed both fathers and mothers to contract several marriages without incurring any financial
loss or detriment; but from the time of Theodosius the
Great more thought has been given to this question; we
ourselves have made many enactments on the subject
and have now decided that it is necessary to rectify not
only the enactments of previous emperors but also our
own; for we are not ashamed, if we discover better solu-
tions not merely than those enacted by others but even
than those previously enacted by ourselves, to legislate
afresh rather than wait for the law to be subsequently
rectified by others.'... (*ii*) We adhere to the law that goes
back to the Twelve Tables 'whatever disposition of his
own property each individual has made, let that be law.'
(*iii*) Marriage is marriage with or without a marriage
settlement; what has been bound can always be un-
bound. ... (*v*) Whatever property either party to a marriage has willed to the other must go to the legatee,
whether the union is ended by death or by one party
taking monastic vows. (*vi*) Marriage may be dissolved if
one party is impotent ... or (*vii*) has been a prisoner or
captive for five years; but not (*viii*) if one party is sent to
the mines, for that implies reducing a free-born citizen to
slavery, a thing we do not allow.... (*x*) If on the other
hand a party has been married professing to be a free citizen and is subsequently discovered to be a slave, we decree that the original marriage is no marriage at all. ...
(*xii*) A wife may be divorced if without the knowledge or
in spite of the protests of her husband she goes off to un-
seemly convivialities with other men, or without reasonable pretext spends her nights away from home against
her husband's will, or delights in attending race meetings
or theatres (including stage plays or the like and fights
between men and beasts), or plots against him with
poison or sword, or lays violent hands on him.

44 (537). Notaries must not leave to irresponsible

subordinates the drawing up of wills. Justinian to the Praetorian Prefect John: A case which we recently heard has provided the occasion for this present law. A document was produced on the part of a certain woman which contained a statement not written by her, as she was ignorant of letters, but drawn up by a notary and having the signature of a registrar to testify to the presence of the woman and of witnesses. Later, when a dispute arose about it and the woman asserted that what the document stated was not what she had directed, the magistrate who was hearing the case sought to ascertain the facts of the matter from the lawyer who had drawn up the document, and called in the registrar. He declared that he recognised the signatures but did not know the contents, since he had not personally received her instructions but had left one of his clerks to do so; nor had he been at the final signing but had left that to another. The clerk who had been present at the signing appeared, but said that he too did not know the facts, for he was not the man who had drawn up the document; he could only inform the court that it had been completed in his presence. The clerk however who had received the original instructions was not to be found.'

84 (539). 'The fact that nature is constantly changing (as has been said frequently in previous prefaces and will be frequently repeated hereafter as long as nature goes her way) leads us to constant new enactments.' The novel proceeds to deal with the case of a man who has had children by three successive wives, the third of whom survives him and then has children by a second husband. If one son or daughter, issue of one of these marriages, dies, how should his or her share of the inheritance be portioned out among the surviving heirs? The novel tells us.

89 (539) completely re-enacts the law dealing with illegitimate children: they may be made legitimate... (ii) if males, by making them *curiales*, if females, by marrying them to *curiales*. (iii) Bastards so legitimized are to have full rights of succession except that they are not to have better treatment than lawful offspring (if any); but if

made legitimate on these grounds they cannot renounce curial duties. (*iv*) Such legitimized sons or daughters are to have no rights of succession to property of their father's relations, cognate or agnate, nor have such relations any claim on the son's estate. (*v*) The father's right of willing his property is conditioned by whether his heirs, natural or testamentary, are *curiales*. (*vi*) If the offspring are all bastards, their claim on the estate holds only if they have become *curiales*; if none of them has, he is to be regarded as having died childless. ... (*ix*) No deficiencies on the part of the mother, even if they make a lawful marriage impossible, are to prevent the legitimizing of natural children; for originally all children were free (*liberi*), and we are only returning to the law of nature when we restore to that state those who are not. (*x*) This may be done after the father's death if the children can produce evidence that such was his intention; the children are to regard this as a gift from their father and the emperor, *i.e.* from nature and the law. ... (*xii*) Valens, Valentinian and Gratian allowed natural children, if there was also lawful offspring, only one ounce (*i.e.* 1/12) of the inheritance, a concubine without children, if there was no lawful wife, 1/24. ... (*xv*) These concessions do not apply to the offspring of incest or other damnable unions; but the enactment of Constantine of blessed memory, that the illegitimate offspring of certain very high officials are not to be recognized as natural children, is hereby annulled.

90 (539) prescribes who can be witnesses, when their oral evidence can be taken in lieu of the written word, how many times they can be recalled, under what conditions they can be summoned from one prefecture to another, when they can be compelled to give evidence etc. The relevance of this novel to the subject of wills and property is shown by the preface which explains that its immediate cause was an incident in the prefecture of Bithynia. Witnesses had sworn that a testatrix had signed a will; but it came out in examination and was finally admitted by the witnesses that she had died while the will was being drawn up and that the sign of the cross had been traced by putting a pen into the hand

of the dead woman and guiding the dead hand to make the holy sign.

94 (539). Children's mothers are to be exempted from the law preventing interested persons from acting as guardians. 'But since we are much concerned to avoid oaths by the great God being rashly taken and then broken, we have thought it necessary to amend the law which requires mothers when about to become guardians of their own children to swear on oath that they will not enter on a second marriage; for we have found that this oath is broken almost as often as it is made.'

101 (539). *Curiales* (see above p. 104) may will or donate property to persons who are not *curiales* only on condition that the legatee becomes a *curialis*. A legatee may not take over property willed to him on these terms until he has actually become a *curialis*.

107 (541). On wills made by parents in favour of children. 'The ancient law so favoured wills of this description that it accepted them even if they were so obscurely drawn up as to need diviners rather than interpreters of the law to determine what they meant.' The new law prescribes the form under which such wills must be drawn up: *e.g.* the names of the children must be clearly written out in full in the testator's own hand, and also details of the intended distribution; numerical fractions are likewise to be written out in full and not indicated by arithmetical signs.

109 (541). Heretical wives are not to enjoy the privileges as regards dowries allowed to the orthodox, but they may acquire them by renouncing their heresies.

117 (542). Mothers and grandmothers and other relations, after providing for their children as required by the law, may will the residue of their property as they please.

118 (543) lays down the laws of inheritance in cases where a person has died intestate. It supersedes earlier laws on the subject, which contained many contradictory instructions. (See Bury II pp. 404–5).

129 (551). 'So long as the Samaritans boldly rose against the Christians ... we chastened them with many

punishments and in particular by not enabling them to make wills nor, if intestate, to pass on their property to their kin except only if their kin were of the Christian faith; and we forbade them to make legacies or gifts in any case where the proposed recipient was not of the orthodox faith, though even then we did not observe the same strictness in our actual practice. (*i*) But now, seeing them returned to more reasonable ways ... we make this present enactment.' The new regulation still practically excludes persons of the Samaritan faith from inheriting, but gives them every opportunity of doing so by becoming orthodox.

134 (556, see also under section A).... (*vii*) Any creditor seizing as security or compensation for non-payment of debts the child of his debtor is to pay the child or his father double the amount of the debt claimed and be subjected to corporal punishment.... (*ix*) No woman is to be imprisoned as a result of any purely financial suit; if convicted in a serious criminal suit she is to relegated to a nunnery, not a prison, lest it should lead to an outrage on her chastity.... (*xi*) If parties divorce one another for reasons the law does not allow, then both are to be sent to monasteries and their property divided between these monasteries and their heirs; those who abet such divorces are to receive corporal punishment and be banished; but if either party, before the sentence is carried out, consents to return to the married state, the sentence is to be revoked. (*xii*) If anyone convicted of adultery escapes through the connivance of the judges or by any other means and repeats his offence, he is to receive the extreme penalty after being previously tortured; the woman is to be chastised and permanently relegated to a nunnery. (*xiii*) But since we are bound to have regard for the frailty of the human race, we mitigate corporal punishments to a certain measure and hereby forbid the cutting off of both hands or feet ... and order that one hand only be cut off ... For a case of theft we are absolutely averse to the criminal losing any limb whatsoever or being put to death. Let him be chastised some other way. By thieves we mean those who commit such offences by stealth and

without arms. Those who commit assaults by violence, in a house or on the road or on the sea, we order to be subjected to the penalties prescribed by law. And to mitigate not only corporal punishments but also those which consist in loss of property, we order in the case of those convicted of offences for which the laws prescribe confiscation of property or death as the penalty that their property shall not go to enrich the magistrates or their staff or even, as earlier laws prescribed, be assigned to the public treasury ... In cases of treason however the old law is to be strictly applied.

136 (535) deals with the complaints of moneylenders that existing laws do not adequately protect them in their beneficent activities.

138. Moneylenders have no further claim on a debtor if they have already received twice the amount lent.

153 (541). Andrew, priest and *apocrisiarius* at Thessalonica, reports that people there abandon their newborn infants, leave them to be brought up by the church, and then claim them as their slaves. Such foundlings are to be permanently free, and parents who so abandon their infants are to be severely punished.

156: Those who direct the affairs of the church in Apamea inform us that certain women on their estates have married farmers from elsewhere and demand that both the husband and the offspring should belong to them. This demand ignores our recent law that in such cases the offspring be divided between the two estates, the odd child, if there is one, going to the estate to which the mother belongs.

159 (555). A rich man of the rank of *illustris* has left his large estates to various heirs with instructions where the property is to go if and when these heirs fail. This novel takes up the case and defines how far a testator can bind his heirs in the second and subsequent generations.

With these novels that deal with the family as property owners we may group two other series, the first of which deals with private property without introducing the family, the second with immorality as a threat to family life and the safety of the empire.

To the former of these groups belong:

32–34 (535), addressed, 32 and 34 to the governor of Moesia Secunda or Haemimontus Thraciae (*i.e.* the Balkan districts of the lower Danube), 33 to the Praetorian Prefect of Illyricum. All three deal with the same subject: 'A terrible thing is happening that goes beyond all bounds of impiety and greed, and we have decided to remedy it by a law of general application ... We hear that there are certain individuals in your province who have dared, taking advantage of the failure of the crops, to make loans to certain farmers on the security of a small measure of the same and then, when this was not forthcoming, to seize all their lands instead, so that some of the farmers have fled, some been starved to death, and a terrible devastation has ensued that is no less disastrous than a barbarian invasion.' The novel proceeds to prohibit absolutely any such seizure of a farmer's land. Moneylenders who go beyond what the law allows will lose their right to press even their legal claims.

36 (535). Romans in Africa are given permission to reclaim ancestral property there. A time limit of five years is prescribed for the establishment of these claims and provision made to prevent fraudulent claims.

106 (540) regulates the terms on which loans may be made on sea-borne cargoes and confirms the long-existing practice as established by examining on oath shipmasters and those who make loans to them.

160. The people of Aphrodisias possess large public funds. Certain rich individuals have agreed to take them over and pay the city an annual rent or interest used to pay for heating the public baths and for other public works. These individuals are now appealing to the law which says that debts are automatically cancelled when the debtor has paid double the amount he received. They claim that they have now paid that amount and may now retain these public funds and have no further obligation to the city. We hereby decree that our law concerning debts and moneylenders does not apply to

this sort of case. If hereafter any individual who has taken over public funds in this way attempts to discontinue the proper annual payments to the city, he will have to pay double for having shown himself a bad citizen when he had the opportunity of being a good one.

Of the Novels that seek to repress immorality

51 (537) prohibits employers of women on the stage from making them take an oath to continue in their immoral profession. Women induced to take such an oath will be doing their duty to God by breaking it. Employers inducing a woman to take such an oath are to be heavily fined and the fine to go to the woman to help her start a new and more moral way of life.

77 forbids swearing and blasphemy, 'since it is owing to offences of this kind that famines, earthquakes and pestilences occur.'

141 (559) bids homosexual perverts abandon their evil ways and confess their sin to the patriarch of Constantinople before the coming Easter. Otherwise they will be punished with all the rigour of the law. The novel mentions the fate of Sodom and Gomorrah, and appears to be inspired by the fear that this sin, if not confessed, may bring a like fate on Constantinople.

154. An extraordinary report has come to our ears, that the inhabitants of Mesopotamia and Osroene dare to contract unlawful marriages ... We can hardly credit it; but considering the various invasions which that region has endured and the rustic character of the population, it is not impossible; and for the same reason we forbid inquiries into the past. But if anyone, after the enactment of this law, contracts such a marriage, he is to be severely punished by the loss of all his property and a portion of his body and in specially serious cases of his life, no matter what his status. Any official who fails to enforce this law will likewise be subjected to the extremest penalties, including the loss of his post and his property.

In his concern for property the emperor was no doubt constantly thinking of the interests of the owner as he conceived them. But he was also no less constantly and deeply concerned with it as the source of the taxes of which he was always in such pressing need. Only two novels deal with this subject, probably because the desperate financial situation gave him little chance of making enactments to restrain his tax collectors and lighten the load of taxation that was ruining his subjects. Both reflect these two contradictory and irreconcilable motives.

128 (545). The basis on which taxes are to be levied shall be determined each year, and copies of the schedule determined on shall be circulated throughout the empire to the officials concerned. Various measures are to be taken to see that the taxes are collected on this basis and that abuses are avoided; e.g. ... (*vii*) Nobody can be called on to pay an impost on land gone out of cultivation except for the period when he has been responsible for such payment; ... (*ix*) extra payments are not to be exacted to cover the expenses of forwarding the taxes collected to headquarters; ... (*xi*) the means and occasion of tax collecting are not to be used for securing satisfaction of private claims; ... (*xiii*) nobody engaged in tax collecting may plead the right of asylum against taxpayers who claim that they have been injured by him.

147 (553): to Areobindus, Prefect of the East. Many have approached us and pleaded for remission of taxation, and we have not sent them away unsatisfied. But deeming it mean and unworthy of our majesty to make these piecemeal concessions, we hereby decree a general remission of arrears. But there shall be no refunding of payments already made, and ... (*ii*) there are to be certain other exceptions.

The civil service, the church, the family as possessors and transmitters of property, these three topics between them furnish the material of the great bulk of the Novels and dominate the picture that may be formed from them of life under Justinian. To complete it we may quote from a few miscellaneous Novels that illustrate some of the other subjects that occasionally occupied the attention of the emperor and his legislators.

63 (538). In this our royal city one of the most pleasing amenities is the view of the sea; and to preserve it we enacted that no building should be erected within 100 feet of the sea front. This law has been circumvented by certain individuals. They first put up buildings conforming with this law; then put up in front of them awnings which cut off the sea view without breaking the law; next put up a building inside the awning; and finally remove the awning. Anyone who offends in this way must be made to demolish the building he has put up and further pay a fine of ten pounds of gold.

64 (538). We have been receiving many complaints about the misdoings of gardeners in this blessed city and its suburbs. They form a union which underestimates the value of gardens when the owner is letting them out and tremendously overestimates the value when the owner is taking them over again (and paying compensation for improvements). The prefect of the city is to put an end to this abuse.

85 (539). Arms are to be manufactured only in state arsenals for state purposes and on no account to be sold to private individuals.

116 (542). Soldiers are not to be diverted from their military duties for employment by civilians whether in their homes or on the land.

122 (544). Artisans, labourers, sailors and the like are forbidden to demand or accept increases of wages. Offenders are to pay the treasury three times the amount concerned.

130 (545). Of the passage of troops through cities: they are to be maintained, fed and quartered without harm or loss to the civilian population; special officers are to see about securing supplies and quarters for the troops, and supplies are to be received in kind, the officers taking one fifteenth as their remuneration.... (*ii*) They are not to demand commodities not to be had in the neighbourhood. (*iii*) If anyone has contributed more than his due, he is to be refunded. (*iv*) The taking of money in lieu of or in addition to supplies is prohibited; offenders are to be punished by paying back twice the amount. (*v*)

Any civilians who are not given a quittance for their contributions should appeal to the local magistrate or bishop, and their complaint is to be forwarded to the praetorian prefect.... (*ix*) Billeting in occupied private houses is forbidden.

165. The law (Nov. 63 above) that no building must be erected within 100 feet of the sea to obstruct the sea view applies to the side view as well as the front.

If the *Novels* were our only source of knowledge as to the government of Justinian, we might well picture it as a highly efficient and benevolent bureaucracy, constantly on the watch for defects or abuses, constantly taking steps to correct them, and often with engaging frankness admitting failure. 'Laws do for the business of life what medicine does for diseases; consequently the effect is often the opposite of that intended, and accordingly we hereby abrogate Novel 9.' These words come from the preface to Novel 111 (A.D. 541). But to correct the impression that failures were put right by this simple process of making or abrogating laws we have two other most important documents which give us a very different and much less favourable picture. The first of them, the *de Magistratibus* of John Lydus, has already been dealt with in Chapter VI. We have seen that Lydus takes a most gloomy view of the administration, which he depicts as in a state of rapid decline. According to him the state services were being ruined and rendered lamentably inefficient by ill-judged economies, and the civil service generally was falling into the hands of men without the education essential for competent officials. We have seen that Lydus' criticisms are those of an ultra-conservative civil servant who shows no understanding of the immense difficulties with which the emperor was struggling; but even so they make it clear that there was a serious lag between aspiration and achievement in even the wisest and most practical of Justinian's measures.

The other main document that has to be collated with the *Novels* is the history of Procopius and more particularly his *Secret History*. This is reviewed in the next chapter,

but we may anticipate here and notice that Procopius
has not a good word to say about the administration
of the empire or those who were most concerned in it,
whether he is speaking of prefects like John the Cappadocian, jurists like Tribonian, or the emperor himself.
All are represented as not merely inefficient or corrupt
but positively malevolent. How Procopius came to see
his contemporaries in the extraordinarily distorted light
that pervades the *Secret History* is discussed below, where
it is argued that there must have been something radically wrong to make so able a man write with such perverted bitterness. Whatever our interpretation of Procopius, we can hardly collate these three documents, the
Novels, the *de Magistratibus*, and the *Secret History*, without
being forced to the conclusion that the emperor was far
more successful in detecting where things were wrong
than in finding effective remedies. Even if we allow him
much more success than Lydus or Procopius suggests, yet
even so, taking him on his own valuation, the *Novels*
themselves show only too clearly the limitations of his ob-
jectives. The narrow outlook that we found in the *Code* is
reflected in the *Novels*. There is the same excessive preoccupation with the rights of private property and with
sexual aberrations as the one unpardonable form of sin,
the same over-emphasis of Christian dogma at the expense of the Christian qualities. Where the latter do occasionally intrude, it will often be found to be due to the
influence not of the gospels but of the enlightened paganism of the great pre-Christian emperors and the men who
worked for them.

The problem of combining conservatism with progress
is fundamental to all good statesmanship in any civilized
society. But those who hold that conservatism of the best
kind is the opposite of mummification must admit that
the past weighed far too heavily on Justinian in almost
everything he undertook. If his whole conception of the
world was not wrong, Christianity had brought into it
something new and vivifying, but it is hard to see the
effect of any really new and vitalizing influence in the
well-intentioned tinkering with the traditional law of

Rome which is what his efforts actually amounted to. The last great attempt to make a new world by the union of the Graeco-Roman and the Christian traditions failed not only because external conditions were against it, but also and still more because the men who made it knew not what manner of spirit they were of. Heresy hunting and the savage suppression of deviationists are sure signs of something radically wrong either with the gospel on whose behalf they are invoked or with those who use such methods to propagate it. Justinian's legislation to enforce orthodoxy makes depressing reading. All the same it would be wrong to end this chapter on a note of unqualified condemnation. Perhaps the most attractive thing about the *Novels* is the way that admissions of fallibility are constantly breaking through. Those who find their inspiration in the prophets, sacred or secular, will not discover in the legislation of Justinian any fresh source of the divine fire, but they may be helped to a more sympathetic understanding of an age that knew not the prophets and sought salvation in the law.

G

CHAPTER IX

The Writers

*

> 'To the people of the world generally I venture to
> think that Palaeolithic man has more meaning than the
> Greeks.' From a paper entitled "Education and the
> Study of Man" published in *Antiquity*, 1943, p. 118.

> 'In the beginning was the Word.' St John (translated
> from the Greek).

WHEN the old Classical education, with its concentration on literature and language, began to be challenged
by the introduction into our schools and universities of an
ever widening range of new subjects, much resulted that
was pure gain. The truth was rediscovered that sermons
may be found in stones as well as books. Unfortunately
the ground thus won was largely offset by that which was
abandoned. The fact was forgotten, and in some quarters
still is, that we can never have anything but a superficial
knowledge of any age or people unless they have left us a
written record of how they lived and what they thought.
The word, and above all the book (or bible, to use the
Greek word for it) is the one medium by which we can
really recover the living past. The ancient Egyptians
have left us, thanks to the exceptional climate of their
country, temples, pictures, sculptures, furniture, abundant specimens of their handiwork of every sort. They
have even left us their own bodies wrapped in the cloth
in which they were buried. The one thing they have not
bequeathed to us is a bible. The Hebrews on the other
hand have left us a bible and very little else. Yet who can
deny that the Hebrew legacy means infinitely more for
us than all the temples and statues and mummies and
pyramids of the Egyptians? It is true that the great arch-
aeological discoveries made during the last few generations in Egypt, Mesopotamia and Crete and indeed over
the world generally, have widened and enriched our

historical background wonderfully. But it is also true that
they have tended to blind some of us to the fact that the
supreme achievement of man is speech, that the study of
man begins and ends with the word, and that an age or
race which has not left us its thoughts in written records
has failed to hand on to us the one thing needful.

What gives the age of Justinian its intense historical interest is the fact that it was a literary age in the full sense
of the term and that we are fortunate enough to have preserved from it a whole series of writers who reflect and
record the life and thought of their age from a variety of
angles. Some account has already been given of two of
them, John the Lydian and his *De Magistratibus*, Justinian
or his legal experts who were responsible for the *Institutes*
and the *Novels*. The historians have been constantly
quoted, but only from the point of view of the events that
they record. The purpose of this chapter is to give a more
connected account of these historians and to attempt
some appreciation of their significance, as also of Justinian's poets. Though much less important they are not
without their interest.

A. PROCOPIUS

By far the most important of the historians is the remarkable man whose detailed account of events down to
the year A.D. 552 has been the basis of those previous
chapters that dealt with Justinian's wars and his great
attempt to restore the empire to its ancient borders, and
whose *Buildings* is our chief literary source for Justinian's
architectural activities, which form the subject of the
next chapter. His introduction to the history of the wars
has already been quoted (above p. 18). Other extracts
have shown that he had a considerable gift for clear coherent narrative and for the portrayal of character. With
all deference to the pre-historians this capacity for drawing vivid character-pictures is a matter of supreme importance for any serious study of man. It is the possession
of this great gift in an outstanding degree that distingu-
ishes all the epochs of history that have a vital significance

for us, such as those of Homeric Greece, Thucydidean Athens, Ciceronian Rome, Shakesperian England or the France, Russia and England of the great nineteenth-century novelists.

The honesty and veracity of Procopius when writing objectively of events he had himself witnessed or could ascertain from eye-witnesses is generally admitted and need not be here put to any meticulous tests. But the historian himself is a figure of such exceptional importance for an understanding of Justinian himself, that the rest of this study of our author will be devoted mainly to a brief account of the facts he tells us about his own life, of his reactions to the emperor himself, and of the remarkable use he makes of the classical style of the great historians of the fifth century B.C. in which the Byzantine convention expected him to write.

When early in A.D. 527 Belisarius was promoted to be one of the generals in the war that had recently broken out between the Roman empire and Persia, Procopius tells us that he was chosen as Belisarius' adviser. How old he then was we are not told; but as he appears to have survived Belisarius and Justinian, who both died in A.D. 565, he must still have been a youngish man. We have already noticed (p. 26) the part he played, after the armada had reached Sicily, in securing information about the Vandal dispositions in North Africa. In 536 A.D. we find him escaping from a mutinous army in Africa to join Belisarius at Syracuse. In the spring of 538 he is in Rome during the siege by the Goths, and is sent by Belisarius on a special mission to Naples (above p. 42). The last event which he states that he witnessed personally is the great plague that devastated Constantinople in A.D. 543. (*Wars* II. xxii–xxiii).

From then on it seems probable that he was no longer acting as Belisarius' special adviser or holding any other privileged post that gave him any inside knowledge of what was going on. Everything suggests that he became a disappointed and disillusioned man, and that the disappointment was twofold: there was a sense of personal frustration and there must have been also a deep feeling that Justinian's undertakings in Africa and Italy had not achieved the brilliant results that they promised at the outset. The first rapid conquests had been followed by long and disheartening campaigns to maintain them, during which the emperor found himself involved in a second costly and indecisive Persian war while still forced to keep large armies in the field against Gothic kings in Italy and Moorish rebels in Africa. And though at last an indecisive peace was patched up with Persia, before that happened disasters such as the capture and destruction of Antioch had shaken the whole empire. There seems little doubt that Procopius had come to the conclusion that things of this sort needs must be at any famous victory. The world's great age was not going to begin anew nor the golden years of Classical Rome and Athens to return. I am inclined to think that Procopius' disillusionment was the more bitter because, in spite of a certain sardonic humour that runs through the *Wars*, the historian had at first half-persuaded himself that the empire was really embarking on a glorious crusade. We must remember that, as the wars dragged on, Justinian was growing old. In 548 A.D. he lost his masterful wife, and with her he seems to have lost much of his hold on both men and situations. He began to appoint commanders who spent most of their time disobeying instructions and quarrelling with one another. At the end of his reign he even fell into the damnable heresy of aphthartodocetism.

Some hints of Procopius' change of attitude may be detected in the references to Justinian that occur from time to time in the *Wars*. They contain no complete portrait of the emperor; but that is only natural. Justinian as emperor saw no active service and is always in the background, while Procopius is attached to the commander personally conducting operations. Such allusions as there are do indeed often sound rather critical; but the criticism is always more or less comprehensible. When the commissariat goes wrong, as it is bound to do occasionally on large distant campaigns, the minister in charge of such matters is naturally blamed and Justinian is implicitly blamed for trusting him. When the Nika riot broke out it was the empress who never for a moment lost her nerve. Praise of Theodora's part implies criticism of Justinian's. But the emperor could hardly take amiss a panegyric on the wife to whom he was devoted. In the later books criticism becomes perhaps more obvious, as for example when things were going wrong in Italy and Procopius complains that the emperor to whom the armies looked for guidance was absorbed in a study of theological controversies (VII. xxxv. 11). A little later (xxxvi. 6) our historian suggests that the emperor was neglecting Italy because some other business had cropped up and he had ceased to be interested. It would hardly be gathered from these statements that one of the main problems in this all important undertaking of winning back Italy was the knotty and almost insoluble one of reconciling the theology of Rome with that of Alexandria and Constantinople, or that the 'other business' which distracted the emperor's attention from Italy was the fact that hordes of Slavs were on the march for Constantinople itself.

The note of despondency is particularly marked in Procopius' comments on the crowning mercy that he records at the end of the last book of the *Wars*, namely the final expulsion of the Goths from Rome and the recovery of the imperial city for the empire. 'Then indeed it was most plainly shown that when men are doomed to disaster even what seem to be successes always end in destruction, and that when they have got their heart's desire such success may bring ruin in its train. Thus for the senate and people of Rome this victory proved to be still more the cause of ruin. It came about like this. When the Goths fled and abandoned their hope of remaining masters of Italy, they used the occasion of their retreat to despatch all the Romans who came their way. And the barbarians in the Roman army treated as enemies all whom they encountered when entering the city ... It so happened too that Totila, when he left the city to encounter Narses, had assembled the children of distinguished Romans and selected up to 300 of those who struck him as exceptionally handsome and given their parents to understand that they would be his guests, though in truth intending them to be hostages. Totila at the time simply ordered them north of the Po. But Teias now found them there and put them all to death' (VIII. xxxiv. 1–8). So ends Procopius' account of the final recovery of Rome and realization of Justinian's great dream.

His second published work, the *Buildings*, takes us into a different atmosphere. It was written and published after the *Wars*, to which it makes frequent references. It is frankly a panegyric, and its subject, Justinian's buildings, takes us right away from the failures or half-successes recorded in the *Wars*. We need not accuse the author of intentional disingenuousness. In the mood of disillusionment which seems increasingly to betray itself in the *Wars* he may well have been glad to obey an imperial command, or have sought to recover the imperial favour, by turning to the constructive achievements that are one of the unquestionable glories of Justinian's reign. No need for the author here 'not to conceal the shortcomings of even his greatest friends' (I. i. 5). The *Buildings* is a work in six books. Book I describes in detail the churches, hospitals, penitentiaries, palaces, cisterns and other buildings erected or restored by the emperor in Constantinople; Book II takes us to the Eastern frontier provinces and describes the cities built as bulwarks against Persian invasion or restored after they had been destroyed by the Persian invader; Book III deals similarly with Armenia and the Caucasus, IV with the Balkans from Dacia to Greece, V with Asia Minor and VI with Egypt and the rest of North Africa. The work is mainly descriptive and contains a mass of precious information as to the material achievements of the empire under Justinian, with occasional geographical and anecdotal excursuses that recall the historian of the wars. But the purpose of the whole work is plainly a lavish panegyric of the emperor. In the preface we are told how insignificant were the services that Themistocles rendered to Athens or Cyrus the Great to Persia compared with those of the Emperor Justinian. He had 'driven out of the empire the barbarians who from times long ago had been oppressing

it, acquired many new provinces and built many new
cities; finding the church erring and straying in diverse
directions from the orthodox faith, he had closed all the
roads that lead into error and had brought it to pass that
it should all stand firmly on the one foundation of the
true faith; finding the laws obscure through their un-
necessary multiplication and confused through the way
in which they contradicted one another, he had purged
them of their multiplicity and permanently removed
their contradictions; he had voluntarily enriched the
poor and needy, and in short wedded the state to the life
of happiness' (B. 1. i. 6–10).

This panegyric is for the most part no more illuminating than any similar eulogy addressed to any other ruler
possessed of dictatorial powers, and it shares with the
rest of them that dreadful lack of humour which must in
this case be attributed to the genre that our author is here
writing in rather than to his own original character. But
it does give some idea of the main lines of achievement
that have to be equated with the emperor's personal gifts
and temperament if we are to form a picture of the man
himself and his reactions on his contemporaries. And in
one section, that dealing with the great church of Sancta
Sophia, it does more than this. When he tells us there of
the feeling of peace and exaltation that comes over the
worshipper every time he enters this great church he
seems to be relating a personal experience (B. 1. 17–78,
see further below p. 223). In certain moods this complex
character could find in the glorious building an escape
from the disappointments and disillusionments of the
devil-ridden world outside.

But the historian had other blacker moods which he
has also recorded with appalling candour. For what gives
Procopius an almost unique interest is that he has left us
two versions of the history of his times. One is to be found
in the *Wars* and the *Buildings*, both written for public con-
sumption and published during the lifetime of the
writer and the people he wrote about. The other version
which we get in the work known as the *Anecdota* or *Secret
History*, cannot have been published – it can scarcely have

been privately circulated – till after the death of all the persons principally concerned. For it is a violent and virulent attack on the leading personages of the period and everything they ever did. The writer himself in his preface divides his work into two parts; Part I, he tells us, will deal with the villainies committed by Belisarius and his wife Antonina, Part II with those of the Emperor Justinian and his consort Theodora. The work is valuable incidentally as a supplementary storehouse of possible facts, but its chief interest is subjective or perhaps it might be more precise to say pathological. If only for this reason the most appropriate place to consider it is in this chapter, which deals with the historian himself, rather than in any which deals more objectively with the events and characters of the age.

The characters of Theodora and her entourage, including Antonina and her husband Belisarius, are the subject of Chapter X. We may therefore concentrate here on Procopius' treatment of Justinian himself. It is perhaps the most revealing part of the whole work. Early in the *Secret History* Procopius gives us his one attempt at a full-length portrait of the emperor. It illustrates admirably the tone of the whole work.

'In person he was neither particularly tall, nor stunted, but of moderate stature; not thin however, but slightly plump. His face was round and not uncomely, and even after two days' fasting his complexion was ruddy ... Of his character I could not possibly give a precise description: he was at the same time malevolent and gullible, the type that people describe as being both fool and knave. He never spoke the truth himself, but was always crafty both in word and act, and yet always easily at the mercy of those who wished to deceive him. His character showed indeed an unusual blend of foolishness and maliciousness ... He was full of dissimulation, treachery and affectation; he secretly nursed resentment, was double-faced, cunning, a past-master in the art of acting a part; his tears were always ready, not in response to pleasure or suffering, but because he could always turn them on to help the requirements of the occasion. He was always

lying, not just casually but on paper and with the most
solemn oaths, and that too to his own subjects. He would
break promises and oaths as soon as he had made them,
like the worst of slaves when terrified by threats of torture. As a friend he was faithless, as a foe implacable. He
had a consuming passion for murders and money. He
was quarrelsome and interfering, easily persuaded to evil
though no advice ever turned him to what was good;
quick to devise and execute everything mean, whilst in
the case of anything good he thought even the mention
of it distasteful. Such being Justinian's character, how
could anyone portray it adequately? For these vices he
displayed, and many others worse than these, in a super-
lative degree. It seemed as though nature had taken all
the wickedness of all mankind and planted it in the soul
of this one man' (viii. 12, 22–27).

Before discussing this unflattering picture let us turn to
one or two examples of the way in which Procopius proceeds to develop it. This for instance is what he has to say
in the *Secret History* about Justinian's wars (*H.A.* xviii):

'Now that Justinian was not a human being but a sort
of demon in human form may be inferred from the im-
mensity of the evils that he wrought upon the human
race ... To tell the full number of the persons that he did
away with I do not think would be ever possible for anyone in the world or even for God ... But reckoning up all
the regions whose lot it was to be made desolate of their
inhabitants, I venture to say that he destroyed myriad
myriads of myriads. Libya ... he so utterly devastated
that one may go a long journey there and find it a difficult and notable matter to come upon one single man.
And yet of Vandals who bore arms there had been
80,000 there ... and of the Libyans who lived in the
cities previously and worked the land or plied trades connected with the sea, as I have chanced to note from wide
personal observation, how could anyone in the whole
world be competent to calculate the multitude? Still
more numerous by far than these were the Moors in these
parts, all of whom with their women and offspring were
utterly destroyed. Many too both of the Roman soldiers

and of those who attended them from Byzantium lie buried in the earth there. So that if anyone affirms that five million men perished in Libya, I do not think that his statement would be adequate to the fact.'

'The reason of this was that when the Vandals had been defeated he ... did not take measures that his possessions should be protected by the firm good-will of his subjects ... but imposed certain most burdensome taxes that had not previously existed, and claimed all the best of the land; he excluded the Arians from the mysteries that they celebrated among themselves; he fell into arrears with the pay of his troops, and in other ways made himself offensive to them. Hence the rebellions which broke out and ended in great disaster. For he could never abide by established usages but was a born meddler and disturber of all things.'

'And Italy ... was rendered in all directions still more destitute of men than Libya ... All the crimes he committed in Libya he committed there also.'

'And the Persians and Chosroes made three invasions of the rest of the Roman empire, destroyed the cities and ... made the land destitute of its inhabitants wherever it came to pass that they swooped down ... Chosroes was indeed of an evil disposition himself, but as has been stated by me in the proper connexion, our emperor supplied him with all the grounds for war. He did not think fit to suit his actions to the occasion, but did everything out of season: in times of truce and peace he was always with crafty intent fastening on his neighbours causes of war, while in times of war he grew negligent with no reason and carried on his active preparations with excessive caution out of meanness; instead of interesting himself in this, he would contemplate things above and develop a curiosity about the nature of God, neither abandoning the war, because he was a bloodthirsty tyrant, nor succeeding in getting the better of his enemies, because out of petty meanness he did not take the necessary steps. And so while he was emperor the whole earth was pretty well saturated with human blood both of Romans and of very nearly all the barbarians.'

'All this befell all mankind in the days of this devil incarnate; and he was accountable for it as being placed on
the throne.'

The same tones are heard in the *Secret History* version
of the emperor's foreign and financial policy: 'All the
barbarians he presented with large sums of money, letting
no opportunity pass, both those of the east and of the
west, of the north and of the south, as far as those who
dwelt in the Britains and all over the inhabited world,
peoples whose tribes we had not previously so much as
heard of: we first saw them and then learned their several
names. For they of themselves, learning the man's disposition, flocked to him at Byzantium from every land;
and he with no hesitation but rather delighted ... that he
should be able to squander the wealth of the Romans and
fling it away on barbarian creatures or the sea surge, constantly each day sent away one of them with rich gifts.
And in this way all the barbarians became complete
masters of the wealth of Rome' (*H.A.* xix. 13–16).

Such is the account in the *Secret History* of one important side of Justinian's foreign policy. There is no hint
either of the difficulties or of the hopes that dictated and
inspired it.

The chapters on the emperor's methods of raising
money are no less one-sided and unsympathetic. The
whole system of the imperial taxation of the period is
much too complicated a subject to be dealt with incidentally. Our author's attitude may however be quite well
illustrated from some of the emperor's more occasional
efforts at raising money. A rich man named Maximilian,
so the *Secret History* tells us (xxix. 17–25), died leaving a
daughter who inherited his riches and a wife already provided for since she had inherited a fortune from her own
father, a certain Anatolius. Shortly after, the daughter
died also, leaving no child, and her fortune would legally
have reverted to her mother. 'But Justinian,' Procopius
continues, 'at once laid hold of all her money, making
this remarkable utterance, that since the child of Anatolius was now an old lady it was not holy for her to be enriched with the wealth both of her father and of her hus-

band.' Procopius cannot conceive that there could be anything to be said for an emperor who challenged the absolute right of even the most excessively rich to all their excessive riches.

One small and special class which suffered periodically from the emperor's zeal to raise money were the members of his own body-guard. These troops were called scholarians. From the account in the *Secret History* they were evidently less useful than ornamental. To appreciate Justinian's treatment of these toy soldiers it should be remembered that the position was purchased and the purchase money recovered in the form of high pay, not to speak of social status. This is how they were treated. 'Against those included among the scholarians he devised as follows: when it was expected that an army would be sent against Libya or Italy or the Persians, he sent orders for them too to prepare to go on active service although he knew quite well that they were entirely unfit for it. And they, fearing that this might happen, renounced in his favour their pay for a fixed period. This experience befell the scholarians repeatedly' (xxiv. 21).

On the whole however Procopius' criticisms in the *Secret History* of his emperor's policy may be unfair, but they are at any rate comprehensible. It is different when we come to his purely personal attacks; not that the virulent hatred they display is by any means an extinct emotion. But the form in which it attacked Procopius differs markedly from the modern varieties, at least as they may be observed in any country which enjoys any measure of political freedom. For historians this manifestation of pure hate is one of the most illuminating things about his writings. Take for example these reflections of his on the character of the royal pair Justinian and Theodora:

'For this reason they seemed both to me and to most of us not to be human beings at all, but some sort of malicious demons ... who having taken counsel together how they would be able most quickly and most easily to destroy all human beings and all human works, clothed themselves in human form and becoming devils incarnate in this manner convulsed the whole world. This one might infer from many things and in particular from the power which they displayed. For the diabolical differs from the human in being immensely more powerful. Now of the many men who in the course of history have been by chance or natural powers extremely to be feared, some have laid low cities, others countries or the like. But the destruction of all mankind and the whole inhabited world no beings but these were able to achieve' (xii. 14–16).

'Certain of his attendants, who were waiting in the palace late at night, men of irreproachable character, believed that they saw in his place a strange and diabolical phantom. One of them declared that Justinian suddenly rose from the royal throne and was pacing the room (for he used never to remain sitting for long), when suddenly his head disappeared, though the rest of his body seemed to be pacing up and down. For a long time my informant stood stupefied, thinking his eyes were at fault; then, to his amazement, the head returned to the body and he saw the figure become whole again' (xii. 20–2).

'Another said that once he was in the presence of Justinian, who was seated, when suddenly his face became like a lump of shapeless flesh: there were no eyes, no eyebrows in their proper places, no recognizable features at all. Then after a time he saw the shape of his face return. These things that I describe I did not see myself, but I have heard them from those who declare that they saw them' (xii. 23).

'And surely,' he continues, 'this man must have been some wicked devil, seeing that he never took his fill of food, drink or sleep, but would just casually taste a few morsels of what was set before him and then pace the palace all through the dead of night' (xii. 27). (It is in this context that Procopius tells the story quoted in Chapter VII of the monk who saw the Prince of the Devils sitting on Justinian's throne where his courtiers saw only the emperor.)

When Procopius wrote that Justinian must have been an incarnate devil because he had an extraordinary control over his appetites, he was plainly in a very bad way. We naturally ask whether his troubles had not affected his mind. There is little doubt that he was perfectly sane; but to prove his sanity we must look a little more closely into the mental condition of his contemporaries.

The real mental trouble with these Byzantines, the trouble that puts a great gulf between even their intellectuals and those of Classical Greece and Rome, was that they were dominated by the belief that both in politics and religion they had attained the ultimate verities. Nobody dared criticize the Roman imperial system, and it was growing more and more perilous to criticize the doctrines of the orthodox church. It is probably impossible to suppress freedom of thought completely. Procopius himself in his less morbid moods provides some interesting illustrations of its survival. One of the most remarkable has already been quoted in Chapter VII, namely the passage (*Wars* v. iii. 5–9) where he stigmatizes as 'a sort of mad folly' the attempt to define the nature of God. But what is most remarkable about that and all his criticisms is their extreme conservatism. Theologians are condemned for claiming to know more than is humanly possible about the Divine nature; but nowhere do we find radical and constructive criticisms. Radical changes are as inconceivable to Procopius as to Justinian himself.

But interesting as is the passage just referred to for its matter, it is still more so for its form. No better example could be found of the way in which the Classical tradition influenced the writer's range of ideas and at the same time afforded him a safe vehicle for their expression. The passage is a palpable adaptation of Herodotus and exemplifies what was perhaps the only way in which criticism could still be suggested and conveyed with comparative safety. A writer's claim to elegance might almost be measured by his skill in quoting or adapting the Classics. Byzantine Greek, like Classical Latin but most unlike Classical Greek, was a learned language. Historians were expected to be highly reminiscent of Herodotus and Thucydides and as far as possible to describe current events and contemporary conditions in the language of the Classical historians. This convention makes it sometimes hard to disentangle the thread of fact running through a piece of narrative, as may be seen by taking Procopius' account of the great plague at Constantinople and collating it with that of Thucydides describing the great plague at Athens. It is a convention that often leads to much artificiality. For instance, as there are, for obvious reasons, no references to Christian saints in Herodotus or Thucydides, St Peter tends to appear in Procopius as 'Peter, a man regarded, if any other, as holy by those who are called Christians.' But that this same convention was not without its usefulness will hardly surprise anyone who has ever sought to acquire or to impart the fine art of Greek prose composition. It forced on the writer of history a posture of detachment which sometimes resulted in a certain amount of the real article. And where any shred of free thought survived, the classicising language provided it with a safe disguise. When the description of the setting out from Constantinople of the great armada that was to win back Africa for the empire recalls, as it often does, the setting out of the Sicilian expedition in 415 B.C., the suggestion is almost inevitable that both expeditions were equally ill-advised. There can be no doubt that our author's classical paraphrases of current theological controversies are deliberately intended to convey acute and telling criticisms of the prevailing dogmatism. But clear thinking is not easy when clear speaking is taboo, and even the best natural gifts for clear thinking are warped and withered in an atmosphere fundamentally hostile to clear and free thought.

There was a time when the claim of Procopius to be the author of the *Secret History* was questioned. It was argued that the man who in the *History of the Wars* showed himself to have so much in common with the great Classical historians could hardly have sunk to such a pathological production as the *Secret History*. But critical historians have always pointed out that both in language and in matter there is really nothing suspect. And recent psychological investigations are all in favour of the authenticity of the work. It is in fact a copy-book illustration of the

evil effects that result from the repression of fundamental
natural activities. Men of independent mind, such as Procopius most certainly was, must have been acutely afflicted with a sense of powerlessness in the face of the despotism, intellectual and political, under which they
lived. Perhaps some supreme political genius might have
challenged the whole autocratic Caesaropapistical system
root and branch. But no such genius arose. Probably the
atmosphere was too stifling for his growth to have been a
possibility. A commonplace civil servant like John the
Lydian vented his hatred on such persons as John the
Cappadocian, the unscrupulous praetorian prefect who
succeeded to some extent in relieving Justinian's financial embarassments by oppressive taxation and by ruthless axing of the civil service. Procopius, who had been
the adviser of the great Belisarius and had moved in the
highest society, or at any rate seen the highest circles at
close quarters, was filled with impotent hatred of the
highest in the land – of Belisarius and Antonina and still
more of Theodora and Justinian. Some of his remarks on
the royal pair are amusing for all their bitterness, as when
he says that they never employed good men because
'whenever they unexpectedly found a gentleman among
their servants they grew dizzy and uncomfortable' (xxii.
35). In the same vein is the account of Junilus, who had
never as much as attended an elementary school but was
promoted to be quaestor and whilst holding that office,
which he did for seven years, experienced no shame at
putting up for public sale letters written by the emperor
and never hesitated to shake hands with anyone he met
at the rate of a gold stater a shake (xx. 17–19).

Normally, however, these distorted descriptions have a
purely pathological interest. But this in itself is a matter
of the utmost historical significance. Procopius is undoubtedly an able historian and one with a real gift for
character drawing, but he has left us no true portrait of
the emperor who made so gallant and able an attempt
to preserve and restore both politically, materially and
spiritually the great empire of which he was the supreme
head. All we have from him is the material from which

to make one by an elaborate and rather deadening process of dissection and reconstruction. But it is precisely in this fact that the value of his picture as a historical document is to be found. No student who reads Byzantine history even at its best can fail to be convinced that a government or society which allows no open criticism and no real freedom of thought is committing social and political suicide. Unfortunately, however, for those who believe in political and social freedom, Byzantine history also shows that this suicidal process may be a matter of centuries or even millennia. And so long as it lasts it will continue twisting and perverting the minds of those who live under it, even as that of the good Procopius was twisted and perverted by the sense of impotence and frustration that came upon him when he found that he could no longer follow blindly in the steps of the good Justinian.

B. AGATHIAS

(The detailed references below are to the page and line
of the Teubner text *Historici Graeci Minores* Vol. II)

The narrative which Procopius in his *History of the Wars* carried down to A.D. 552 was continued as far as 558 by Agathias, a writer with a very different background and a very different character. In the preface to his history he tells us that he must follow the practice of historians by stating who he is and whence he came. 'My name', he informs us (135. 29f), 'is Agathias, my home Myrina (some 20 miles north of Smyrna), my profession Roman law and pleading in the law courts.' He must have been born early in Justinian's reign; for in A.D. 554, when a series of earthquakes occurred at Byzantium and many places in the Roman empire and even Alexandria felt a slight shock, he was in the latter city and records his personal impressions. 'I happened myself to be staying there pursuing my legal studies, and was alarmed in spite of the disturbance being very slight; for I reasoned that their buildings were neither strong nor thick nor of a nature to stand even a slight shaking ... for they are constructed with a thickness of only one stone' (204. 30f.).

It is typical of our author that he proceeds to a long disquisition on the cause of earthquakes. Chances of displaying erudition are always seized, and this chance the more so since did not the great Thucydides (III. 89) allow himself one of his rare digressions on this same topic? About the same time he had occasion to make a voyage to Byzantium and on his way saw the utter devastation caused by one of these earthquakes in the island of Cos: the dust from the ruins made the air stifling (206. 24f.).

The five books of Agathias' history fall geographically into three parts. The first (I–II Chapter 14) deals mainly with events in Italy and the incursion into that country of the Frankish adventurers Butilin and Leutharis; the second and longest (II Chapter 18–v Chapter 2) with campaigns against the Persians in the regions south of the Caucasus; the third (v Chapter 3–end) mainly with events in and round the capital, including a great earthquake, the restoration of the cathedral of Sancta Sophia after the damage that the earthquake caused it, an outbreak of plague there, and a great inroad into the Constantinople district, Greece and the Thracian Chersonese of a swarm of Cotrigur Huns, to meet whom Belisarius was called on for the last time to take the field. This last section is prefaced by an account of the earlier history of the Cotrigurs and ends with the internecine conflicts which Justinian succeeded in stirring up between them and their neighbours the Utigers after he had bribed them to return to their own country, which lay between the Dnieper and the Don.

The scene of the greater part of Agathias' narrative is thus either Italy or the regions north and east of the Black Sea, with none of which he appears to have had any personal acquaintance. All his life after the boyhood spent at Myrina and the student days in Alexandria seems to have been passed in Constantinople as a practising lawyer. He complains that these legal preoccupations made it hard for him to do justice to his history. But the difficulty as he sees it is not that it disqualified him from claiming, as Procopius and Thucydides do, that he had been an eye-witness of the events that he records. His complaint is that he was left with insufficient time to study the classical models so dear to the Byzantine man of letters.

'I should like if it were in my power,' he tells us, 'and I hold it to be of the utmost importance, to blend, as they say, the muses with the graces. But my pursuits drag me in the opposite direction ... My history, this great and most solemn task "that o'er all tasks besides hath precedence" as the Boeotian lyre would put it (Pindar *Isth.* 1. 2), is reduced to a mere pastime in life's course ... I ought to have special leisure for perusing the learned writers of old with the aim of making them my models, and to be investigating and sifting carefully all the knowledge that can be anywhere collected, and to be keeping my mind open and free touching these matters. But here I am sitting in the royal porch studying and unravelling from sunrise to sunset masses of documents full of legal business. I am excessively vexed with these distractions, and I am vexed again if they are not there to distract me. For it is impossible for me adequately to satisfy my needs without this disagreable labour' (236. 8–237. 6).

The passage is indeed very revealing. The historian according to Agathias should no doubt collect and test his material; but first and foremost he must study the styles of his great predecessors. Agathias was in short a man of letters in the most restricted sense of the term. His earlier literary efforts had all been poetical, and there must be many classical scholars to whom he is known exclusively by his contributuons to the Greek anthology (see below, section D of this chapter). Some account of his poetical career is given by Agathias himself in the preface to his history. He had always, he there tells us, admired historians. They are such a very useful class of writers, since few people would live the heroic life if they did not hope that it would win them immortality in the pages of some historian. 'But I did not think that I ought personally to undertake this task ... since I chanced from childhood to have been more inspired by the heroic style.

I loved the sweets of poetic elegance and I have composed a few short poems in hexameters under the title of
Daphniacs, embellished with certain love stories and full
of that sort of witchery. And it seemed to me earlier that
it would be praiseworthy and not without its attractions
if I collected and published in an orderly arrangement
the more modern and recently composed epigrams which
had not yet attracted much attention and had merely
been passed on haphazard in certain circles by word of
mouth ... But since it so happened that in my lifetime
great wars have unexpectedly broken out in many parts
of the world, and that there have been migrations of
many barbarous nations ... and movements affecting
practically all humanity, I was led to fear that it might
be a sin for me to leave unrecorded, as far as I was concerned, achievements so important and marvellous and
so likely to be of use and profit to posterity' (133–134).

It was not entirely an inner voice that prompted
Agathias to turn to history. He was strongly encouraged
to do so by many friends and in particular by Eutychianus the younger, 'a man holding the highest rank
among the imperial secretaries'. Eutychianus pointed out
to Agathias that 'he need not be frightened off from
writing history by the fact that he had not hitherto tried;
... rather he should consider that history is not far removed from poetry; indeed they are brothers and kins-
men and perhaps to be distinguished from one another
only by the fact that one is written in metre' (135. 18–
23). One other fact of a very different nature may be
quoted from this most self-revealing preface: 'I was not
led to turn to the writing of history till after Justinian had
died and Justin the Younger had succeeded to the imperial throne' (137. 22–4).

C. MENANDER PROTECTOR

(Detailed references are to the page and line of the
Teubner *Historici Graeci Minores* Vol. II).

Agathias plainly intended, when he continued the history of Procopius, to carry it down at least to the end of

Justinian's reign. It stops abruptly seven years earlier in
A.D. 558. But Agathias in his turn was continued by a
third historian, Menander, who is generally distinguished
from his namesake, the great writer of comedy of the early
Alexandrian age, by the title of Protector. The *protec-
tores* were a contingent of the emperor's bodyguard, but
by the sixth century A.D. the position seems to have been
purely honorary and not to have implied any military
qualifications. Menander concerns us here less than his
two predecessors for two reasons: we have only fragments of his history, and he himself played no part in the
times of the great emperor. He only began writing history, presumably when still a young man, after the accession of the emperor Maurice, seventeen years after Justinian's death. But he was almost certainly born in Justinian's reign, and his father belonged to Constantinople,
so that he was in a position to write with some authority
of Justinian's last years; and the picture he has left us of
his own early days throws interesting light on the literary
world of the period.

'My father Euphrates', he tells us, 'came from Byzantium. He had received very little education in letters.
Now Herodotus, a kinsman of mine, sampled the education imparted by the laws, though he afterwards abandoned the study of the subject. But I thought that a man
ought not to be without an acquaintance with the laws ...
and I did in fact attain it to the best of my abilities. But I
did not practise the profession; for it did not appeal to
me to plead causes ... and by cleverness of speech to
appropriate the thoughts of this or that person. And so,
dismissing serious pursuits and choosing the worst of
courses, I went gaping about and loved the brawls of the
colours and the horse racing and pantomimic dancing ...
But when Maurice had assumed the imperial power ...
and by offers of money incited and encouraged those who
were rather blunt of wit, I reflected that I must give up my
senseless round of idleness. So I set about writing this history, determining to begin after the death of Agathias
and to start my history' (where his ended) (Teubner 1.2–
2. 13).

So much for Menander himself. But in the longest and most important of his fragments, that quoted at some length in Chapter V above, about the peace conference of A.D. 562–3, he tells us something of the first-hand source from which he drew, which was no other than Peter, the leading Roman envoy. His own version, he says, is based on the voluminous report published by Peter himself. 'Nor did I,' he continues, 'substitute one set of words for another or translate occasional vulgarities of expression into my best efforts at a more Attic idiom. I had no desire to transpose what was actually said, and had reached me, I have reason to suppose, in an accurate form, into another mode of speech, and by smoothness of statement to make known not what was said but my capacity as a rhetorician, especially when I was giving the reports of a truce between two such very great monarchs and states. But should anyone wish to know all that the King of the Persians and Peter on that occasion said on every point, let him read it in the collected works of Peter himself. For he reports in detail all that Chosroes and the Roman and Persian ambassadors both said and heard, in the actual words of the speakers, whether they chanced to be dictated by flattery on either side or whether the statements were made in all seriousness or in irony or by way of taunt or jest ... For a huge volume has been filled with these reports, and filled, I think, with a truthful record, unless Peter has indulged in a little boasting for the benefit of his own reputation ... I have drawn from it what was requisite and set it forth in brief' (32. 8–33. 13).

Menander was plainly very proud of the way he had summarized Peter's report of the conference. Peter himself, he tells us in another fragment, died shortly after returning from it. All the characters most concerned in the proceedings had thus been dead for something like twenty years when Menander took up his task. Peter's work was published and accessible, memories must have still been fresh, whilst motives for distorting or suppressing the truth must have mainly disappeared. We may be unable to accept Menander's claim to be guiltless of verbosity, but there is every reason to believe that his recording of Peter's memoirs is essentially true.

D. THE POETS

(i)

The 'more modern and recently composed epigrams' which Agathias collected and published (above, p. 187) were the compositions of a group of verse writers who were carrying on a tradition that went back for over a thousand years. The word epigram has not the connotation in Greek that it has acquired in more recent times. The Greek epigram is merely a very short poem, nearly always in elegiac couplets, written for some particular occasion or suggested by some particular incident or object. Some of the earliest were written to be engraved on tombstones or on monuments dedicated to some god. Agathias was not the first to publish a collection of such epigrams, nor was he the last. Meleager had collected his 'garland' some six hundred years earlier and supplementary collections had been made in the two centuries following. We owe the preservation of all that we have of these various collections to a still later collector named Cephalas, probably of the tenth century A.D. This anthology of Cephalas has come down to us in a manuscript that was once housed in the Palatine library at Heidelberg and is generally known as the Palatine anthology, to distinguish it from a still later collection made in the fourteenth century by a certain Planudes. Thus the history of the Greek epigram may be said to go back almost to the time of the foundation of Byzantium and to have ended only shortly before its fall.

Of some 3,700 poems contained in the Palatine anthology just one-tenth (376) come from Agathias' collection and are the work of Agathias and his contemporaries. The writers seem to have been highly placed officials – Paul the Silentiary, Julian ex-prefect of Egypt, Macedonius the consul, Arabius, Leontius and Eratosthenes who are described as lawyers (*scholastici*), Rufinus who held the position of *domesticus* and Johannes Barbucallus who is described as *grammaticus*. In the *Anthology* the poems are grouped in books according to the subjects – Love, Death, Dedications, Wine and Jest, Miniature Word-Pictures and Moral Tales and the like. All are represented in Agathias' collection.

The love poems often have themes familiar in our own literature. Agathias for instance (v. 261) is anticipating Ben Jonson when he writes of the kiss within the cup

> If you but touch the bowl with your lips it is hard to be sober.
> Who could refuse such a cup offered by bearer so sweet?
> Surely the bowl is a ferry-boat bearing the kiss you set on it,
> Which, when it comes with its charge, tells of the grace it received.

Paulus Silentarius is still further inflamed by a jug of water which his lady-love pours over him when he serenades her (v. 281). Another beauty affects him by the varieties of her hair-dressing much as Julia did Herrick by the variations in her clothes (v. 260). Agathias and his imprisoned mistress kiss the two ends of her girdle like an earlier Pyramus and Thisbe (v. 285). Several poems are addressed to faded beauties now deserted by their lovers (Macedonius v. 271, Agathias v. 273). They read like sequels to Herrick's 'Sweet be not proud'. But the old and wrinkled Philinna is told by Paulus that her autumn excels another's spring (v. 258). The poem might form a happy epilogue to 'Believe me if all those endearing young charms' of Tom Moore.

Of the sepulchral epigrams a few are personal and show real feeling, as that of Agathias on his gifted sister Eugenia (vii. 593), or those of Julianus on a young wife who died at the age of sixteen (vii. 600, 601) or that on a girl of fourteen who died shortly before she was to have been wedded (vii. 568). Agathias on the death of a pet partridge strikes a different note. It had met its end by having its head bitten off by the cat, and he prays that the earth may lie heavy on his pet lest the cat drag its body from the tomb (VII. 204).

Amongst the favourite topics of the descriptive and moralizing epigrams are bridges (IX. 641), inns (IX. 648–50), private houses (IX. 651–4, 667), gardens (IX. 663–5), public baths (IX. 620, 624, 625, 630, 631), latrines (with moral reflections) (IX. 642–4, 662), mosquito nets (IX. 764–5), a water clock (IX. 782) and famous works of art like Myron's cow (IX. 793–8).

All these epigrams are entirely secular and pagan. But the first of the fifteen books of the Palatine anthology is devoted to Christian epigrams and two or three of the 123 poems that make up the book are from Agathias' collection. One (I. 34) by Agathias himself, on an image of an archangel, praises the artist for forming an image of the invisible and incorporeal. 'No longer is the worshipper confused in his veneration, but he trembles before the image imprinted within him as if it were the real presence.' In another (I. 35) Agathias and three friends offer the archangel an ikon of himself to celebrate the fact that they have completed the fourth year of their legal studies.

With occasional exceptions these epigrams, whatever their subject, are just conceits. The language is that which had been used for similar epigrams on the same set of subjects for many centuries. But that is not to deny them a certain limited sincerity. In an age like the present, with its acute reaction against the past, it is not easy to realize how profoundly traditionalism was in the very blood of the educated Byzantine. His own emotions and experiences, serious and trivial alike, took on a fresh significance from the simple fact that they had been those of his predecessors in earlier generations. Hence it was natural for him, when he sought to give them expression, to turn to the words and the forms in which they had been expressed by men of former ages. We get a better understanding of the spirit in which Justinian's jurists undertook the compilation of the Code and proceeded to administer it, when we think of them in their more domestic moments, writing these pretty archaistic trifles and then proceeding to make a corpus of them.

The conceits which abound in them are no less significant. When Dr. Ede, Dean of Worcester, died early in the
seventeenth century, his handsome tomb in Worcester
cathedral was inscribed with a set of Latin hexameters
that begin

'Ede quis es.' 'Ede.' 'Ede cur hic.' 'Quia praefuit aedi.'

There is no reason to think that the people of Worcester
felt that there was anything unfeeling or disrespectful in
adorning the tomb of their departed dean with this
learned *jeu de mots*. What such conceits do generally indicate is that the writers are living in an age which takes for
granted what it regards as the fundamental verities.
When the depths cannot be stirred there is all the more
incentive for playing with the surface.

(*ii*)

The manuscript which has preserved for us the Palatine
anthology contains also one considerable poem by
Agathias' friend and fellow epigrammatist Paul the
Silentiary. Like the epigrams it is an occasional poem,
but the occasion was no less a one than the ceremony
that celebrated the restoration of Sancta Sophia in A.D.
562 after the collapse of the roof in 558. It opens with an
address to Justinian, by God's grace and the prayers of
the late empress victorious over all the earth and preserved from the assaults of conspirators at home (whom
he has treated with marvellous mercy and mildness).
The poet then leaves the palace and proceeds towards
the church and, arrived before it, addresses the patriarch.
These prefatory lines (1–134) are in iambics. Then in
hexameters he bids the clergy rejoice that their church is
restored to them, urges old Rome to rejoice that her
daughter now outshines her, and praises the emperor
who alone had remained undismayed when the disaster
occurred. How fortunate that it happened while he was
still on the throne to inspire the work of rebuilding. Next
the priests are summoned to open the doors of the church,

the assembly enters, and the description proper begins.
The actual building is described in detail (354–611), then
the various marbles of which it was built and the mosaics
with which it was adorned (617–67), then the silver
iconostasis and the altar with its tabernacle and silk cur-
tains (668–805), and finally the multitudinous lamps that
lit it by night so that it became a beacon to ships upon the
sea (806–920). God save the emperor and God save the
patriarch (921–1029). This ends the main poem, but it is
followed by a second, written for recitation on the same
great occasion, describing the ambo or pulpit newly constructed for the restored church. It too has a preface in
iambics (1–29). The description that follows and the final
invocation of the Trinity are in hexameters.

The poem must have given immense satisfaction to its
writer. The Greek hexameter had been given a new
character a generation or two earlier by the remarkable
poet Nonnus, and Paul uses the Nonnine form of the
verse not without effect. His vocabulary too is impressive
and abounds in words and formations and phrases that
seem faintly but not altogether familiar to those who
know only classical Greek and bear witness to the poet's
own familiarity with his predecessors of all periods from
Homer's onwards. What the audience that first heard it
made of it we can only conjecture. We can however feel
fairly sure that if they mostly found it rather beyond
them the poet was not disconcerted. The occasion called
for all the charm of all the muses, and that is what Paul
must have felt that he had provided. In substance too the
poem follows ancient and highly respected models. Its
two themes are the details of the fabric and furnishments
of the great building and extravagant praise of the emperor, a blend which classical students are familiar with
from the *Silvae* of Statius. Anyone with any feeling for
literature will find Procopius on the great church (below,
Chapter XI, p. 222f.) infinitely more moving and impressive than Paulus. But all the same it cannot be denied
that the verse writer has conveyed in his poem much of
the outlook of educated Byzantines of his age. It is a piece
of good fortune that has preserved for us this composition,

which takes us back to the very occasion when the emperor went in state to celebrate the restoration of his great church, which still stands in all essentials as it was on the day when Paulus called on the priests to open its doors.

(iii)

The 4,670 hexameter lines of Corippus' Latin epic the *Johannid* are our main source for the history of the final pacification of Libya by John Troglita (see Chapter II, end). The details of these operations do not here concern us. What is of more immediate interest is the way they are recorded by the Latin poet. John is represented as setting out with instructions from the emperor which repeat almost word for word Virgil's famous lines on the mission of Rome.

> . . . tu prisca parentum
> iura tene, releva fessos, confringe rebelles. (1. 146–7)
> (Do thou hold fast by the ancient laws of our sires,
> comfort the weary, crush the rebellious).

And the emperor goes on to declare that his 'pietas' bids him always tame the proud and spare the vanquished, *parcere subiectis, gentes domitare superbas* (1. 148–9). John is in fact commissioned to be another Aeneas. His son Peter goes with him, and when they pass the Troad John tells him the tale of Troy and the young Peter imagines himself another Ascanius (1. 170–207). John like Aeneas, has supernatural enemies and protectors. On the voyage to Libya he is visited by a fallen angel, *malignus angelus ... claro deiectus Olympo* (1. 253–4), who tries to frighten him from going forward with his enterprise; and just as Juno is countered by Venus in the *Aeneid*, so when John is assailed by the fallen angel a heavenly spirit comes to his aid, descending from Olympus to guide him on his way. John, like Aeneas, encounters a fearful storm. It subsides only when he has prayed to God and explained to Him that his mission is to end the war and slaughter that is going on in Libya, and that he is doing the will of his master Justinian who in turn is the servant of God and doing His will (I, 271–322). As in the *Aeneid*, the events that preceded the hero's landing in Africa are recounted as a narrative within the narrative, told (III. 54–IV. 246) by a veteran general. The story includes the earlier history of one of John's chief opponents, the Moorish chief Antalas. Prodigies attended his birth and his father consulted the oracles of Ammon and Apollo. This leads (III. 85f.) to a description of the priestess in the throes of inspiration and prophecies of coming troubles, both reminiscent of the Cumaean Sibyl in *Aeneid* VI.

These examples are perhaps enough to give some notion of the way that Corippus approaches his subject. He has himself epitomized it in the elegiac preface to his poem.

> Aenean superat melior virtute Johannes,
>   sed non Vergilio carmina digna cano.
> (Aeneas is surpassed by John with his superior virtues,
>   But the song I sing does not compare with Virgil's).

No one will dispute the truth of the second line of this couplet. But the *Johannid* has its qualities, and they are qualities that it shares with nearly all the writings of the period and it is thanks to them that the age of Justinian still lives for us. It is a valuable record of facts; it gives us something of the atmosphere of the period; and it is an admirable example of the traditionalism which, with all its limitations, has rendered the world a priceless service by preserving through ten centuries of partial eclipse the legacy of Greece and Rome.

CHAPTER X

Theodora, Antonina, and John the Cappadocian

*

In a famous passage on Athens in the days of her greatness Wilamowitz-Moellendorf observes that only one female character played a leading part in Athenian history and that that one character was a goddess, the patron goddess of the city, Pallas Athene. The German historian touched on one of the fundamental weaknesses of Athenian civilization, and our first impulse is to contrast unfavourably the condition of things in the city state of Athens with that which prevailed under the Roman empire, where the empress or empress-mother is so often, both in old Rome and New Rome, one of the most forceful and arresting figures of the period, from the days of Agrippina to those of Irene. The antithesis is in many ways unfortunate, for nearly all these forceful women illustrate the danger of power falling into the hands of persons with a masterful temperament but inadequate political education. But if we allow that the study of power exercised by those unqualified to do so is one of the most instructive that history has so far provided us with, then it may fairly be claimed that the career of Theodora is worthy of our most serious attention. For of all the long series of masterful empresses, whether consorts or sovereigns in their own right, none is so arresting as the consort of Justinian. She is in the foreground of every picture of the period.

This pre-eminence she owes almost entirely to Procopius, whose account of her in the *Secret History* is perhaps the most scandalous record ever left by one who was unquestionably a notable historian. This record has much to say about her enemies and confederates, and in particular about her great enemy John the Cappadocian and about another woman, Antonina the masterful and capable wife of Belisarius. Like Theodora herself, both John

and Antonina were notoriously uneducated, and in the
case of all three the picture supplied by the *chronique
scandaleuse* of the *Secret History* can be tested and supplemented from other sources. It is indeed essential to remember that the picture is entirely coloured by Procopius' virulent vituperations; but, as argued in the previous chapter, it is essential also to remember that this
appallingly frank exhibition of venom is in itself evidence
of the first importance as to the influence exercised by
this remarkable woman.

Her origins were humble and extremely disreputable;
for like Nell Gwynn she had spent her early years on the
stage in a period, like that of Restoration England, when
the stage was the antithesis of respectability. For this part
of her career we naturally have to rely almost entirely on
the *Secret History*. 'There was at Byzantium a certain
Acacius, keeper of the wild beasts for the faction of the
Greens, with the title of feeder of the bears. This man fell
sick and died while Anastasius held the imperial throne,
leaving three children, all girls, named Comito, Theodora and Anastasia, of whom the eldest was not yet seven
years old' (ix. 2-3). Their mother, in extreme destitu-
tion, married the man who was expected to succeed to
her late husband's post. But an internal intrigue amongst
the Greens led to another applicant being appointed,
whereupon the mother caused the three destitute children to appear as suppliants in the circus. The Greens absolutely refused to listen to their entreaties; but the Blues
had also recently lost their keeper of the beasts and
appointed the suppliants' new step-father to fill the
vacant post. When the children grew up their mother
sent them on the stage, since they were all good-looking
(ix 4-8).

All three children were highly successful, but Theodora most of all. Their performances were of the Folies
Bergères order, and the narrative goes on to describe the
acts of extreme indecency both on and off the stage by
which Theodora made herself notorious. According to
Procopius her technical accomplishments were as meagre
as were those of Nell Gwynn according to Pepys: 'she

was no flute player nor harpist; she was not even a
trained dancer, but simply sold her favours to every
chance comer ... Afterwards she went on the stage and
took a regular part in the actors' performances, appear-
ing in certain kinds of low comedy: for she had a ready
wit and a gift for mockery' (ix 12–13). 'Later, when
Hecebolus, a man of Tyre, became governor of Penta-
polis (Cyrenaica), she went there with him to minister to
his vices. But she had some quarrel with the man and was
quickly expelled from there, with the result that she was
soon in absolute want and was reduced to supplying her
needs by prostituting her person as she had been accustomed to do before. She first went to Alexandria and then,
after touring all the East, got back to Byzantium' (ix.
27–8).

We may perhaps discount the more lurid parts of this
narrative, which refer to days in which Theodora was
still obscure. The story has become the subject of innumerable romances, some frankly pornographic, some
wildly idealized, as for instance Mr. Masefield's Theodora, where the stained glass features of the Ravenna
mosaic are applied to the actress of this early period. But
the account in the *Secret History* has all the marks of a fundamentally true picture seen through jaundiced eyes. It
suggests that Theodora had her heart in neither of her
professions, neither in that of prostitute and exhibitionist
nor in that of actress, but that her early experiences had
made on her a profound impression. The circus factions
which had played so decisive a part in her earlier experiences had become for ever an overmastering reality,
and so too had the threat of poverty and obscurity to
which she had been so constantly exposed. Everything
attributed to her in these early days becomes convincingly comprehensible if we assume, as all the evidence points
to having been the fact, that her one unshakable resolve
was to escape from all this; and for this end she chose and
unswervingly followed the one way open to a woman in
her position. Two details of her subsequent career confirm the fundamental truthfulness of this earlier narrative. When the actress had become empress she was

H

constantly concerned in a very special way with the lot of
unfortunate women; and on one occasion when she wished to punish an eminent patrician she staged a performance to discredit him that gives us some idea of what
the low comedy must have been like that she had so excelled in in her unregenerate days (xv. 24–35).

Soon after Theodora got back to Byzantium she became the mistress of Justinian and secured over him the
ascendancy that was to last till the end of her life. He was
not yet emperor and did not yet dare to marry her or to
ennoble her by advancing her to the rank of patrician.
The old empress Euphemia was the obstacle. Though
she was illiterate and uneducated like her husband Justin and prudently kept clear of all matters of state, she
was 'far from being a bad woman' and refused to allow
the ex-circus girl to be publicly acknowledged as the
future empress. Theodora was content to accept large
sums of money from her devoted lover and to join with
him in allowing the Blues to indulge in greater excesses
than ever before (ix. 29–49). But directly Euphemia was
dead Justinian persuaded his uncle Justin to amend the
law which prohibited senators from marrying courtesans,
and Theodora became Justinian's lawful wife. As such
she became empress when he became emperor in A.D. 527.
(ix. 53–4). Procopius deplores how not a single senator
or priest or soldier protested at having to swear allegiance to her and how the common people riotously
clamoured to be called her slaves (x. 6–8). We may leave
unexplored the motives which led to this acquiescence
on the part of the government, the church and the army;
but it is at least possible that when the common people
acclaimed her it was because they remembered that she
had once been one of themselves, and that her elevation
gave them positive satisfaction. Our historian seizes this
occasion for one of his reflections on the mysterious ways
of fortune (x. 9–10) and also, very appropriately, to give
us a picture of Theodora's personal appearance. 'She
was fair of face and charming as well, but short and inclined to pallor, not indeed completely without colour
but slightly sallow. The expression of her eyes was always

grim and tense' (x. 11). This description may be compared with the mosaic portrait of her in S. Vitale at
Ravenna (pl. 13). Nothing is added to these two records by the description of a statue of her in *Buildings*
1. xi. 8, a piece of courtly flattery entirely lacking in
definition.

No less appropriately Procopius gives us at this point
his views on the remarkable way the emperor and empress worked with and for one another all through their
long years of partnership. 'For a long time all believed
that both in their views and their practices they were
always directly opposed to one another. Later however it
was recognized that this belief had been deliberately
built up by them in order that their subjects should not
with one accord rise up in revolt, but should be all divided in their views on them' (x. 14). This policy, the historian goes on to argue, was practised by the royal pair
with signal success in relation to both the main interests
which divided their subjects, namely the circus factions
and theology.

It was on the momentous occasion when the two circus
factions for once in a way combined in the famous Nika
riot of January A.D. 532 that Theodora gave the supreme
exhibition of her quality. This was an event that affected
everyone in Constantinople, and for Procopius' account
of it we have to turn to his *History of the Wars* (1. xxiv).
The chapter in question has already been quoted from
when giving an account of the circus factions (Chapter
VII (*b*)). The riot began as one of the ordinary demon-
strations of rowdiness. 'The city authorities were leading
away some of the rioters to execution, when the two factions came to an understanding and truce, seized the condemned men, and then, breaking into the prison, set free
all who were confined there for sedition or any other mis-
demeanour. The officials were all killed off-hand: respectable citizens fled to the mainland opposite and the
city was put to the flames just as if it had fallen into the
hands of an enemy ... The watchword used by the
crowds was Nika (conquer) and from it the incident got
the name by which it is still known' (xxiv. 7–10).

Meanwhile the emperor and empress had shut themselves up in the palace (xxiv. 10). Here they learned that
the rioters had turned their fury against two of the chief
imperial ministers, the praetorian prefect John of Cappadocia and the quaester Tribonian. The emperor 'wishing
to win over the people, immediately dismissed both from
office' (xxiv. 17). The riot, however, continued un-
bated, and on the fifth day it took a still more serious
turn. Justinian had with him in the palace where he was
sheltering Hypatius and Pompeius, the nephews of the
late emperor Anastasius. He now ordered these unhappy
men to leave the palace, and they were forced under protest to do so. The fact became known to the rioters, and
the next morning they dragged Hypatius from his home
and proclaimed him emperor. The situation had indeed
developed ominously, and those of Justinian's counsellors
who were still in the palace seriously debated whether
they should stand their ground or take to flight in their
ships.

This was the moment at which Theodora made the
speech that saved the situation. Procopius does not pre-
tend to quote her actual words, but claims to give the
gist of what she said. 'As to whether it is wrong for a
woman to put herself forward among men or show daring
where others are faltering, I do not think that the present crisis allows us to consider whether we should hold
one view or another. For when a cause is in the utmost
peril there seems to be only one best course – to make the
very best of the immediate situation. I hold that now if
ever flight is inexpedient even if it brings safety. When a
man has once been born into the light it is inevitable that
he should also meet death. But for an emperor to become
a fugitive is a thing not to be endured ... If you wish to
flee to safety, emperor, it can easily be done. We have
money in abundance; yonder is the sea; here are the
ships. However ... as for me, I hold with the old saying
that royalty makes a fine winding sheet' (xxiv. 33–7).

The magnificent arrogance of this speech is surely
something beyond the range of Procopius' invention. It
recalls Clytemnestra in her superbest mood, and the

words 'yonder is the sea' may be an intentional reminiscence of the words of the Mycenean queen in the *Agamemnon*, though we may doubt whether this echo derives from Theodora herself or from her learned chronicler. However that may be, the speech of Theodora decided the issue. It put fresh heart into her audience. The household troops were still disaffected and hanging back to see how things would go. But the faithful Belisarius with his personal retainers and Mundus with a force of Herule barbarians were ordered to fall on the rioters who were crowded in the hippodrome just outside the palace. Thirty thousand are said to have perished in the massacre that followed. Hypatius and his brother were killed the day after, and their bodies, like those of so many later victims of emperors and sultans, were thrown into the sea (xxiv. 40–56). 'The emperor confiscated their property and that of all other members of the senate who had supported them. Later however he restored to them all, including the children of Hypatius and Pompeius, both the distinctions they had previously enjoyed and all of their wealth that he did not happen to have presented to any of his friends' (xxiv. 57–8).

'This was the end of the Nika revolt.' It was not however the end of the career of the two ministers who had been dismissed on the second day of the outbreak. One of the two, the quaestor Tribonian, whose name is for ever associated with Justinian's codification of the laws, does not here concern us. The other, the praetorian prefect John of Cappadocia, does. There was a deep personal enmity between him and Theodora, and it is to the history of their feud that we must now turn. Like Theodora herself, John was a person of humble origin. 'He knew nothing of humane letters or of a liberal education, since he had only been to an elementary school and had learnt there nothing except to write and even that badly. But by sheer natural ability he became the most powerful man I know of. He had an exceptional capacity for seeing what was required and for finding a solution to difficulties. But he was the greatest scoundrel in the whole world and he used his great gifts for scoundrelly ends ...

Anyhow, after amassing a great fortune in a short time he
broke out into a life of unbounded drunkenness. The
time till lunch he spent robbing the emperor's subjects of
their property; the rest of the day he devoted to drinking
and vice ... He ate till he was sick. He was always ready
to steal and still more ready to fling away and squander
what he had stolen ... He gave no thought at all to God;
and if ever he did visit a church as if to pray and keep
vigil, he did not behave in the least like a Christian, but
putting on a rough cloak proper for a priest of the old
faith which people are now accustomed to call Hellenic,
he would repeat all through the night certain unholy
words which he had previously rehearsed, that the
emperor might be brought still more under his influence
and he himself be immune from harm by anyone'
(xxiv. 12–15, xxv. 10).

This is Procopius' estimate of the Cappadocian in his
public history. We can see how useful he can have been
to Justinian in the desperate task of financing the empire. We can see also how naturally he might antagonize
and alarm his rival upstart Theodora: it is not beyond
possibility that the combined outbreak of the two factions was partly engineered by her for the purpose of getting rid of this unpleasant rival. The empress may well
have been less aware of the use he served the emperor by
his skill in extracting taxes than of the harm he did both
to the emperor's reputation by the way he extracted them
and to her own by the way he called attention to the danger of associating with members of the lowest classes.

If the Nika riot was a plot to get rid of John, it was a
failure, for John was soon restored to his old office and
continued to hold it for ten years (i. xxv. 1–3). For these
ten years the feud between the empress and the prefect
seems to have gathered in intensity. 'The empress detested him above all men; and he, when he offended
her by his wrong doings, never resolved to court her with
flattery and ingratiating behaviour, but openly set about
plotting against her and slandered her to the emperor,
neither respecting her position nor deterred by the extreme affection that the emperor bore her' (i. xxv. 4).

Finally the empress decided to kill him. John learned of her purpose and took extraordinary precautions, spending sleepless nights though he employed thousands of retainers to guard him, a thing which had been allowed to no prefect before him. He also resorted to sorcerers and oracle mongers, who declared to him that he should one day attain the imperial power (xxv. 5–8). It may safely be assumed that these doings of John got to the ears of Theodora by the same sort of channel that brought her own to those of John. It must have become more and more clear to her that Justinian must be rid of this dangerous rival.

She found her opportunity when Belisarius returned to Constantinople fresh from the conquest of Italy to take up again the command against Persia, leaving behind him in the capital his wife Antonina, who normally accompanied him on his campaigns. Antonina indeed played no small part in the history of the wars; we have already had more than one occasion to mention her (e.g. above, pp. 25, 50). The part she played in the palace intrigue which overthrew the Cappadocian makes less pleasant reading; but it is no less an essential part of the history of the period, and throws much light on the complex character of Theodora herself, for it shows how two notable women of very different characters but of very similar antecedents reacted to very similar circumstances. Before following any further this very unpleasant intrigue it will be helpful to turn again to the *Secret History* and the account there given of Antonina's early career. The material is abundant, for it will be remembered that the half of the work which is not devoted to the villainies of Justinian and Theodora deals with those of Belisarius and Antonina.

Like Theodora herself, Antonina was a woman with a past. 'Her grandfather and father had been charioteers who raced in Byzantium and Thessalonica, her mother a prostitute employed at the theatre. She herself at first lived a life of vice and depravity and associated with sorcerers like her parents ... but later she became the lawful wife of Belisarius, after having already become the

mother of many children. She accordingly resolved from
the start to live in adultery, but was careful to conceal
her conduct, not that she was ashamed of her practices or
had anything to fear from her husband (... for she kept
him in subjection by much resorting to magic), but because she dreaded being punished by the empress. For
Theodora used to storm and rage against her exceedingly. But when she had got her under control by helping
her in her direst need, first by destroying Silverius in a
way which will be told in a later passage, and afterwards
by compassing the fall of John the Cappadocian, as I
have described in a previous work, thereafter she had no
scruple about committing every sin more boldly and
without concealment' (*Secret History* i. 11–14).

The services that Antonina had rendered the empress
in the matter of Silverius are not, as Procopius here promises, recorded later. Silverius was a pope who had the
double misfortune of having been elected while the
Gothic usurper Theodatus was King of Italy and of being
opposed to the empress's schemes for appointing monophysite sympathizers to high positions in the church at
Constantinople. We know from elsewhere that he was
deposed by Belisarius on the charge of having had trea-
sonable communications with the Goths, and that he was
banished to an island where he died in mysterious circumstances. The sort of part that Procopius would have
pictured Antonina as having played in the Silverius affair
can be imagined from his account of her plottings against
John the Cappadocian as recorded in the *Wars* (i. xxv.
13–30), to which we may now return.

John had a daughter Euphemia whom her father loved
exceedingly since she was his only child. By cultivating
this young woman assiduously Antonina won her friendship; and then one day when she had her by herself pretended to confide in her that she and Belisarius were extremely unhappy at the ungrateful way that Belisarius
was being treated by the emperor. Euphemia was delighted, for she shared her father's fear and hatred of the
empress, and replied that Antonina and Belisarius were
to blame for putting up with this treatment and not using

their power. To this Antonina made answer that it was impossible for any general to succeed in a revolution unless he had friends at court to help him. If only they had Euphemia's father with them, then indeed they could set about their project with a good heart. Euphemia fell at once into the trap and promised to report to her father what Antonina had told her. John was delighted and thought he now saw his way to bring to fulfilment the prophecies that he should one day take the emperor's place. He wanted an immediate interview with Antonina, but she sent word to him by Euphemia that a meeting in the city was sure to be observed and rouse suspicion, but that in a few days she would be starting to join her husband on the Persian front. If John came and waited on her at her first stop outside the city, that would seem perfectly natural, and they could then make all necessary arrangements. John agreed and Antonina reported to Theodora all that she had done. Theodora passed on the information to Justinian, and took the further precaution of herself sending two high officials, Narses and Marcellus, with a adequate force of soldiers to the place where the interview was to be held, instructing them to kill John at once if they overheard him talking treason. She did not inform Justinian about this step, but it is said (so Procopius informs us) that he got news of it from some other quarter and actually sent a message to John to warn him not to attend the rendezvous.

But 'it was fated that things should go ill for John.' He did meet Antonina, was overheard by Narses and Marcellus agreeing to take part in this bogus conspiracy, and was at once attacked by them. But John too had brought a bodyguard with him, and in the scuffle that followed he succeeded in escaping. Procopius declares his belief that if John had gone straight to the emperor he would have suffered no disagreeable consequences. But his nerve failed him and he sought sanctuary in a church in the city. From there he was removed to Cyzicus, on the south coast of the Sea of Marmora, and forced to take holy orders; but he steadily refused to take duty as a clergyman, and though his property was all confiscated, the emperor allowed him to recover much of it, while much of his wealth never fell into the hands of the treasury at all since it had been amassed and hoarded secretly. 'The Romans,' Procopius comments, 'were literally disgusted that one who has shown himself the worst of devils should be so undeservedly enjoying a happier life than he had lived before. But God, I believe, was only preparing for him an increase of his punishment' (*Wars* I. xxv. 13–36).

It came about like this. The Cyzicenes had a very unpopular bishop, and when Justinian took no notice of their complaints about him they took the matter into their own hands and murdered him in the market place. John had had no part in the murder, but as might have been expected he had had frequent differences with the proud prelate. He was arrested on suspicion, stripped of all his possessions and shipped off to Antinopolis in Egypt, supporting himself on the journey by begging his food. 'And this is now the third year that they have been keeping him in confinement there ... This is the retribution that ten years later overtook John the Cappadocian for his treatment of the State' (*Wars* I. xxv. 37–44). And this was the plight in which he still was when Theodora died in A.D. 548.

After her death Justinian summoned him back to the capital. And there Procopius finally leaves him. 'Of his former honours he did not succeed in recovering anything whatsoever ... Yet the man often dreamed that he would come to the throne. For the divine power loves to dangle extravagant hopes of dazzling success before the minds of men whose understanding is based on no solidity of character.' Characteristically enough, in the same passage as this last penetrating observation on the essential weakness of so many dictators, Procopius goes on to suggest that the prophecy concerning John's imperial destiny had actually been fulfilled at the time of his first humiliation. 'When John had been shorn and forced to accept the priestly office, he had no priestly vestment and so was compelled by those in charge of the proceedings to put on the mantle and tunic of a priest named Augustus.' This assumption of the mantle of Augustus, Procopius suggests, was the literal fulfilment of the prophecy (*Wars* II. xxx. 49–54). In this way Theodora triumphed even in death, for it appears to have been his unfortunate ordination that was the main obstacle to his again assuming any high secular dignity. He was not living in the age of Wolsey or Richelieu.

Procopius is admittedly a biased witness as to John's character, but his evidence is corroborated by a very different authority, the learned and very conventional John Lydus, whose testimony is the more valuable because he was himself an official in the bureau of the praetorian prefect and came from Lydia, where one of John the Cappadocian's most notorious subordinates, another Cappadocian John, made himself detested. Here is what Lydus has to say about the prefect.

'There was a certain John who came from Mazaca – Tiberius Caesar had renamed the city Caesarea ... This man, being enrolled among the scriniarii of the master of the soldiers, craftily wormed his way, like the Cappadocian that he was, and won the friendship of the emperor; and promising to achieve incredible things for the state he was promoted to the position of logothete; then from that position, which he used as a stepping stone, he was raised to the rank of *illustris*; and since it had not yet been realized what sort of character he was, he was pushed all at once into the high office of prefect. For neither before nor after did the emperor, being a good and just man, endure to entrust the post to bad officials ... In this manner therefore the wicked Cappadocian attained to power and wrought public disasters, first of all introducing bonds and fetters and stocks and irons, establishing inside the praetorian court a private darksome dungeon for the punishment of those under his jurisdiction, like a cowardly Phalaris displaying his strength only on his slaves. There he confined his victims, exempting nobody, whatever his station, from his tortures ... and releasing them only when they were stripped of their possessions or dead. The witness to these doings is the whole people; and I know of them from having been an eyewitness of the proceedings' (*de Mag.* III. 57). Lydus goes on to describe how he had seen an old man named Antiochus, a friend of his, tortured to death in an attempt to extract information about some money he was accused of concealing.

The honest Lydus makes it very clear that the brutal and unscrupulous Cappadocian was employed because of the emperor's desperate need to raise more money by taxation, and he at least implies that John succeeded in this immediate aim. But he also makes it clear that John's extortions had a disastrous effect on the population, driving crowds of ruined men to swell the proletariat in the city. 'For these causes ... they all left the lands that had supported them, and preferring rather to idle than to do sober work – naturally enough since they were not even allowed to do the latter – they filled the imperial city with useless crowds. Laws were multiplied to deal with their various offences, reintroducing offices which had for long been in abeyance ... And when these officials proceeded with extra energy against the offences of the people, the multitude rose and combining in an ill-starred agreement fired nearly all the city' (III. 70). The rising here referred to is the Nika riot, and Lydus goes on, with numerous learned and rather tedious digressions into ancient history, to describe the destruction that was wrought, the disappearance of John, and the excellent conduct of his successor Phocas. What more concerns us here is the evidence he gives that even before the Nika riot and John's first disgrace his ascendancy had already been attacked by Theodora. This comes out clearly in his account of the state of things before the rising.

'When the accursed enemy of the laws' (i.e. the Cappadocian) 'had got so far, God turned upon him, resolving to give over the cause of these evils to the treatment he himself meted out, persuading him that

> There is a Justice and a Nemesis
> Brings evil to the evil.

Our most gracious sovereign knew nothing of all that was going on, since owing to the scoundrelly Cappado-

cian's unlimited power everybody, though wrongfully
treated, testified in his favour and indulged in the highest praises of him before the emperor. For who indeed
would have ventured merely to mention his name without praise? Only his consort, who surpassed in intelligence all men who have ever lived and ever kept a
watchful eye out of sympathy with the wronged, could
not endure any longer to look on while the state was
being brought to ruin. So armed with no moderate language she went to the emperor and informed him of all
that had hitherto escaped his eye, and how there was a
danger not only of his subjects being ruined by these evil
doings but also of the throne itself being shaken before
very long. So naturally the emperor, being a good man
and slow to punish the wicked, was involved in desperate
difficulties. He could find no way of removing the
wrecker of the constitution. John was in such a position,
as a result of maliciously confusing the situation and ob-
scuring the taxation system and involving it in hopeless
and irretrievable disorder by the muddle he had made of
what are called the assessments, that it was never possible to put an end to his period of office. No member of
the senate nor in fact anyone concerned with justice
would venture to take over this administration. All the
same the emperor helped his subjects as far as was
humanly possible' (III. 69).

The evidence of Lydus as to the doings and character
of John the Cappadocian is admittedly that of an enemy.
At the end of his account of the Nika riot he turns to his
next theme with the words (III. 72) 'So this was the end
of the first period during which the wicked Cappadocian
held the post of Lord High Brigand.' Lydus had every
reason to hate his fallen superior. There was the bleeding
white of his native Lydia, the humiliation of having to
look on and say nothing while his friends and other respectable citizens were tortured, and for a man such as we
have seen Lydus to have been, the distress caused by the
way that John disregarded the traditions of the civil service. We have seen that Lydus traced the decline and fall
of the service to the abolition some generations earlier of

compulsory Latin. John dealt Latin a still severer blow. 'There was an ancient law that all proceedings of any kind whatsoever in the office of the prefect ... should be conducted in the Latin language: it was from the breaking of this law, as has been said, and in no other way, that all the steps of our degradation proceeded. But all business conducted in Europe necessarily preserved the ancient practice owing to the fact that the population, though mainly Greek, spoke the language of Italy; and this was specially the case with public officials. This was changed by the Cappadocian for a mean, old-womanish form of speech, not from considerations of lucidity but in order that inability to speak anything except the common language that is on everybody's lips might be no bar to those who in accordance with his aim were daring to fill positions for which they were in no way fitted. For in his deeds and his written orders John was revolutionary and did all he could to upset ancient practice' (III. 68).

It is important to have this full picture of John if we are to understand the relentless enmity of the two women who conspired to bring about his downfall. Antonina's behaviour to John's daughter Euphemia could not have been baser or more heartless, and Theodora was perfectly ready to join in this despicable plot, though in many ways the two women were diametrically opposite. Antonina had passed from the stage to the camp. As the wife of Belisarius she recalls in some ways the weather-beaten consorts of some of our own generals and admirals of the eighteenth century who must have been in Jane Austen's mind when she drew her picture in *Persuasion* of Mrs. Croft, the English admiral's wife. But there was a coarseness in Antonina's character equally remote from Mrs. Croft's unaffected dignity and from the grand manner of the empress. Witness the story (*Secret History* i–iii) of her very elemental intrigue with Belisarius' godson Theodosius, who, terrified at her advances, fled to a monastery at Ephesus. He was tracked down there by Antonina and forcibly brought back to Constantinople, where he shortly after died of dysentery. Antonina was bitterly opposed in this affair by Phocas, her son by a previous union. In revenge she abetted his cruel torture by the empress who had special need at this time of Antonina's friendship. She treated with revolting cruelty (i. 21, 26, 27; ii. 12) a slave girl and two boys who had given evidence against Theodosius. She never forgave Belisarius' subordinate Constantine, who had frankly told him he would have done better to punish his wife than the young man she had seduced, and later she caused Belisarius to put him to death (i. 24–8, cp. *Wars* VI. viii; see above, Chapter III, p. 43).

When Belisarius was recalled from the Eastern command and disgraced by the emperor, Antonina became the still closer friend and intimate of Theodora (iv. 13–31). Procopius quotes this fact as a reproach; but we may doubt how far the reproach was merited if we judge Antonina by her own standards. It seems far more likely that she realized that this was the one way of ensuring her husband's safety. Procopius holds up against her the fact that when she had secured Belisarius' partial pardon and he asked to be given again the supreme command in the East, Antonina would not hear of it. She may have been mistaken in her opposition, but it is equally likely that she had the shrewdness to see how dangerous it would be for Belisarius to hold so high a post at his own asking, and how much safer it would be for him to be sent again to Italy, as in fact he was, at the emperor's orders, to carry on the war there at his own risk and expense, with the much humbler title of Commander of the Royal Grooms.

Theodora was different. She had none of the natural coarseness and vulgarity of Antonina. The court, and especially the court of Byzantium, was her spiritual home. Royalty was for her not only 'a fine winding sheet'. It was the breath of life. Everything shows that Procopius was recording her truly when in the same fateful speech of hers at the time of the Nika riot he makes her say: 'May I never put off this purple or outlive the day when men cease to call me queen' (*Wars* I. xxiv. 36). Only one habit from her earlier vulgar days seems to have persisted.

'She had a way of turning even the most serious of matters into comedy when it so pleased her, as though it was a performance on the stage' (*Secret History* xv. 24).

We are all what we have made ourselves, and this protective weapon of mockery, which Theodora had doubtless found invaluable when she was making her way from the stage to the throne, had become too much a part of her to be completely laid aside. But normally the result upon Theodora as empress of the extreme publicity and forced exhibitionism of her earlier days was an extreme inaccessibility. 'Even high officials could not get access to her except after long and wearisome efforts. All were always kept waiting like menials in a small and stuffy room all the time ... When after many days of this waiting some of them were summoned to an audience, they were merely admitted in fear and trembling and quickly dismissed after prostrating themselves and kissing her feet. They were not permitted to say a word or make any petition unless she bade them' (xv. 13–16). Theodora was only exacting the respect that was normally demanded by a Byzantine sovereign from all who were admitted to the presence: Louis XIV in all his glory did not exact a more rigorous etiquette. She certainly enjoyed it, but her insistence on receiving it helped too to emphasize the affability of Justinian himself. 'Even the most humble and obscure were allowed not merely to have audience of this tyrant but even to discuss things with him and have private interviews' (xv. 12). This contrast in accessibility offers yet another instance of the way that the imperial pair supplemented one another.

It was probably part of Theodora's aloofness that 'she paid more attention to her person than was needful though less than enough to satisfy her own desires. She went very early to her bath, left it very late, and proceeded to her breakfast only after these ablutions. After breakfast she rested' (xv. 6–7). But in this particular connexion it must be remembered that she was a woman of iron tenacity who had led a most exacting and exhausting life and that she died of cancer. The protracted baths and protracted rest and even the pose of aloofness which enabled her to avoid exhausting interviews whenever she felt desirable may have been in part dictated by the simple physical necessity of conserving her energies.

In ruthlessness and savage cruelty she matched Antonina. When, four years after the murder of the bishop of Cyzicus, she got hold of two young men who were said to have been implicated and could not persuade one of them to incriminate her enemy John the Cappadocian, she tortured him almost to the point of death and then cut off his right hand. The other was more compliant and gave the desired evidence, but he too, though he escaped the torture, had his right hand cut off (xvii. 41–4). It is hard to see why. After the Council of Chalcedon when a former protégé of hers named Arsenius helped Paulus the patriarch of Alexandria to reform the church of Alexandria in a sense unfavourable to the monophysites whom the empress supported, she had him impaled (*Secret History* xxvii). When on the stage she had had a son named John. The boy lived in Arabia with his father till the father died. He then came to Constantinople and claimed his mother's protection. 'When he arrived and she had seen him, she handed him over to one of her servants whom she usually entrusted with matters of this kind. How the unhappy lad was put out of the way I cannot say; but nobody to this day has succeeded in seeing him, not even since the death of the empress' (xvii. 16–23).

The most distinguished of all the victims of Theodora's ruthlessness, if we are to believe Procopius, was a woman whom she never saw and who had never done her any harm at all, the Gothic queen Amalasuntha, to champion whose cause Justinian started his fateful Gothic war. We have heard in the history of that war (above p. 37) how she was put to death at the immediate order of her Gothic rival Theodatus. The account of Theodora's alleged part in the murder had best be given in Procopius' own words. 'Amalasuntha, anxious to escape from her position amongst the Goths, had decided to start a new life and was planning to cross over to Byzantium ... But Theodora reasoned that the woman was a high-born

queen, exceedingly good-looking and remarkably resolute in contriving ways of securing what she wanted. She
regarded with suspicion her grand manner and out-
standingly virile bearing, and feared at the same time
her own husband's instability of character. She became
inordinately jealous and resolved to plot against the
woman till she had killed her. So she immediately induced her husband to send Peter to Italy as ambassador
with no associate. At his send-off the emperor instructed
him as I have recorded at the proper place in my history,
where it was impossible for me to reveal the true facts for
fear of the empress. But she gave him only this one in-
struction, to do away with the woman as soon as possible
... So he, on arriving in Italy ... induced Theodatus to
make away with Amalasuntha. And as a result he gained
both the office of magister and unrivalled power and
hatred' (*Secret History* xvi. 1f.).

We may indeed doubt whether there was any need for
Theodora to take any positive steps about the actual
murder. Amalasuntha had enemies enough amongst the
Goths who wanted her out of the way. But what Peter
probably had it in his power to contrive, and might have
done but for Theodora, was to have hurried to Italy
and arranged for Amalasuntha's escape from prison and
flight to Constantinople.

Few, if any, of the charges brought in the *Secret History*
against either Theodora or Antonina can be substanti-
ated; but the whole picture of the two women that is
built up by them seems to me convincing. Both had come
out of great tribulation and both were absolutely determined to defend to the last their own positions and those
of their respective husbands. Each was, perhaps excessively, aware of the weaknesses of the man whom she had
married, but equally aware that she had married greatness and that her own fortunes were bound up with
those of her husband: so much so that the two must in
both cases have seemed inseparable. It is easy to see how
the arrival of Amalasuntha in Constantinople would have
seemed to Theodora to threaten her ascendancy over the
emperor and therefore to threaten the safety of Justinian

himself. As for John of Cappadocia, his ambitions were a direct threat to the emperor and for that reason a direct threat to Belisarius, the most loyal servant an emperor ever had. The collaboration of the two wives in compassing his downfall was on this showing a natural corollary. What is startling to those whose lives have been cast in gentler surroundings is the ferocious cunning that they employed to achieve their aim. The fact that John's daughter Euphemia was their dupe and played what proved to be a purely passive part should not blind us to the fact that she too was ready to plot treason and murder on behalf of her father. The ruthless cruelties of these Byzantine ladies form an interesting counterpart to those of Vandal and Gothic kings that we have already encountered or to those of Frankish sovereigns as recorded by Gregory of Tours; so too do John's own private torture chambers (above p. 209). All alike are the normal by-product of any system that allows individuals unbridled power. That is perhaps their main interest.

CHAPTER XI

The Buildings

*

'Solomon, I have surpassed thee'. Justinian on
Sancta Sophia.

WHEN Procopius cast censure aside and turned to un-
diluted eulogy of the age he lived in and recorded, the
theme he chose was that of the great building programme carried through by Justinian all over his empire. His motives for writing this panegyric have been
frequently explained, nearly always with excessive sim-
plification of the workings of that curiously twisted mind
which we have tried to analyse in a previous chapter.
One fact is beyond dispute. In an age when conservatism was the watchword, innovation a term of reproach,
and originality a word that had passed out of the vocabulary, Justinian and his great architects Anthemius and
Isidore created in the church of Sancta Sophia a building which is still one of the outstanding landmarks in
the whole history of architecture. Most fortunately we
still have this magnificent cathedral much as the emperor left it. And further to help us to realize what we
owe to Anthemius and Isidore we have numerous notable churches of the period and of the preceding century
to suggest what Justinian's architectural efforts would
have been like if in building also he had persevered in the
prevalent conservatism. Great churches had been
erected all over the empire from the days of Constantine,
when Christianity became the official religion. They were
of two familiar types, both adaptations of earlier pagan
models. The commonest was the basilica, fundamentally
of the same plan as our larger mediaeval parish churches :
the building forms a long rectangle with aisles marked off
by two rows of pillars, to which is added an apsidal chancel. The pillars were modelled on the classical orders

where they were not lifted bodily from earlier classical buildings. The roof was of wood, generally open so as to show the timbers that supported the external covering. The other, less common, type was round or polygonal with a domed or vaulted roof and generally a circular aisle formed by a ring of pillars beneath the central dome. Both types had a long history behind them and were destined for a long survival. The rectangular basilica was an adaptation of a common form of secular Roman building used as law-court or exchange: it remained in plan, though with all sorts of developments in style, the normal shape for the West European church. The round or polygonal type had been used in pagan times for temples and for tombs and persisted for centuries after Justinian as a church type: see, e.g., the round churches at Cambridge and Northampton and the Temple Church in London. In mediaeval England, in its simplest form with no pillared aisle it became the accepted model for the cathedral chapter house (Westminster, Wells, Salisbury, York, Southwell, etc.). In South Europe another variety of this simplest form was favoured for baptisteries (Pisa, Florence, Parma, etc.). A fine secular example of the aisled type is Gibbs' camera at Oxford which forms part of the University library. Examples of both main types of church, the basilican and the round, earlier than the time of Justinian may be found illustrated in any handbook: e.g. at Rome the basilican S. Maria Maggiore and S. Lorenzo fuori le Mura and the round mausoleum church of S. Costanza, at Salonica the basilican Eski Djouma (H. Paraskeve) and S. Demetrius and the simple round church of S. George.

For those who have been brought up in a country like England or France where the mediaeval churches fit so perfectly into the landscape to delight the eye and refresh the spirit, these Roman basilicas seem very prosaic efforts; it is a question whether their appeal is not fundamentally historical. The one artistic contribution that they make to architectural history is perhaps their use of mosaics on the walls and particularly in the half domes of their apses. Even from this aspect they fall behind their

eastern counterparts. Another distinguishing feature of
the Byzantine church of even pre-Justinian days is the
sculpture of the capitals. Here the deep undercutting and
the lavish use of the drill produce effects of light and
shade that recall the mouldings of the best Early-Eng-
lish Gothic.

What churches of Justinian's own reign were like when
they merely carried on the existing tradition may be seen
at Ravenna in the basilican church of S. Apollinare in
Classe (pll. 9a, 10) and the octagonal S. Vitale (pll. 9b,
11) both erected shortly after the recovery of the city
from the Goths. S. Vitale is further notable for the magnificent mosaic portraits (pll. 12, 13) of Justinian with the
high officials of his court and Theodora with her ladies.
Ravenna is the city where the architectural developments of the period can be best followed. Justinian's
S. Apollinare in Classe can be compared with the earlier
S. Apollinare Nuovo, erected by the great Theoderic,
while S. Vitale may be contrasted with the fifth-century
baptistery begun by Bishop Ursus and completed by Bishop Neon. With Justinian's S. Vitale at Ravenna we may
compare also the church he erected at Constantinople
to SS. Sergius and Bacchus known sometimes as Little
Sancta Sophia (pl. 6a, b).

If this was all that Justinian's age had done for architecture, it would have been on the level of the rest of its
achievements, a matter of maintaining standards and
introducing minor improvements. His basilican churches,
like their predecessors, for all their detailed merits, are
excessively simple in plan and execution. His round
churches, like round churches generally, are not big
enough to be really impressive. Neither can produce on
us the effect of our own great mediaeval cathedrals,
which so many still find so inspiring thanks to their com-
bination of fine craftsmanship displayed in an infinite
variety of detail with a vast and elaborate design that
makes the visitor feel that he has escaped from the world
without and can lose himself here in another. George
Herbert could find heaven in Salisbury cathedral. Even
he could hardly have done so in some of the churches

just mentioned, at least not in any sense in which the experience is the direct result of the architecture.

The Cathedral of the Holy Wisdom (Sancta Sophia) at Constantinople (pll. 4 and 5) is another proposition. It is in every sense of the word a great church. When we enter it from the lovely west gallery (Jackson *Byzantine and Romanesque Architecture* pl. xv) we see a great nave that stands comparison with any in Europe. Magnificent colonnades rise from the floor on either side of us, and above these are equally magnificent triforium galleries, while above these again, where we look for the clerestory, are rows of windows admirably disposed for letting in the light. One aspect of this first view that will at once impress the beholder and would have filled with envy the great architects of cathedrals like Salisbury or Ely or even York is the width of the nave. Disregarding the aisles we are in a great hall 100 feet wide and considerably more than twice that length. The corresponding measurements of Salisbury cathedral or Westminster abbey are about 40 by 400 feet, of York, our widest mediaeval cathedral, about 50 by 480 feet. Our builders understood how to make the most impressive use of the resultant effect of immense length, as everyone knows who has sat right at the back of any of these glorious buildings with the high altar and the great eastern screen or stained glass window almost infinitely remote but still intimately connected with him by the long arcades and vaulted roof. It is hardly fanciful to say that this experience, which must be familiar to every Englishman with any feeling for his country's architectural inheritance, explains one trait of our national character at its best, the feeling that the back seat, even if it is not always the one he is called to, is from some points of view the best and certainly one that he may from time to time reasonably demand the privilege of occupying.

No such feeling is evoked by the great church of Sancta Sophia, though Jackson is certainly overstating it when he says (*ibid.* p. 96) that at Sancta Sophia there is no mystery and the whole design is obvious at a glance. The whole design is indeed obvious at a glance, but there is very much that only gradually reveals itself: we can step out again into the narthex, walk round the aisles, or explore the magnificent galleries on the triforium level that are an essential part of the church. Here in North Europe we are apt to identify mystery with gloom, and forget the mystery of light which was one of the great discoveries of the Greek Pindar. Sancta Sophia is above all things the church of light and colour with the two interdependent. The lighting comes not only from the very many windows below the roof level but most notably of all from the forty lights that run round the bottom of the dome as close together as are the windows in King's College chapel at Cambridge and catching the sun at every hour of the day. And in Sancta Sophia we have a building with an exceptionally wide and open central nave, and a very low-pitched dome that does not form as it were a centre of darkness, while dome and floor pillars and walls are all of varied coloured marbles or of bright mosaics which instead of absorbing the light reflect it and even, so the ancient panegyrics assert, increase it.

This effect of light was one of the great qualities of the church in the eyes of Procopius. 'It is flooded with sunlight, both direct and reflected. You would imagine that it was not merely illuminated from without by the sun but that radiance springs also from within it. Such a superabundance of light pours on this holy temple' (*B.* i. i. 29–30).

The great domes of St Peter's at Rome and St Paul's in London are incomparably superior to that of Sancta Sophia if viewed from the outside; but internally they make an impressive break in the vaulting of nave and choir. They are in fact only magnificent developments of the lantern treatment of the central tower of some of our great mediaeval churches such as is seen at its most striking at Ely or at St Ouen at Rouen, but occurs also at York and Durham, Lincoln and Peterborough and in others, though by no means all, of our great churches. But Sancta Sophia is entirely different. There the great flat dome is the main element of the roof; and this predominance of the dome is enhanced by the pendentives

which help to support it and by the system of part domes,
one great above a group of three smaller, that crown
the apsidal design of the east end. Procopius is not ex-
aggerating when he says 'all these elements, marvellously
adjusted to one another, poised in mid air one above
the other and supported only by those adjacent to them,
produce a total effect of the most perfect harmony: they
do not allow the eye of the beholder to dwell long over
any one of them but each in turn attracts his gaze and
leads it on without effort to itself' (*B.* i. i. 47).

This appreciation of Justinian's great church by a
critical contemporary is sufficient answer to Jackson and
other modern critics. Procopius goes on to praise it further in language that has a curious likeness to that of the
Salisbury poet about the cathedral that he so loved.
'Whenever anyone goes there to pray ... his heart is
lifted up to God and finds itself in heaven, deeming that
He is somewhere nigh and loves the place that He has
Himself specially chosen to abide in. And this happens
not only when he visits it for the first time; every time he
goes there everyone gets this same impression, as if each
visit were his first' (*B.* i. i. 61–2).

But to return to the actual structure. It was a great
architectural adventure when our early Gothic architects, whose fathers and predecessors had timidly roofed
with flat wooden boards the central naves of such splen-
did interiors as those of Peterborough, Ely or St. Albans,
produced the great vaulted roofs of Gloucester or Salisbury. But compared with the achievement of Sancta
Sophia even these are unenterprising. What makes
Sancta Sophia so exciting a building is that its architects
were not only great artists but also great and adven-
turous engineers.

The names of these architects were Anthemius of
Tralles, a city some thirty miles inland from Ephesus, and
Isidore of Miletus. The building that they raised is sufficient monument to their genius. Procopius justly calls
Anthemius 'the man most learned in what is called
mechanical science not only of the men of his own time
but of all men for many generations back' (*B.* i. i. 24).

The voice of the imperial panegyrist begins to obtrude only when he goes on to suggest that God had specially raised up these two master craftsmen to work for the emperor and that the emperor's discernment in discovering their ability was as marvellous as the ability that he discovered.

The Greek word used by Procopius to describe Anthemius' occupation is not *architektonike* (architecture) but *mechanike*, which would naturally be taken to mean engineering. The Loeb editors argue that Procopius employs this word in order to imply that the master builder was the emperor, or alternatively God Himself. This explanation seems rather far-fetched. Sancta Sophia was no ordinary piece of building and Anthemius no ordinary builder. The scheme of Procopius' *Buildings* makes it natural for the historian to ascribe to the two real architects a very subordinate place. How his contemporaries regarded Anthemius may be better inferred from Agathias, who describes him (v. 6. p. 357) as one who reached the summit of mathematical science and whose subject (*techne*) was 'the inventions of engineers who apply geometry to solid matter and make copies and as it were models of things that are'. He came of a very gifted and versatile family. One of his brothers was a literary celebrity who became the tutor of many of the most distinguished families in Constantinople, another a most successful lawyer, two others no less successful physicians, the one in his native Tralles, the other in Rome. Anthemius himself was remembered not only for the remarkable buildings of which he was the architect but also for his actual experiments in applied mechanics. On one occasion he had a quarrel (Agathias v. 6–7, pp. 358–9) with a certain eminent lawyer named Zeno who occupied a flat in Constantinople just above his own. When Anthemius got the worst of it in a wordy dispute, he arranged a set of pipes in one of his rooms with the top funnel-shaped ends applied hermetically to the ceiling, which was of course the floor of the room above. The other ends of the pipes were fitted in a similar way to a set of cauldrons of water which he then proceeded to boil.

The result was a miniature earthquake in the room above,
which caused Zeno and his friends to rush out into the
street and make themselves ridiculous. This practical
joke is said to have been inspired by the architect's theory
as to the cause of earthquakes, which he explained as due
to the action of hot air (steam?) seeking an outlet from
subterranean passages. The apparatus for the toy earthquake was presumably a specimen of our engineer's
models of things that are.

This revealing anecdote is introduced into Agathias'
history when he is recording the great earthquake of A.D.
557, which seriously shook Sancta Sophia and made it
necessary to reconstruct the great dome. The reconstructed dome, the one we now see, is not the work of
Anthemius. Both he and Isidore were now dead, and the
reconstruction was entrusted to a younger Isidore. The
new dome is said by Agathias to be not so impressive as
was the original but very much safer (v. 9, p. 362. 10 –
15). Anthemius had not built for safety. Procopius records how there had almost been a collapse when the
original dome was being constructed, and how the architect thought it prudent to consult the emperor as to how
to deal with the alarming situation, which the emperor of
course triumphantly did (B. 1. i. 68–72).

'Adjacent to the great church is that named after Irene
which had been burnt down along with it and was now
rebuilt by the emperor and vastly enlarged. It is now
second to scarcely any of the churches in Byzantium except only Sancta Sophia' (B. 1. ii. 13). S. Irene still
stands complete. It measures about 150 by 100 feet,
which gives us some idea of the dimensions of churches
of the second rank at the time. Its dome rises from a
drum as does that of St Paul's in London. As domes rest-
ing on drums were a later development and the church
is known to have suffered severely from an earthquake in
A.D. 740, S. Irene as we now see it cannot be regarded
as an uncontaminated example of Justinian's work. But
architects are inclined to regard it as preserving at least
the general design.

One other of Justinian's buildings in Constantinople

may still be seen much as he left it, namely the great underground reservoir of which we have this account in the *Buildings*: 'By the Imperial Portico ... there is an immense court, extremely long and adequately broad, with colonnades on all four sides ... Excavating this and one of the four porticoes that surround it, that namely which faces south, to a great depth, Justinian constructed a reservoir to conserve for use in the summer the superfluous water that was being wasted in the other seasons' (*B*. i. xi. 12–13). There are two great underground cisterns still preserved that claim the honour of being the one described. Diehl in his *Manuel d'Art Byzantine* (I p. 157) identifies it with that known as Bin Bir Derek. It is a magnificent vaulted crypt (pl. 7) with 212 columns of double height, the upper and lower shafts of each column bonded together by a ring of wood, measures 64 by 56 metres, and is compared by the great French Byzantinist with Sancta Sophia itself for the breadth and audacity of its design. The identification of Procopius' building is determined by topographical as well as stylistic evidence, and other experts claim that he is describing the Yere Batan Serai (pl. 8), the other of these two palatial crypts. (See Dewing in his edition of the *Buildings* pp. 90–1, n. 1; Bury I pp. 73, 77.) Which identification is the right one hardly matters. Either is adequate evidence of quite exceptional skill in designing a really noble structure to meet a vital need of city life. One of the essential services of a great city, its water supply, has been made the occasion for the construction of an architectural masterpiece entirely suited to its purpose.

Of the city as a whole as it appeared in the reign of Justinian we can form no full picture, for of the secular buildings, baths, law courts, palaces, squares and the like, there is little left. But we can safely assume that it must have been as impressive in the sixth century as it is at the present day, when it is doubtful if any city makes such a overpowering impression as Constantinople seen from the sea at the dawn of a summer's day with the low sun lighting up the domes and minarets of the mosques on its seven hills and the long sweep of its walls and

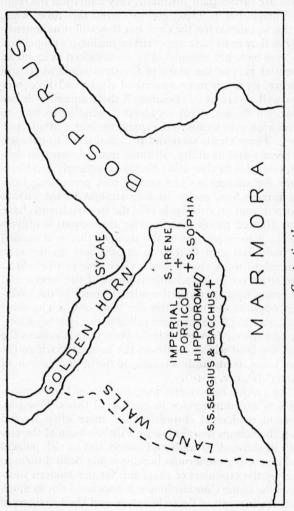

Constantinople

towers. One of these domes is that of Sancta Sophia; the
walls are earlier than Justinian: they date from the reign
of Theodosius II (A.D. 408–50) and the time when
Attila was menacing the city: but they still stand essentially as they must have appeared in Justinian's reign. And
the seas have not changed. The sea is indeed as much an
essential part of the glory of Constantinople as it is of
Venice, its much more advertised rival; and Procopius
was well aware of it. 'Besides all these amenities it has
above all the sea, nobly set about it, winding its way in,
narrowing into straits and expanding into a great open
sea ... Three straits surround it ... and serve to enhance
its beauty and its utility, all three most pleasant for sailing, desirable to view and offering exceedingly good har-
bours for anchorage. The central one, proceeding from
the Euxine Sea, makes its way straight to the city to
adorn it, and on either side of it the two continents have
their allotted places. Confined by their coasts it quivers
and as it were prances at the thought that it is carried
by both Asia and Europe as it advances on the city.
You might think that it was a river that you beheld ...
The strait on its left ... affords views of the woods and
charming meadows and the other features of the mainland opposite, on which the city looks out ... The third
strait, starting from the place called Sycae, extends a long
way on the city's north side ... Thus the sea crowns the
city, the land which continues the boundary where the
seas cease being only enough to weld the crown of
waters' (*B*. I. v. 2–10).

The unique beauty and magnificence of Constantinople was a commonplace in mediaeval times. Few passages of mediaeval chroniclers are more often quoted
than the famous description by Villehardouin of the city
with its stupendous walls and towers and its rich palaces
and incredibly numerous churches rising behind them as
seen by the crusaders of 1203. But for the modern west-
erner the name Constantinople is associated not so much
with the marvels of its architecture and the loveliness of
its surroundings as with vexatiously insoluble political
problems. It is well to be reminded of this other and let us

hope more lasting aspect. In a far profounder sense than is the case with Venice Constantinople is the city where the sea weds the land; and as Procopius also points out, it is the city where Europe stretches out to embrace Asia. It is indeed the imperial city *par excellence*, still awaiting the great hour of destiny marked out for it by its founder. In a memorable speech at Strasbourg after the 1914–18 war a representative of that great city claimed for it the mission of interpreting France to Germany and Germany to France. The mission remains though it has since then been made infinitely more difficult. That of Constantinople is of the same nature but on a still greater scale. It is not merely a Greek city, still less a Turkish. It stands there as a challenge for the realizing of mutual understanding between two continents which cannot be abandoned merely because it has baffled sixteen centuries of our civilization.

The greater part of the *Buildings* (Books II–VI) deals not with the capital but with towns rebuilt and fortifications restored or newly constructed all round the immense frontiers of the sixth-century Eastern empire as well as with the many buildings restored or raised further back from the frontier. The largest part deals with this matter of frontier defence, naturally enough when we remember Justinian's aims and ideals.

Book II starts with Daras, the great frontier city-fortress some 150 miles north-west of Niniveh that plays so prominent a part in the Persian wars (above, Chapter IV). Procopius goes into some detail as to the way the walls of Daras were rebuilt. The curious reader may turn to the relevant passages (*B.* II. i. 14–27, and Dewing's note on the passage in the Loeb edition). One problem that repeatedly confronted Justunian's architects and engineers was that of rivers and water as friend and as enemy of besieged and besiegers. It presented itself at Daras. Water is essential to a city. But a good supply of water usually implied a river, and a river would supply besiegers as well as besieged; also, in a country where the rivers descend from not very distant mountains, floods might be a deadly menace to the fortifications themselves.

How Justinian's experts dealt with the problem at Daras is described in *B.* II, ii-iii. 25. The problem at Daras was particularly difficult and we may note that it was referred to Justinian himself. Before sending back his happy solution of it the emperor consulted Anthemius and Isidore, the architects of Sancta Sophia.

From the Euphrates region Procopius takes us to the much tried city of Antioch in Syria. Here again we find the emperor's experts dealing drastically with the mountain-fed rivers and other natural features and completely replanning the whole city, the greatest in all his Asiatic dominions. Palmyra also was among the cities in this region which the emperor provided with new walls, a new water supply and a new garrison (II. xi end).

Book III takes us to Armenia and begins with an excursus on earlier Armenian history. In this buffer state Justinian rebuilt Martyropolis fifty miles east of the Upper Tigris in the direction of Lake Van, Theodosiopolis (Erzerum), Kitharizon, half way between Daras and Trapezus (Trebizond), Satala, half way between Kitharizon and Trapezus, and Melitene on the Upper Euphrates, south-west of Kitharizon. This brings Procopius to the Tzani, whose part in the Caucasus campaigns has been recorded above (Chapter V). We are given a further account of their habits and history, of their wild mountainous country, and of the forts and roads which the emperor constructed to ensure that the now pacified and christianized Tzani 'should not at some time change their manner of life and revert to ways of barbarism'. From the Tzani we are taken to Trapezus on the Black Sea, where Justinian built an aqueduct and restored the churches; from Trapezus to Lazica where Justinian's policy fluctuated between the fortifying of strongholds against the Persians and the dismantling of these same fortresses to prevent their becoming Persian strongholds; and from Lazica to the Sea of Azov and the Crimea. Here the emperor 'finding that the walls of Bosporus and Cherson were completely dilapidated, turned them into marvels of fine workmanship and strength'. Bosporus and Cherson are now famous as Kerch and Sevastopol.

One part of the Crimea stood outside these building activities of Justinian. This is how it came about. 'There is by the sea there a land called Dory, inhabited from of old by Goths who did not follow Theoderic on his march into Italy but voluntarily remained where they were and even to my days are in alliance with the Romans. They serve with them in expeditions against their enemies whenever it is the emperor's pleasure. They amount to about 3,000 men, excel in military operations and are expert farmers on the land and the most hospitable of all mankind. The actual land of Dory lies high but is neither rough nor hard but good and fertile and yields the best of crops. No city or fort was built by the emperor anywhere in this land, since the inhabitants will not endure to be shut up within any enclosure but love to spend their life in the open country. But wherever in this district there seemed to be an easy way open to aggressors, he built long walls to block the gaps, thus removing from the minds of the Goths all anxiety about attack' (III. vii. 13–17).

On the west coast of the Euxine, not far from the modern Bulgarian city of Burgas, lay the ancient spa of Anchialos. 'There are springs of hot water here gushing up not far away from the city and creating natural baths for the people there. This place had been unwalled from ancient times and neglected by previous emperors, though such numerous savage tribes were settled near it that invalids used to visit it and seek its benefit at great peril. Justinian now built walls round it and enabled them to take the cure in safety' (III. vii. 20–3). This account of the fortification of a popular watering-place only 150 miles from the capital closes Procopius' survey of the Black Sea and the third book of the *Buildings*.

Book IV brings us to the European frontier and more particularly to the regions bounded by the Danube and the Adriatic, which between them, according to our historian, make South-east Europe a sort of island. The starting point of this section is Skoplje or Uskub in modern Serbia (about 150 miles north-north-west of Salonica). Justinian was born near the site of this city, which

I

he founded to commemorate the fact under the name of Justiniana Prima. Procopius claims that it is geographically proper to begin this section of his work with the birthplace of the founder of the civilized world. The city was provided with an archbishopric, an aqueduct, churches, lodgings for magistrates, arcades, market places, fountains, streets, baths and shops too many to enumerate. Sardica (Sofia), Naisopolis (Naissus, Nish) and Justinianopolis (Adrianople) are among the many other Balkan cities where the emperor did much building.

In Greece he devoted special attention to Thermopylae, the vital pass from Northern to Central Greece, elaborately fortifying the pass itself, the small towns in front of it and all the many mountain paths near it, and building granaries and cisterns to supply the garrisons of the forts with food and water. Athens, Corinth and the cities of Boeotia also had their walls repaired. Only the cities of the Peloponnese, south of the Isthmus of Corinth, were left unwalled. But the partly fallen walls across the Isthmus itself were rebuilt, and fresh forts constructed and garrisoned. North of Thermopylae lies the great mountain-ringed region of Thessaly. Here the city walls were reconditioned by the emperor like those of Central Greece. They included those of the pleasant little town of Larissa, which was so ruthlessly destroyed in 1941.

From Thessaly we are taken to the great island of Euboea; but at this point there is a gap in the MSS and we find ourselves suddenly in Macedonia (iii. 21) in the three-pronged peninsula that lies south-east of Salonica. At the northern end of the western prong (Pallene) lay the city of Cassandria, which a thousand years before under its original name of Potidaea had been what Salonica now is and had long been already in Justinian's days, the chief port of the north-west Aegean. Justinian rebuilt the walls of this city and also the ruined cross wall that had once blocked the way into this prong. This undertaking is specially praised by Procopius because 'time had brought the buildings here to such a state of decay that a tribe of Huns not long previously had fearlessly demolished both the cross wall and the city as if by way of pastime, although they had never assaulted a city since the creation of man' (iii. 22). The open country near Salonica itself had likewise been completely at the mercy of the barbarians till Justinian built a strong new fort by the mouth of the River Rhechius (Vardar).

The country so far reviewed in Book IV formed the prefecture of Illyricum and corresponds roughly with modern Yugoslavia south of the Save, Albania and Greece, though Sofia, as we have seen, is included while the coast strip of Greece east of Mt Athos is not. The survey of this region ends with a list of all the other strongholds that Justinian built or reconstructed in the interior of the prefecture. 'It will be not amiss,' Procopius explains, 'to give just a simple list of them, in order to avoid overloading my narrative with crowds of names' (iv. 3). The list that follows contains nearly 400 entries, of which ninety-two are classed as new foundations, the rest as restorations.

The first four chapters of the fourth book of the *Buildings* are a rather grim commentary on the state of the Pax Romana at the time they were written; for the buildings recorded in them are almost all fortifications against enemies from outside the frontier and all of them lie away from the frontier right in the empire. It is only with Chapter V that we come to the great line of frontier defences running down the Danube, the line that had collapsed so disastrously in the previous century at the time of Attila's invasion and had never since been adequately reconditioned. As restored by Justinian the line had its western end at Singidunum. This ancient Celtic city, which still bore its Celtic name, is the modern Belgrade. 'This city the barbarians had captured in the course of time and at once razed to the ground ... But the Emperor Justinian completely rebuilt it and set a very strong wall round it and made it once again a city of great note and account' (v. 13–15). Some fifty other strongholds on the Danube where it forms the frontier of Illyricum are next listed as having received the emperor's attention, including Pontes, where the Emperor Trajan,

conqueror of Dacia and thus in a sense the founder of
Rumania, had built his famous bridge across the river,
and a town with the familiar Celtic name of Bononia
(still preserved by its more famous namesakes Bologna
and Boulogne). A further twenty-four fortified places were
built or restored still farther down the Danube, sixteen in
Moesia, the rest in what Procopius calls Scythia, the
modern Dobruja.

The rest of Book IV is devoted to Thrace, and here, as
with Illyricum, our author begins at the centre of things,
'fixing on the regions round Byzantium as the surest
foundation of our history, since the city dominates Thrace
by reason not only of its strength but also of its geographical position, standing like a kind of European citadel
and acting as a bulwark to guard the passage of the sea
that separates it from Asia' (viii. 2). The words just
quoted may remind us that Constantinople may be regarded as a barrier as well as a bridge.

In these Thracian homelands Justinian built a fine new
road from the suburb of Strongylum to a place called
Rhegium. Previously this road had been so rough that 'if
by chance there was a fall of rain, it became a swamp'
(viii. 5). Before Justinian built his new road, those who
got safely past the mud had next to traverse a narrow
causeway between the sea and a lake which lay just behind it. The crossing had been made by a wooden bridge
that often collapsed and drowned those who happened to
be on it. This perilous wooden structure was now replaced by a fine arched bridge of stone. The next city on
this same road, Athyras, was supplied with a reservoir
and had its walls repaired. Beyond Athyras lay a place
called Episcopia. Here Justinian 'observing that the
place was at the mercy of hostile attacks and that as a
result these regions were entirely unprotected, built a
fortress. Its towers he constructed not in the usual way
but like this: a series of buildings project from the circuit
wall, very narrow where they start from it but reaching a
great breadth where they end, and here a tower is built.
This makes it impossible for an enemy to approach very
near the main wall, since when they get between the

towers they come under cross-fire from the garrison and
are destroyed. The gates are placed not in normal position between the towers but at an angle in the narrow
part of the projections, concealed from behind and invisible to the enemy. In this undertaking Theodore the
Silentiary, a man of exceptional ability, was the emperor's chief assistant' (viii. 20-4). We may observe
once more how very close to the capital these defences
were found necessary. The danger was indeed chronic;
Procopius goes on to describe the booty that was to be
gathered by marauders from the luxurious villas that
wealthy citizens of Constantinople had built themselves
in the suburbs of the capital. The emperor Anastasius
had thought to meet this danger by building long walls
from the Propontis (Sea of Marmora) to the Euxine
(Black Sea) some forty miles from the city. 'But this step
only proved to be the cause of greater disasters; for it was
impossible either to render so extensive a structure im-
pregnable or to detail guards for all of it. Whenever
the enemy swooped on any section of these long walls
they overpowered all the guards with no trouble and
falling unexpectedly on the rest of the population they
wrought indescribable havoc' (ix. 7–8). Justinian rebuilt these long walls on an improved system, making
each tower a separate strong unit. Procopius however
refrains from any prophecy as to the effects of this
improvement.

West of the long walls, on the shores of the Sea of Marmora, Heraclea and Rhaedestus (Rodosto) had their walls
repaired and Heraclea had its aqueduct and a royal
palace there restored. Rhaedestus had in earlier times
been a prosperous port, but more recently it had been
abandoned by traders as being too much exposed to
raids by barbarians. After Justinian's restoration the
port was again frequented by traders and it became also a
place of refuge for the whole neighbourhood during the
raids which still occurred. At the west end of the Sea of
Marmora lies the Thracian Chersonese (Gallipoli Peninsula). The ancient wall at the neck of this peninsula
had recently been broken through by the barbarians.

Justinian completely rebuilt it from its foundations, raised
its height and provided it with a covered way above the
battlements, and widened and deepened the moat in
front of it. The individual cities on the peninsula also had
their walls repaired or new ones built if they had none before. Ciberis was further provided with baths and guest
houses, Callipolis (whence the name Gallipoli) with
granaries and wine cellars (IV. x).

Still farther west, on the North Aegean, Aenus at the
mouth of the Hebrus (now the Maritza, boundary between Greece and Turkey) and Anastasiopolis likewise
had their walls strengthened and restored. This whole
district had been particularly liable to be overrun by
Huns and Sclaveni, since the mountains to the north of
it had been inadequately fortified. The cities in this
mountainous region of Rhodope and the Balkan (Hae-
mus) range were reconditioned by Justinian, among them
Adrianople, about seventy miles up the Hebrus at the
point where the river turns abruptly south, and Philip-
popolis, likewise on the Hebrus some 100 miles west of
Adrianople; 'and he established innumerable fortresses
all over Thrace and thereby secured that the land, which
was previously exposed to the incursions of the enemy, is
now never ravaged at all' (xi. 20). Chapter xi, the last of
Book IV, closes with a list of these fortresses. There are 180
of them, grouped geographically. The list bristles with
problems, unsolved and perhaps often insoluble. But the
importance of place names for historical studies is being
more and more realized and has been brilliantly illustrated in recent work on the dark age of Western Europe.
For students with a turn for geography and topography
who have some acquaintance with the languages of
south-east Europe these lists in Procopius offer a fascinating field of research. Meanwhile we must be content
to point to their great length. That in itself affords a
striking illustration of one of the outstanding features of
Justinian's character, namely his restless and unbounded
energy.

With Book V we enter a much more peaceful atmosphere. It records the emperor's buildings in Asia Minor

and the Palestine area, where invaders seldom penetrated at this period. At Ephesus a great new church was
built to St John (i. 1–6; see the plan in Dewing's edition
p. 47); on the island of Tenedos, just south of the Dardanelles, a granary 280 by 90 feet to facilitate the
transport of corn from Alexandria to the capital. In
Bithynia at Helenopolis, birthplace of Constantine's
mother Helen, a wonderful aqueduct which supplied
water 'that met the requirements of the population not
only for drinking but also for bathing and all the other
forms of luxury indulged in by people who have a lavish
supply of water' (ii. 3), also baths, churches, a palace,
arcades, and lodgings for officials. Nearby the river
Draco had its course regulated, and a road was constructed through the mountains. At Nicaea, famous in
the history of theology, monasteries were built for men
and women, the palace and baths restored, and lodgings
for the *veredarii* (postal officials) rebuilt near the bridge.
At Nicomedia (Ismid), still in Bithynia, Justinian restored the baths and at the time when the *Buildings* were
being written was constructing a bridge over the rapid
river Sagaris (iii. 7–11). This bridge is known from other
sources to have been built A.D. 559–60, a fact which
establishes the date of Procopius' treatise. A marshy
stretch of the road that ran from Bithynia into Phrygia,
the district south of Bithynia, so bad that travellers over
it were frequently drowned, was reconstructed with large
stone paving and made completely safe. At Pythia in
Bithynia there were hot springs much used by the people
of Constantinople, 'especially by those suffering from some
ailment'. Justinian gave this spa his most lavish patron-
age: he built a royal palace there, new baths and an
aqueduct, and enlarged the church and infirmary. At
Syceae in Galatia, south-east of Bithynia, the river was
rapid and dangerous and liable to rise suddenly in spate
and drown travellers. Justinian built a strong bridge over
it and a new church west of the bridge to be a refuge for
those passing that way in the winter season. Ten miles
down this stream was a town called Juliopolis whose
walls on the river side were being undermined by the

current. Justinian prevented this from going any further by building an embankment.

South and east of Galatia lay Cappadocia, the most easterly of the provinces of Asia Minor. In this region defence against the Persian peril was Justinian's main concern. The walls of Caesarea, because of certain natural features, had been built to take in much more than the area actually inhabited. Justinian now shortened them and stationed an adequate garrison in the town. The town of Mocesus in the same province he removed bodily from its low-lying site to one 'at the top of a steep incline impossible to reach if anyone tried to attack.' Thus strongly fortified the city was made the capital of the province and Justinian built there 'many churches and hostelries and public baths and all the other buildings that indicate a wealthy city' (iv. 15–18).

In Cilicia, the south-east region of Asia Minor, between the Taurus mountains and the sea, nature again becomes the chief problem. At Mopsuestia the bridge over the lovely river Pyramus had grown extremely dangerous. Justinian restored the ruined parts, 'ensured again the safety both of the bridge and of its users and enabled the city once more to wear without peril the crown of beauty which the river brings it' (v. 4–7). The high-arched bridge over the Sarus at Adana (between Mopsuestia and Tarsus) had grown equally dangerous. To make it safe the river was temporarily diverted whilst the piers were restored. At St Paul's city of Tarsus the mountain-fed river Cydnus had recently caused so disastrous a flood that it had carried away the bridges and flooded the houses to their upper stories. In the *Secret History* this flood is quoted as an instance of the malign influence of the emperor; but here in the *Buildings* Procopius describes how the emperor had a new channel constructed for the river, so that henceforth only half its waters flowed through the city in the old channel, and built a new bridge over it far broader and stronger than the old, 'so that life in the city has been freed of fear and peril for all time'.

With Chapter VI of this book we skip from Tarsus

straight to Jerusalem. Here Justinian built to the Mother of God a magnificent church (which has now completely disappeared) on the highest hill in the city. The top of this hill was not big enough for his plan; so a vast substructure as high as the hill itself was raised to form the foundations of the east end of the church. Forests had to be scoured to find rafters long enough to span the roof. The site, we are told, made it impossible to bring up from any distance columns of the size and quality requisite for so magnificent a building. 'But when the emperor was getting distressed at the impossibility of the task, God revealed to him in the nearest hills a kind of stone suitable for the purpose. Either it had lain hidden there all along or had just been specially created. For the tale is credible either way to those who attribute the cause to God ... For to God there can be nothing whatsoever that is impracticable or impossible' (vi. 19–20). Attached to the church are two hospices, one where strangers may put up who are stopping in the city, the other a rest house for sick paupers.

Like Uskub and Constantinople, Jerusalem causes Procopius to stray from strict geographical order. We now retrace our steps northwards to Neapolis (Nablus) in Samaria. An excursus on the woman of Samaria and the bloody feuds between Christians and Samaritans in the reigns of Zeno and Anastasius leads up to a description of the fortifications built by Justinian to protect the church where the Samaritans had committed their outrages. Lastly we are taken to Mount Sinai. 'On this mountain dwell monks whose life is nothing but a sort of strict training for death. They love the loneliness and take full advantage of it. These monks had nothing that they sought after. They are above all human passions ... But the emperor built them a church which he dedicated to the Mother of God, so that they might be able to spend their lives there in prayer and devotions. This church he built not on the mountain top but far below it; for it is impossible for a man to pass the night on the mountain peak since the roar of thunder and certain other portents are heard constantly all through the night, striking with panic even the strongest and most resolute of men. Here it was that Moses, they tell us, received the laws from God ... And at the foot of the mountain the emperor built a very strong fort and stationed there an important garrison so that wild Saracens might not be able to take advantage of the district being uninhabited and use the place as a base for invading with all possible secrecy the districts towards Palestine' (viii. 4–9).

The closing chapter of the book lists thirty-eight monasteries in the east, mainly in Palestine and Syria, which the emperor either restored or supplied with wells or reservoirs or hostelries or poor-houses.

Book VI takes us to Africa by way of Egypt. But Egypt itself is very summarily passed over. One of the few buildings recorded is a wall round the granary at Phiale, a quarter of Alexandria where the grain was stored that was brought down from the cornlands of the Nile. The walls were necessary because 'it often happened that the grain was destroyed there through the people breaking out into riot' (i. 1–5). Procopius here repeats the view that Africa begins only west of the Nile, the river forming the boundary between the continents. One day's journey from Alexandria, at a place called Taphosiris, Justinian raised many buildings including residences for the chief officials and baths. From Taphosiris we pass directly to the other side of the Libyan desert, where in Cyrenaica, 'twenty days journey for an active traveller', Teucheira (Tokra) received a new town wall, Berenice (Benghazi) walls and a public bath, Ptolemais (Tolometa) an aqueduct, and forts were built to protect the country folk from desert marauders. The Jews of Boreium were converted to Christianity (it is not stated how), and their ancient temple converted into a Christian church (VI. ii).

In what is now Tripolitania, Procopius has again not much to record in the way of buildings. At Leptis Magna (Lebida) Justinian rebuilt the walls but with a restricted circuit. Part of the older walls had got buried under the sand, and there he left it. The ancient palace, built by the emperor Severus, who was born there, and died at York in A.D. 211, was also restored, and five churches

built (iv. 1–5). Nearby at Sabratha (Tripoli Vecchia)
he built walls round the city and 'a very notable church'
The rest of the section on this district describes the peculiar behaviour of the sea in the Syrtes and the conversion
of the natives to Christianity (iii. iv).

'After Tripolis and the Syrtes let us proceed to the rest
of Libya' (i.e. what is now Tunisia and Algeria). 'We
must start with Carthage, which is the greatest and most
notable of the cities there' (v. 1–2). It was the only city
whose walls Gizeric had not dismantled. It was renamed
Justiniana. These walls were repaired and a moat dug
round them. Churches and arcades were built and a public bath well worth seeing as well as a monastery so constructed as to be also an incomparable fortress.

In the province of Byzacium, south of the Carthaginian
province of Africa Proconsularis, Hadrumetum (modern Susa), which had been the constant victim of raids
by the Moors, became a strong walled city (vi. 1–7). Farther south along the coast Caput Vada (Ras Kaboudia),
where Belisarius' troops had first landed, was likewise
fortified, 'and the yokels there have cast away the plough
and live like civilized people ... They haunt the city
square all day long, hold public meetings to discuss their
needs, engage in trade with one another and in all the
other activities that are the mark of a great city' (vi.
15–16). The inland cities of Byzacium were similarly
fortified, as were also those of the Mt. Arausius (Jebel
Auress) region, amongst them Tamugade (Timgad), and
others farther west in Moorish territory that had never
been controlled by the Vandals, and also Trajani Forum
in Sardinia. Finally Septem (Ceuta) on the African side
of the Straits of Gibraltar was strongly fortified and garrisoned and a notable church built there to the Mother of
God. Thus Justinian 'attached the empire's gateway to
her and made the fortress capable of withstanding the
whole human race' (vii. 14–16).

'I have now recorded to the best of my powers all those
of Justinian's buildings that I have been able to learn of
either by viewing them with my own eyes or by hearing
of them with my own ears from those who have seen

them. But I know full well that there are many others that I have failed to mention either through their escaping my notice from their very number or because they remained entirely unknown to me. So if anyone will take the trouble to explore them all and insert them in my account he will gain the reward of having done what needed doing and of having made a name for himself as one who appreciates fine work' (vi, vii. 18–20: finis).

The *Buildings* is certainly the least interesting of all Procopius' writings. But I have summarized it fairly fully for more than one reason. The actual building programme is important for an appreciation of the emperor's aims, and too brief a treatment of it is bound to result in a one-sided view of them. Incidentally the treatise throws much interesting light on life and conditions in Justinian's empire. The elaborate lines of frontier fortresses and fortified cities explain themselves. But it is very revealing to read that so many parts of the empire far removed from the frontier needed protection of this sort against the raids of foreign foes. So too with the frequent mentions of bridges and roads, of aqueducts and reservoirs, of public baths and storehouses for food and water, of magistrates' quarters, hospices, and asylums for wayfarers and for the sick. It is interesting too to note how often these buildings had to be designed to master the natural difficulties caused by swamps and floods and precipices. How far Procopius is sincere in the praises that he lavishes on the emperor for these achievements must always remain a matter of personal opinion. One of the great disadvantages of being an absolute sovereign is that praise from a subject has always a suspicion of insincerity. Apart from this, the constant references to the sad state of things before the new buildings were erected admit of a double interpretation. They make it quite plain that things had been wrong previously. They leave it less certain that things had now been put right. It must be left to each reader to collate the evidence of the *Buildings* with that of Procopius' other works and form his own conclusions about the character of our historian.

But for other less subtle and complex characters this work of reconstruction must have appeared entirely good and boundlessly stimulating. For them the great building plans of Justinian must have had something of the inspiration which Virgil had found in Augustus' great back-to-the-land campaign which is the real subject of the *Georgics*. It is against this sort of background that we have to set the work of Justinian's great engineer architects. We have seen them in Constantinople living in surroundings that may fairly be compared with those of the gifted group of men who in Charles the Second's England founded the Royal Society. Anthemius' mastery of mathematics and his amusing experiments with steam are much in the spirit of the first days of the Royal Society as we glimpse them in the pages of Pepys or Evelyn. There is no specific evidence connecting the great architect personally with Procopius; but the pages of Procopius are enough to show that it was possible at this period to have a very lively and varied interest in all sorts of phenomena, natural and historical. And we do know that Anthemius and his colleague Isidore were consulted when the river at Daras caused so serious a problem (*B.* II. ii–iii, see above p. 229f.). In the *Buildings* the two architects are said to have had their suggestions overruled by the emperor, who himself proposed a more excellent solution. But we may reasonably assume that this version of what happened needs to be taken with a certain reserve, and that Anthemius was, as our ancient authorities state, an engineer as well as an architect, and that he was living in an environment that allowed his genius full play and development. For political idealists or even for political dissentients the atmosphere was stifling, as is abundantly illustrated from the *Secret History*, and creative work impossible. But for a man such as Anthemius seems to have been, whose social needs could be satisfied by playing ingenious mechanical practical jokes on his neighbours, but who accepted Justinian's ideal of materially rebuilding the shattered empire, the environment was entirely favourable for the full blossoming of his remarkable genius. Justinian's repressive

legislation against free thought and the immoralities of
the court had no more effect on Anthemius than the corresponding measures and immoralities of the England of
the Restoration period had on the work of our own Sir
Christopher Wren. Alone amongst the men and women
who surrounded Justinian his great architects were positively creative. They stand in their achievements half
way between the Hellenistic age that produced Archi-
medes and Aristarchus and our own full renaissance.

CHAPTER XII

The Achievement and its Limitations

*

WHEN in his last years Justinian looked back on his life's work, nothing probably gave him such satisfaction as the fact that he was leaving the empire with something like the frontiers that it had boasted in the days of its greatest power and glory. The recovery of North Africa, Italy and the three islands of Sicily, Sardinia and Corsica was indeed no mean achievement. But the three great countries of the far West offered a less satisfactory picture, Gaul under the Franks was outside the empire and we have seen Frankish chieftains actually operating against it. Britain was still more hopelessly lost. Only in Spain could he claim to have achieved anything whatsoever.

The Spanish peninsula has not been mentioned in our narrative of Justinian's wars. Neither Procopius nor Agathias makes any reference in his history to any attempt to recover the peninsula. But parts of southern Spain were in fact won back for the empire late in Justinian's reign, as we learn from two western writers, Gregory of Tours (*Hist. Franc.* IV. 8) and Isidore of Seville (*Hist. Goth.* ed. Mommsen, p. 286). The empire retained these Spanish possessions for some seventy years, so that the references in Gregory (died A.D. 594) and Isidore (died A.D. 636) are to a state of things still existing in their own days. It is doubtless to these conquests that Agathias refers in the poem that he prefixed to his anthology when he bids the west as far as the threshold of Gades (Cadiz) and the Spanish strait fearlessly embrace its beloved Rome (*Hist. Graec. Min.* II. pp. 395–6, ll. 53–7, cf. 82–7). But the silence of the Greek histories and the imperative mood of the poetical allusion suggest that this reconquest was only very partial and precarious.

Britain on the other hand is mentioned several times by Procopius, but no silence could so clearly show as do these passages how completely the island had been lost. Justinian's empire had lost not merely possession of the island but practically all knowledge of it. Britannia, we are told, lies some fifty miles from the mainland on a level with the uttermost parts of Spain (VIII. xx. 5). It is one tenth the size of Thule (VI. xv. 4) but much bigger than Sicily. Belisarius ironically offers it to the Goths when they offer him Sicily (VI. vi. 28), the point of his offer being that Britain is not his to dispose of.

Besides Britain Procopius has something to say about another mysterious island in the western ocean which he calls Brittia. Brittia is only twenty-five miles from the mainland, about opposite the mouths of the Rhine, in the rear of Gaul where it faces on the ocean to the north of Spain ... It is inhabited by three populous nations, the Angili, the Phrissones and the Britons (who have the same name as the island), each with its own king. These peoples are so numerous that every year they send emigrants to the Franks on the mainland. The islanders are unacquainted with horses, and their boats are all rowing-boats. There is a great and ancient wall across the island. On the hither side of this wall the climate is good and the land fruitful, but on the farther side life is impossible (VIII. xx). On the mainland opposite Brittia there are fishing villages. The fishermen who inhabit them have a strange task. Every night they are summoned from their houses by a mysterious knocking at the door. They have at once to obey the summons, go down to the sea, where they find strange boats waiting for them, and row across to Brittia. They see nothing, but their boats are heavily laden and deep in the water. But directly they touch land on the island the boats suddenly lighten. They have been ferrying over to Brittia the souls of the dead.

Various explanations have been offered of these two islands. The Loeb editor accepts Britannia as Britain and suggests that Brittia is Denmark. Bury, in his edition of Gibbon (IV. 157) identifies Brittia with Britain and suggests that Procopius' Britannia is in fact Brittany. The island with the ancient wall, inhabited by Angles, Frisians and Britons, and geographically situated near Gaul and

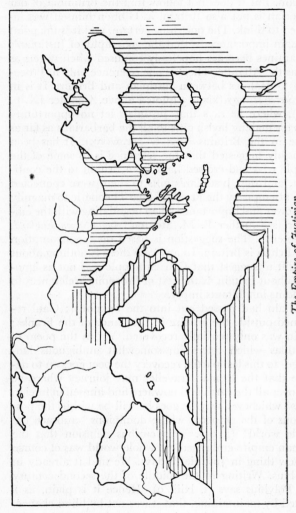

The Empire of Justinian

Vertical shading : The Empire of 527. Horizontal shading : Parts recovered during Justinian's reign.

the mouths of the Rhine, can scarcely be other than
Britain. But it does not follow that the Britannia of our
historian is not also Britain, as Gibbon himself was inclined to think. The one thing certain, and it is the point
of main importance, is that the geography of Justinian's
Byzantines becomes hopelessly confused when it gets as
far as the Atlantic. There is one reference only in Procopius to dealings between Justinian and Britons. It is in
the *Secret History* (xix. 13 quoted above, Chapter IX. p.
178), where he says that Justinian let no opportunity
pass for making lavish gifts to all the barbarians as far as
those in the Britains (τοὺς ἐν βρεταννίαις). It has been
plausibly suggested that the reference is to some of the
people who had crossed back from Britain to the conti-
nent, and that Justinian's gifts to them were connected
with attempts by the Frankish king Theoderic to magnify
his power and importance when negotiating with the emperor (see further F. M. Stenton, *Anglo-Saxon England*,
Chapter 1). The suggestion is based on the assumption
that Brittia is Britain. In any case there is nothing about
the gift to suggest that Constantinople was not as ignorant about Britain as the rest of Procopius' references to
it and its inhabitants imply.

Britain had passed out into the unknown; Gaul remained outside the empire in the hands of the Franks;
Spain was only partially recovered. Yet in the poem of
Agathias which refers (in somewhat ambiguous language) to this last partial recovery the poet goes on to declare that the Roman traveller may journey where he
will over all the earth and nowhere find himself in foreign
parts; whichever way he goes he will be within the possessions of the emperor whose dominions 'embrace the
whole world' (l. 95). This curious delusion that the
Roman empire embraced the whole world was of course
no new thing in Justinian's days. We find it already in
Polybius. Writing in the middle of the second century
B.C. Polybius says (i. lxiii. 9) 'Hence it is plain, as I
started by maintaining, that it was not by blind chance,
as some of the Greeks opine, but as the natural consequence of their training in affairs of such character and

importance that the Romans not only boldly aimed at universal leadership and domination, but actually achieved their aim.' When these words were written neither Gaul nor Britain had been subdued by Rome, and Egypt was still ruled by the Ptolemies. The Roman dominions were in fact of just about the same extent as they were when Agathias made for them just the same claim. Polybius' attitude was natural enough. Since the conquests of Alexander, some two centuries before he wrote, the idea of a world empire had been much in men's minds. It was certainly the aim of Alexander himself, and though after his early death his conquests were never extended and the lands he had conquered were divided out between the families of three of his leading generals, who wasted much of their time and strength in trying each to improve his position at the expense of the others, still this very fact only helped to keep the world in mind of Alexander's aims and achievements. The kings who had partitioned Alexander's conquests were, like Alexander himself, Macedonians, not Greeks. The Romans also were a people neither Greek nor altogether barbarian. The Latin language is a first cousin to the Greek. The Tarquins were, as Polybius tells us, of partly Greek descent, and contacts between Rome and Greece had been frequent, if rather more intermittent, even in the first centuries of the republic. Accepting, as so many thoughtful people of his period did, the idea of a world state, it was not unnatural for an educated Greek like Polybius, moving at Rome in philhellenic circles, to look to Rome rather than to any Macedonian ruler for the realization of his aims.

Polybius' views on the mission of Rome naturally made a great appeal to many Romans, not only to ambitious imperialists but also to the much more numerous class of humbler citizens whose one ideal was peace and quiet. Then at the fateful period when Augustus established his power and restored peace to the Roman dominions after generations of wars, the idea of a universal Roman empire found expression in Virgil, as when he makes Jupiter declare (*Aeneid*, I. 278–9) that he has set the Romans no limit of space or time but has bestowed on them an empire without end, or when Anchises prophesies (*Aeneid*, VI. 781–2) that Rome's empire shall be conterminous with the earth. The same claim is made over four centuries later by Claudian in his famous panegyric of Rome (*In secundum consulatum Stilichonis* 150–60), where he says that she has gathered the human race into one family and that there will never be any bound to her sway.

This geographical error, which identified the world with that favoured fraction of it that fringes the Mediterranean, had unfortunate consequences. It prevented the Romans from ever dealing on equal terms with any communities outside the empire. In practice of course Rome had to have all manner of dealings with the lesser breeds without the law. Persians to the east and the various barbarians who impinged on the other frontiers were indeed the daily preoccupation of the empire, as the history of Justinian's reign sufficiently shows. But a world state can hardly have a coherent foreign policy. Rome never pretended to have one. The ideas that are slowly and painfully and not without many inconsistencies emerging amongst the English-speaking peoples and their friends throughout the world, of communities of nations each recognizing their responsibilities to their neighbours but each within these limits working out their own salvation and making their own particular contribution to the good life, was alien to the Roman ideal.

This last point will become clearer if we turn back to the empire and consider what it superseded. The Roman empire and the Roman peace were not the first of their kind. The vital difference between that of Rome (and her Hellenistic predecessors whose work she continued) and those of Persia, Egypt or Assyria was that Rome had inherited something unique to preserve, namely the legacy of the city states whose development between the seventh and fourth centuries B.C. had opened an entirely new chapter in human history. It was these city states that laid the foundations of everything vital in our modern way of life. No type of community has been so prolific of great men or raised the average of political and intellectual attainment to anything like the same level as that of fifth-century Athens. It is true, as every text-book tells us, that the Greek city states had fallen to Macedon largely as the result of their own dissensions and internecine wars, which had been as great a curse to fifth- and fourth-century Greece as the wars between rival states have been to modern Europe. But it is equally true, and far less often said, that the fatal defect in the outlook of the Macedonian potentates who put an end to the epoch of the city state was their entire unawareness of what they were destroying.

The western, Latin, half of the empire had likewise risen on the ruins of the city state, though here it was victories, not defeats, that brought about the ruin. When the cynical self-seeking adventurers who controlled the late republic were replaced by the benevolent and often beneficent bureaucracy of the Caesars, the change was certainly welcomed, and with reason, by the mass of Rome's subjects. But the new régime was a move still further away from the city-state ideal. Its basic assumption was that the masses are incapable of being educated into responsible citizens. Still less was there any idea of the possibility of a United States of Rome. Nowhere is this brought out more clearly than in Claudian's famous panegyric. The benefits that Rome confers upon her children are 'that the stranger walks in a strange land as if it were his own; that men can change their homes; that it is a pastime to visit Thule and to explore mysteries at which we once shuddered; that we drink at will the waters of the Rhone and the Orontes; that the whole earth is one people' (translation by R. C. Jebb). Stripped of its eloquence this list of benefits boils down to freedom of movement within the boundaries of the empire. Freedoms other than this of movement are not mentioned by Claudian, some of them because they did not exist within the empire, some because he could not imagine their existence anywhere. What Rome as universal mother offered her non-Roman children was the privilege of becoming not good Gauls or Greeks or Libyans but fully qualified Romans. Rome loved her children in her own peculiar way, but she did not trust them. The ideals so magnificently set forth by Thucydides in the funeral speech of Pericles had been quietly abandoned ages before. They had ceased to be even comprehensible.

There is nothing in Claudian's panegyric that Justinian would not have fully endorsed. Some of the lines of Agathias' eulogy are indeed little more than a paraphrase of Claudian. True, the one freedom that the earlier poet so stresses had practically disappeared; but it had done so only as the result of economic conditions which Justinian deplored and would have remedied if only he had known how. For the rest he is entirely at one with the poet. His ultra-paternal legislation and his highly centralized bureaucratic administration are based on an ideal that is the absolute antithesis of everything that the city state had stood for. The effects of this ideal can be well illustrated from the emperor's treatment of the Vandals and Goths. When he intervened in Libya and Italy these two peoples had already passed their most barbarous and destructive stages. Under a few more rulers like Theoderic and Hilderic they might have developed into self-governing communities gradually absorbing something of the Graeco-Roman tradition and making to it their own individual contributions. Perhaps under different circumstances, if for instance Theoderic had left a male successor like himself and Hilderic had been stronger and left a suitable successor, Justinian might have acquiesced. But there can be no doubt that he regarded the troubles that led to his intervention in Libya and Italy and to the overthrow of these two kingdoms and their reunion with the empire as an unmixed blessing for the world, and that he would have done so even if these two peoples had not been heretical. There was no element of growth and development in his conception of a good world. His aims were purely conservative.

While Alexander was conquering the realms of the King of Persia and setting up his military monarchy which ended the life of the free Greek city state, the great Aristotle was writing his manual on Politics. In spite of

Alexander's dazzling successes Aristotle continues to regard the self-governing city state as the one form of community in which it is possible to lead the good life. An eminent modern historian has taken him seriously to task for what he regards as his political blindness. But is it so certain that Bury is right and Aristotle wrong? Is it not at least equally arguable that the modern historian has fallen into the besetting error of students of history, that of being unduly impressed by the *fait accompli?* We cannot give unqualified approval to the empire of Justinian or of any of his predecessors and at the same time hold to the Aristotelian doctrine that man is a political being.

But when all has been said, and it is essential that it should be said, there is still an immense debt that we owe to Justinian and the ideals for which he stood and fought with such untiring tenacity. The light that came into the world with Solon and Cleisthenes and Pericles and the heroes and statesmen of the young republic of Rome had illumined only a small corner of the world. The books that had recorded the new age and the two languages in which that record had been written might easily have disappeared altogether if the empire had not spread and preserved them. The vital part of the message embodied in these writings had lost much of its meaning for the contemporaries of Procopius and John the Lydian. But we owe it to them and the system that they represented and which they served so well according to their lights that it is with us at this day.

This is the great debt that we owe the Byzantines. They have passed on to us a great inheritance which they did their utmost to preserve though they very imperfectly understood it. But we owe them, and the richly documented age of Justinian in particular, another and more intimate legacy in the picture they have left us of a purely conservative community. It is a picture well worth our study. Even in times of growth and development the greater part of the activities of the greater part of mankind must always be conservative; and periods of growth and progress must inevitably be followed by long spells of consolidation that will often seem to idealists to be stagnation. We have had occasion to quote Virgil more than once and to point out that his whole outlook, with its majestic sadness at the doubtful doom of human kind, is distinctly unhelpful, not to say antagonistic, to those who are fired with the desire to make a new world. It is hard to imagine Virgil writing

> Bliss was it in that dawn to be alive
> But to be young was very heaven.

But times when this is the dominant feeling have not been too numerous in the world's history. Even when they come and are not quickly followed by disillusionment, they are bound to be interspersed for every individual with periods of reaction. For everyone therefore in some phases of his life and for many all through it the one essential thing must seem to be simply to carry on. And for such periods, whether in the life of the individual or of a whole community, the record of Justinian's life and times has an enduring value.

Index

*